The Encyclopedia of American

SUPERCARS

By Robert C. Ackerson

Best regards
Bob Ackerson

Bookman Publishing/Baltimore, Maryland

Preface

The time span between 1948 and 1970 encompassed many trends, innovations and events of significance within the American automotive industry. Tail fins began with the 1948 Cadillac and, by the latter years of the 1950's, were to be found, in varying stages of acceptability, on every American-made automobile. Indeed, even in Europe their impact was felt, with Mercedes-Benz for a time apparently feeling the need to conform to the norm.

Roughly at the same time that fins reached their maximum point of elevation, a counter-revolution began that, aided and abetted by political and economic forces of unprecedented scope, has not yet run its full course. This was, of course, the revival of interest in America of the small car. The beachhead was secured by the early postwar Austins, English Fords and Renault 4CV's. Then came the major assault force, the Volkswagen followed by the Toyotas and Datsuns from Japan. But, with the American manufacturers not yet finished with their task of downsizing their products, the outcome of the old import-domestic battle is yet to be written. Imports today control over 25% of the total U.S. car market. With the advent of Chrysler's Horizons, Omnis and K cars plus General Motor's front-wheel drive X and J cars, however, the tide might, as it did in the late '50's, once again swing back in favor of Detroit.

Certainly the international concern about conservation of resources and more efficient automobiles cannot be faulted. Each age identifies a new set of priorities and then acts upon them. Thus, the present becomes delimited from the past which, in turn, becomes a fertile ground for researchers to not only discover the stimuli that lead to the present but also the motivating forces that gave those years their personality and dynamism.

In this way, history both instructs and entertains. The emphasis of this book is primarily upon the entertainment role of history. Clearly, the 20th Century has been the century of the automobile and, surely beyond all doubt, its middle years in America as elsewhere in the world were memorable ones. In Europe, the rise of Italy as a force dominant not only in racing, with its Ferraris and Maseratis, but in auto styling, as well, via the masterpieces of Pininfarina, Vignale and others, was of great importance. The English automobile industry, while in recent time unfortunately oblivious to opportunities, particularly in the American market, was producing two-seaters of amazing variety that, if nothing else, made American sports car racing the colorful spectacle that it was.

Many Americans of the early fifties, more in tune with developments in Europe at that time, failed to fully appreciate the changing character of the American automobile until it was well underway. To the dyed-in-the-wool American sports car enthusiast, the automotive products of his homeland were wallowing, bulging bowls of mush. Indeed, all too often they were. But, upon the introduction of Cadillac's 160 hp overhead valve V-8 in 1949, followed shortly by Oldsmobile's "Golden Rocket" V-8, the die was cast. The performance of American automobiles advanced by leaps and bounds. By 1951, there were Chrysler Firepower V-8's. Four years later, the unforgettable C-300, Chevrolet's 265 cid V-8, the Corvette V-8 and, perhaps the King of the Hill, the Pontiac GTO.

These cars were, to fall back on a cliche, as American as apple pie. Their roots traced back to that marvelous home grown, self-taught talent, the American hot rodder. He first practiced his art on Henry Ford's fabulous flathead, discovering to his delight how to double and triple its output. Once the hot rodders got hold of modern, overhead valve V-8's, there was literally no stopping them. Before long, with the guiding hand of the National Hot Rod Association pointing the way, drag racing became a respectable form of motor sport.

Detroit didn't waste much time in picking up on the postwar performance theme and soon the mid-fifties horsepower race was on, slowed down only temporarily by such obstacles as the 1957 AMA anti-performance edict.

The arrival of the Pontiac GTO in 1964 had an afterburner effect upon Detroit's interest in supercars. The youth market was high, wide, handsome and rich. No manufacturer dared ignore it and, soon, save for just a handful of very expensive European sports cars, there were no production automobiles in the world that could not be out accelerated by ones built in the United States. Save for the Corvette, they are all gone now, victims of changing automotive legislation and, to a degree, of the over-indulgence of their manufacturers. But, while they reigned supreme, the American supercars were machines of unique character, awesome acceleration and top speed potential and, while many of their detractors hated to admit it, often possessing respectable handling. It was indeed a Golden Age, the likes of which will not be repeated.

History has yet to accord the American supercars their proper place in the evolution of the automobile. This book's purpose will be well served if it signals the start of a redress of this oversight.

Certainly, the years in which they were produced were anything but tranquil. Happily, the time span in which the postwar supercars have become collectable is an age when national pride and interest in our recent history is on the upswing. In such an environment, the chances are good that many aging supercars will be saved from the crusher and become future super stars at shows and meets across the country.

While the writing of a book is basically a solitary, lonely act, it cannot take form without the input of people with particular talent and knowledge. Coming from Dick Teague and Larry Mitchell was help with American Motors' performance cars. Judy Siff of Pontiac's public relations department performed a similar task in regard to the Pontiac GTO. My good friend and Chrysler 300 enthusiast, Moe Liedkie, was the source of a valued insight into those grand machines. I would be amiss not to recognize the contribution of Phil Adee, who typed the original manuscript. Thanks, also, for illustrations supplied by Sam Shields, Jr., and Lincoln-Mercury. While I alone have to bear responsibility for any errors contained within, to these wonderful people goes my appreciation and gratitude for their valued assistance and advice.

Special thanks goes to my editor and friend Tom Bonsall who extended deadlines with patience and, when it was all down in print, turned a dream into reality.

July, 1981

"To Grace, Cindy, Lynn and Susan"

Contents

RAMBLER AMERICAN ROGUE

343 CUBES

We don't build them the way we used to. For American Motors to stuff a 343 cube Typhoon V-8 into an innocent-looking Rambler American is guaranteed to cause news. But 1967 looks to be a *driver's* year like no other, and the 1967 American Motors has risen to the occasion. Witness this Rogue hardtop. Its 343 cubes are fed by a 4-barrel Carter to develop 280 horses, and this mill winds up to higher rpm's faster and pays off in quicker shifts. The 4-speed stick is mandatory (as you'd expect in a machine of this caliber), and you can opt for a fat pile of goodies including a special handling package, power disc brakes, Twin-Grip rear axle, electric tach, shoulder belts, and extra-wide-profile red line nylons mounted on 5.5" rims.

So you see, we *don't* build them the way we used to. That's our message. With this added plus: American Motors believes any driver's year must be a safe driver's year. So you get an energy-absorbing steering column, deep-dish wheel, Double-Safety brake system, shoulder belt anchors, and many other built-in safety features. See what a 343-CID Typhoon looks like in any of 7 Rambler Americans, at your American Motors/Rambler Dealer. It just might end up *you* don't build them the way you used to, either!

THE 1967 AMERICAN MOTORS

AMBASSADOR · MARLIN · REBEL · RAMBLER AMERICAN

THE NOW CARS

6

1. American Motors

For all practical purposes American Motors was the last major U.S. manufacturer to enter the high performance circus of the mid-fifties. There was a logical reason for AMC's tardiness; when the wolf is at the door you worry first about survival, fun and games come later. After several lean years, things began to improve for American Motors during 1956. With the totally redesigned Rambler finding favor with many customers George Romney apparently felt there were enough coins in the coffer to spend a few on a super-stock Rambler.

The obvious ingredient in the high performance recipe, a V-8 engine of modern design, relatively low weight and with the potential for future development was not available to American Motors' engineers until late 1956. It's true that both in 1955 and 1956 the big Nash and Hudsons were available with Packard built V-8s but in no way could these cars be perceived as starting points for the creation of an exciting performance automobile. The Packard V-8 possessed potential but its weight and bulk were big disadvantages. Furthermore, the unit-body shared by Nash and Hudson was visually unexciting and not of the character that one would normally associate with a "hot" automobile.

During 1956, however, the introduction of the new 108 inch wheelbase Rambler made it possible for AMC to move in a surprisingly bold fashion, for such a conservative company, into the high performance arena. This car was no styling *tour de force*, but it was new, it was small and, if somewhat over decorated, at least appearancewise, a breath of fresh air from Kenosha.

American Motors' first in-house designed V-8 debuted as the powerplant for Nash and Hudson "special" models roughly midway through the 1956 model run. In a paper presented to the Society of Automotive Engineers, its designers outlined four fundamental criteria that were set for the new V-8 before its development began. Most important was an inherent potential for both greater cubic inch displacement and power output. In its earliest form the AMC V-8 displaced only 250 cubic inches with a bore and stroke of 3½ inches x 3¼ inches and developed 190 hp. There was lots of room (4.75 inches) between bore centers for future expansion and the following year a ½ inch bore increase boosted displacement to a fairly healthy 327 cubic inches. Since AMC couldn't draw upon the economic resources available to the Big Three it had literally no choice but to put all its eggs in one basket with the engine. In other words, not only did it have to possess the ability to be produced in various cubic inch displacements, but its external dimensions had to be small enough to allow for its use in automobiles ranging in size from compact to full size. With length, width and height measurements of 27¾ inches, 25⅝ inches and 14 5/18 inches this latter mandate was met quite nicely. Because of its anticipated across the board use it was also vital that the new AMC V-8 be as light as possible without, of course, sacrificing durability. Thus modern thin wall castings were used yielding a base weight without flywheel or clutch of 601 pounds.

With small valves (1.787 inch intake and 1.406 inch exhaust) and a mild (244° duration) cam that had only 0.375 inches of lift, this engine was obviously not, at least in 1956, intended to be a high rev-high output unit. However,

when mated to the 108 inch wheelbase Rambler chassis and compact body style such deficiencies weren't particularly serious and after its other 1957 models had been introduced American Motors produced such a combination.

On December 4, 1957, Roy Abernethy, then American Motors' vice-president of automotive distribution and marketing, announced the Rambler Rebel. Described by Abernethy as a "distinctive car — both in appearance and performance" the Rebel was available only as a four-door hardtop sedan painted a solid light metallic silver-gray color that was not available on any other AMC model. (Similarly its interor of black seats with vinyl metallic silver-gray bolsters, black carpeting and silver-gray headliner was exclusive to the Rebel) In appearance the Rebel was certainly no worse than most of its contemporaries, at least no double or triple color combinations were offered and its side trim moulding with a bronze-gold anodized insert was reasonably restrained.

American Motors had an infatuation with continental tire mounts in the mid-fifties and apparently felt compelled to so equip the Rebel. This made little sense and probably was a good example of just how much AMC had to learn about performance at this time.

With 58.4% (2085 pounds) of its weight on its front wheels the Rebel's handling was its greatest shortcoming as a high-performance car. Its designers did equip it with a front stabilizer bar, heavy-duty springs, Gabriel "Adjustomatic" shocks with three settings plus a long anti-sway bar at the rear, but the fact remained that the old adage about the problems inherent in making a purse of a sow's ear apply to cars as well as to leathergoods. Thus Ray Brock's advice *(HOT ROD,* August, 1957) that "We recommend that you not try to road race your Rebel" was not idle puffery. If the Rebel misbehaved in the turns it partially redeemed itself thanks to its first class brakes. With only 9 inch brake drums and 150.24 square inches of surface area its credentials weren't particularly impressive, but with flanged drums and 15 inch wheels the Rebel pulled down smoothly from high speeds and did not suffer from serious brake fade.

Aside from its distinction as the first performance car from AMC, the big attention getter for the Rebel was its electronic fuel injection system. Roy Abernethy asserted that the Rebel not only was the first production car so equipped but also had "more power per pound than other six passenger American automobiles." Rambler claimed that the fuel-injected 327 V-8 with solid lifters and 9.5:1 compression ratio developed 288 hp and 350 lbs-ft of torque.

In theory the Bendix Electrojector fuel injection was the model of simplicity. A control "electric brain" or electronic modulator received data from sensors on the intake manifold, and throttle shaft and a thermostat mounted in the water jacket. The modulator correlated this information with timing data received from an electronic wafer positioned in the distributor and, in turn, controlled the amount of fuel entering the combustion chambers through solenoid-operated injectors.

All in all this was a neat setup. Since it was not a mechanical system it was easily adaptable to any engine with a minimal amount of modification. Unlike the system adopted by Chevrolet in 1957, a high pressure metering pump was not needed nor were there any problems with dirt from the fuel tank fouling any system since the injection nozzles were large enough to pass dirt without clogging.

Unfortunately, not only the best made plans of men and mice, but also those of American Motors and Bendix occasionally go astray and in the spring of 1957, when production of Rebels was scheduled to begin a number of flaws were discovered in the Electrojector system. As a result all of the approximately 1500 Rebels built were powered by the 255 hp 327 cid V-8 engine equipped with a four-barrel Carter WCBF carburetor. With ''Flash-away'' Hydramatic the Rebel was a 9.4 second car from zero to 60 mph. With overdrive and a 4.10:1 rear axle this figure dropped to just under 8 seconds.

Apparently AMC was just a little shy about letting its new car mingle with the fearsome creatures from the Big Three in open competition. Instead, selected members of the motoring press were invited to compete on Daytona Beach during the 1957 Speed Week in quarter-mile drag competition with a 255 hp Rebel. Ken Fermoyle of *MOTOR LIFE* was the victor with a time of 17.87 seconds. Ironically, more conventional Ramblers did quite well during the speed trials. Robert Reed's 250 cid V-8 won the standing start one mile run for Class 4 cars (213-259 cubic inch engines) with a speed of 71.785 mph. Reed also won Class 3 (167-213 cubic inch engines) with a six-cylinder Rambler whose speed was 64.795 mph.

American Motors also offered a power pack for the 250 cid V-8 Rambler during 1957 consisting of a four-barrel carburetor and special intake manifold that boosted horsepower from 190 to 208. Its retail price was a modest $29.50.

When American Motors announced its adherence to the AMA performance ban in June, 1957, the fate of the Rebel was sealed. In 1958 the Rebel name was transferred to the Rambler V-8 powered series and with profits rolling in for the first time in its history AMC could hardly be faulted for stressing economy over performance in its automobiles.

This lack of corporate enthusiasm for power and quick acceleration was not, however, total. When production of the big Nash and Hudsons ended after the 1957 models, their place in the AMC lineup was partially taken up by the Rambler Ambassador, essentially an elongated version of the compact Rambler on a 117 inch wheelbase. The styling of the early Ambassadors was not particularly outstanding until 1963 when new bodies with crisp, clean lines and a distinctive appearance were adopted. With a 112 inch wheelbase and a 270 hp version of the AMC 327 cid V-8 the Ambassador became in the view of *HOT ROD* magazine (April, 1963), ''perhaps the most overlooked and underrated performance car on the American road.'' This was pretty strong language from a magazine that was the granddaddy of all drag racing publications. *HOT ROD* backed up its opinion of the Ambassador by detailing the exploits of one Ambassador with a most undiplomatic ability to turn 14.20 seconds — 97 mph quarter-mile runs.

Although the four millionth modern Rambler was built in 1967, there were many in the industry who forecast a future for AMC that was on a par with that facing a sinking ship. When the market for high-performance-sporting automobiles shifted into high gear in 1964 AMC was left out in the cold. Its conservative approach to automobile design had been a big success a few years earlier but by the mid sixties it was steering AMC toward disaster. A quick shake up in the head office brought Roy D. Chapin in as company chairman early in 1967 along with William V. Luneburg as

president. For most of 1967 they fought a rear guard action; staving off immediate disaster by cutting prices on the low-priced American series while implementing a long term plan of recovery. In many ways AMC found itself in a position in regard to high performance automobiles not unlike that of 1957. Both times it was on the outside looking in. However, Chapin and Luneburg were not nearly as hesitant to build a high performance car as Romney had been in 1957. AMC was not as successful as Pontiac in changing its image but throughout the late sixties and early seventies it did turn out a series of imaginative and at times outrageous supercars that undoubtedly were instrumental in its recovery.

If there was a redeeming factor in AMC's coming from behind position, it was that it at least could avoid committing the same errors as its competitors and at the same time capitalize on their successes. Nowhere was this more apparent than in the Javelin. In virtually all its vital dimensions; including rear passenger room and luggage space the Javelin was superior to the Mustang-Camaro crowd. Yet even the most hardened anti-AMC type had to admit that Dick Teague, AMC's styling boss, and his crew had done an exceptional job.

Teague had first demonstrated his ability to create a sporty AMC image change with the Rambler Tarpon showcar. This experimental fastback was first shown at the January, 1964, SAE National convention held in Detroit. If the Tarpon had survived the transition from showcar to production model without losing much of its basic attractiveness there's little doubt it would have been at least a moderate sales success. By using the 100 inch Rambler American chassis Teague kept its overall length down to a reasonable 180 inches. On such a scale its fastback roofline looked good and the motoring press was almost unanimous in praising it as a potential turnabout car for AMC. Unfortunately, a lot of unpleasant things happened to the Tarpon in its transformation into the production model Marlin. The worst was the result of management's decision to mount it on a 112 inch wheelbase and expand its overall size to accommodate six passengers. Instead of boosting AMC's stock value it became the laughing stock of the industry. American Motors it seemed, couldn't produce a good looking sporty car if its life depended upon it and to a large degree it did.

Fortunately, the more enlightened management team lead by Roy D. Chapin, Jr. who became general manager of American Motors automotive division in 1966 and AMC's board chairman and chief executive officer on January 9, 1967 (replacing Roy Abernethy) was far less inclined to tamper with a good design. Teague's styling department was busy at work during this transition time on a number of interesting projects from which were to evolve two of AMC's most successful high-performance automobiles, the Javelin and the AMX. In point of time the AMX which first appeared in non-operational form at the National SAE Convention in Detroit in January, 1966, preceded the Javelin, but since the Javelin was conceived as a higher volume car that would allow AMC access into the highly lucrative pony car market, its production received first priority. However, it's important to realize that the two cars were developed virtually together thus making it possible for them to share many body and chassis components.

It comes as no surprise that Teague used an early Mustang as his target car. What was needed of course was not merely a carbon copy of the Ford pony car but an automobile that was just as sporty but with a styling theme all its own. On this point Teague scored a big success. The clay model submitted to management in late 1965 (carrying a Rogue nameplate) possessed virtually the same silhouette as the final product. Early in 1967 at the Chicago Auto Show a teaser in the form of the AMX III, a silver-gray fastback sports station wagon, provided a preview of the Javelin's very clean and tastefully original split grille work and headlight/parking light arrangement. For a time headlight covers were considered for the Javelin but production costs fortunately cancelled out this gimmick.

Eary Javelin ads, cleverly titled "An unfair comparison between the Mustang and the Javelin" made a fair number of believers out of hardcore cynics who once saw AMC as basically a dumb company producing what were seen, in an era of cheap gas and big engines, as dumb cars. A total of 56,462 Javelins were built in the 1968 model run (AMC had expected first year Javelin sales to run in the 35 to 40,000 car range) not enough, to be sure, to scare Chevrolet or Ford but enough to make the "Hey, Javelin" cry (a creation of the Wells, Rich, Greene Agency that handled AMC advertising) a cliche with highly positive overtones.

Like the Mustang, AMC delivered the base Javelin with a six cylinder engine. Fortunately, for those who preferred something more interesting than a 232 cid-145 hp six both the 290 and 343 cid American Motors' V-8's were also available. Several changes were made in the 343 V-8 that brought it closer to being a high performance engine. AMC wasn't there yet but thanks to redesigned cylinder heads with cleaner intake passages and larger (by 0.025 inches) intake valves, things were improving in this area. With a Carter AFB four-barrel carburetor the 343 cid V-8 developed 280 hp at 4800 rpm and 365 lbs-ft of torque at 3000 rpm. Running with a 4-speed transmission and 3.54:1 rear axle this output enabled the Javelin to record a zero to 60 mph time of 8.1 seconds and run the standing start quarter-mile in 15.4 seconds with a speed of 93 mph.

The 280 hp/343 cid V-8 was available as part of the Javelin "Go Package" which also included dual exhausts, power front disc brakes and E70-14 wide oval tires. The handling features that balanced the power elements of the "Go Package" included a larger diameter front anti-roll bar and heavy duty springs and shocks. The Javelin's suspension was typical both of American cars in general and other AMC cars in particular. In the front high mounted coil springs and unequal-length wishbones were used. At the rear were 53 inch x 2.5 inch leaf springs similar but larger than those of the Rambler American. Rear axle windup was kept within reasonable limits by placing the passenger-side shock ahead of the rear axle with the other shock located behind the axle.

Javelins were given a very minor face lift for 1969. An accent colored central panel spruced up its one piece injection-molded ABS plastic dash and a "bullseye" grille insert were the most obvious cosmetic changes. There were fortunately some more interesting mechanical changes. All column-mounted shift levers were dropped and Javelins with 4-speed transmissions were now available with Hurst shifters. When the AMX was introduced in mid-February, 1968, it was the only AMC car available with a 390 cid V-8. During the 1968 model run, however, this engine was also made part of the Javelin "Go Package" and was readily available in 1969.

The 390 V-8 shared many design features with the 290 and 343 cid AMC engines but its block used a different casting and had heavier cylinder walls. Whereas the two smaller V-8's carried cast iron crankshafts, that used in the

390 engine was a drop-forged steel unit. With a four-barrel Holley carburetor, Edelbrock intake manifold and a 10.2:1 compression ratio its rated horsepower was 315 at 4600 rpm. With 11.9 pounds per horsepower the 390 Javelin needed seven seconds to reach 60 mph from rest. Its quarter-mile time and speed was 15.02 seconds and 94.8 mph.

The 390 engine had to be viewed as somewhat of an enigma. For its size it was a very light engine, weighing without a starter just 582 pounds. By way of comparison, the Ford 390 V-8 weighed 620 pounds, Chevrolet's 396, 771 pounds and Chrysler's 383, 649 pounds. Within the AMC family the 390 also benefited from a weight comparison, offering 100 more cubic inches than the small 290 cid V-8 at a weight cost just 35 additional pounds. The Achilles' heel of the 390 was simply that it was not originally intended as a high performance engine at all! Rather it was created in 1966 as an option for Ambassadors intended for heavy duty uses, e.g. trailer pulling. With a mild cam of just 266° duration and 44° of overlap it was an eager puller but simply ran out of breath above 5000 rpm. This shortcoming was at least partially remedied by the optional high performance cam with a 302° duration and 98° of overlap and stronger valve springs. These changes raised the output of the 390 to a very healthy 347 horsepower. The smaller 343 V-8 had its horsepower increased from 280 to 308 when similarly equipped. Other Group 19 (AMC designation for its high performance parts list) options included a high riser aluminum manifold that supported two four-barrel carburetors, traction arms and a choice of 4-speed transmissions with either wide or close ratios that could be linked to a variety of rear axles ranging from 3.96:1 to 4.44:1.

Three years after the Javelin's introduction American Motors, obviously confident of its status could admit in an ad headlined, "From zero to Donohue in 3.1 years," that "In 1967 we had nothing sporty to offer. Then in 1968 we introduced the Javelin, our first sporty car." AMC then proceeded to inform readers of the early embryonic racing program that while it did bring some success in NASCAR GT racing, was unable to nail down a championship in the far more visible SCCA Trans Am Series. To remedy this deficiency American Motors signed Mark Donohue and Roger Penske to a three year contract. This dynamic duo delivered the goods for AMC, winning the Trans Am title in 1971.

In Trans Am form the Javelin was an awesome racing machine with performance credentials that included a 175 mph top speed, the ability to reach 60 mph from rest in under five seconds and the strength to run the quarter-mile in less than eleven seconds. To commemorate its first Trans Am title AMC produced a small number of Javelins painted in the distinctive red, white and blue color scheme used on the racing Javelins. All these cars were equipped with the 390 V-8 fitted with ram-air induction, dual exhausts and a heavy-duty engine cooling system. Other standard features included the Twin-grip differential, 4-speed close ratio transmission with Hurst shifter, power front disc brakes, heavy-duty suspension, a front air ram and rear deck spoiler.

All 1970 Javelins carried a new front suspension using two ball joints and with relocated springs that were softer but which, thanks to their new position, offered more roll resistance. A larger (0.94 inch) anti-roll bar that was an option in 1969 (when it was used in Trans Am racing) was also made standard.

A number of changes were also made in the 390 engine design. Smoother gas flow was achieved by a new port design, a larger four-barrel Holley 4300 carburetor was fitted to a new intake manifold and thanks to a redesigned exhaust manifold less power was lost to back pressure. With the cold-air hood the 390 now developed 325 hp at 5000 rpm. The smaller 290 and 343 V-8's were dropped from the AMC engine inventory, replaced by bored out versions displacing 304 and 360 cubic inches respectively.

After reaching a peak of 56,462 in 1968, Javelin production slumped to 40,675 in 1969 and to only 28,210 for the 1970 model run. American Motors response to this slippage was to restyle the Javelin with a new, wider body. The new Javelin was far more aggressive in appearance thanks mainly to new front sheet metal that suggested that the Javelin was so low slung that fender bulges were needed to provide room for its front wheels. All of this was more fancy than fact since the same chassis used previously was carried over into 1971. By redesigning the 390 engine AMC just slid under the wire to join the 400 cubic inch club with its new for '71 401 cid V-8. Ironically this combination of big engine and sharp styling with good aerodynamics came at a time when the rethinking of performance parameters began. Production of Javelins lingered in the low twenty thousand range through the 1974 model year which was the Javelin's last.

As an image changer the Javelin served well. A total of 232,715 were constructed in seven model years and enough of these were of the high performance variety to convey the impression that the Javelin had more going for it than just a pretty face.

Rambler Scrambler

In point of time, honors for beginning the first super performance automobile at a budget price goes to the 1968 Plymouth Road Runner. But, if this is so, then the Rambler Scrambler of 1969 was the first bargin-performance car that blantly proclaimed its ability to anyone within three blocks of its location.

If there was ever an automobile whose basic form and origin suggested it as the most unlikely starting point for the creation of a supercar, it had to be the Rambler American. When it was first introduced in 1950, the Rambler's basic appeal was as a well appointed small car whose owner need not be ashamed to park it in his driveway. When American Motors decided to stake its survival to the production of small cars, the 100 inch wheelbase Rambler was phased out in favor of a larger model with more flamboyant styling and a 108 inch wheelbase. Two years later, however, with AMC reporting its first ever profits and the economy car market rapidly expanding, American Motors did something few automobile companies have ever done: they put back in production an automobile that had earlier been dropped. This was, of course, the 100 inch wheelbase Rambler which returned in 1958 as the Rambler American. Only a two-door version was first offered but, eventually, the American line-up included station wagons, convertibles and two-door hardtop models. A year after the larger Rambler models were given new bodies in 1963 (when *MOTOR TREND* awarded its "Car of the Year" title to the entire Rambler line up) the new AMC look was applied with considerable success to the smaller American series.

As noted elsewhere, AMC's major weapons in its arsenal to get back into the marketing mainstream of the late sixties were the Javelin and AMX models. Yet, by making available, first in 1966, its 290 cid V-8 in the little Ramblers and then, in 1967, the 343 cid, 280 hp V-8, AMC converted what *CAR LIFE* once called "the original plain Jane" into a mini-supercar of sorts. It was possible to order these V-8 Americans with an optional hydraulic lifter kit that included a 302° duration cam and a blocked heat-riser manifold kit. With some careful tuning and attention to details, it was also possible to end up with a zero to 60 mph in 7.8 seconds automobile. Even this husky performance paled before that of the 1969 SC/Rambler Hurst, which was more commonly known simply as the Rambler Scrambler. Hurst Performance, Inc., handled the procedure that transformed ho-hum Clark Kent Ramblers into Superman-like Scramblers with a good deal of finesse. Only 1,512 were built but, particularly in the case of drivers of more established supercars, their impact went far beyond what would be expected of such a small number of automobiles.

George Hurst had originally proposed that the ultra-fast AMX models be given the Hurst treatment but, when AMC opted instead for a low priced performance car based on the American, Hurst tackled the job with gusto. As delivered, with a sticker price of $2,995, the Scrambler was equipped with the 390 cid, 315 hp V-8, a close-ratio Warner T-10 4-speed transmission with Hurst shifter, a 3.54:1 limited slip rear axle, power front disc brakes and dual exhausts with glass-pack mufflers. A special handling package with a large anti-roll bar and stiffer springs and shocks was also part of the package as were a heavy-duty clutch, radiator and a flex fan.

Anyone who desired anonymity would not be enamored of the Scrambler's appearance. The only color scheme available was an eye ball spinning red, white and blue combination that, with mag-type wheels and the "world's most outrageous production cold-air scoop" (*CAR LIFE*, May, 1969), left no doubt as to what this car was all about. The Scrambler's visual impression was no illusion. Quarter-mile speeds of 100-plus mph were routine milk runs. The Scrambler and its zero to 60 mph time of 6.3 seconds certainly made believers out of many skeptics.

A successor of sorts to the SC/Rambler (which was produced only in 1969) was the Hornet SC/360 of 1971. Only 784 were built, all fitted with 325 hp, 360 cid V-8's.

Up with the Machine

On October 25, 1969, at the National Hot Rod Association World Championships at Dallas, Texas, the Rebel Machine, replete with arrows, stripes, decals and virtually every other exterior appearance device known to the creators of American supercars, appeared. Like the SC/Rambler, the Machine seemed at first impression to be a satire of sorts, intended to make the sublime of the supercar ridiculous. But, again like its little brother, the Machine delivered the goods on the dragstrip. Special heads, cam and valve train boosted its 390 V-8's output to 340 hp and, thanks to a reworked suspension with the usual stiff suspension plus special springs and shocks that gave it a 2 inch rake, it was a supercar on the turns as well as the straight.

American Motors started the supercar era with an inventory virtually devoid of performance cars. When the days of horsepower unlimited came to an end, AMC had demonstrated many times over that it could learn quickly and well. It never totally shed its conservative image but, nonetheless, it produced a remarkable variety of performance automobiles that successfully broke the Big Three's monopoly on four wheeled excitement machines.

2. AMX

When Roy Chapin, Jr., took over as Board Chairman at American Motors in early 1967 he and his new President William V. Luneburg embarked on a grueling schedule of speech making and public appearances geared to convey the impression that AMC was not about to slip into its grave. This effort to buoy public confidence was buttressed by some hard and fast changes. The Rambler American, which at that time was going nowhere in terms of sales, became, thanks to a price cut, an item of interest to customers who were looking for an economy car. More important, at least in regard to the public's image of American Motors, were advertisements that proclaimed AMC would over the next three years be introducing a new car every six months.

Such a grandiose plan would have taken resources on the scale of the Big Three's unless it involved a good deal of parts interchangeability. This was achieved quite nicely. In the process AMC became adept at literally chopping off rear decks of Hornets and creating Gremlins and transforming Javelins into two-seater AMX's by slicing out twelve inch portions of their midsections.

The actual creation of the AMX was, of course, a good deal more sophisticated than the last sentence suggests, and as the first two-seater American car to go into relatively large scale production since the original Ford Thunderbird and Chevrolet Corvette, the AMX certainly deserves special recognition as a unique modern high performance automobile.

In actual chronological sequence, the AMX preceded the Javelin, being first displayed in January, 1966, at the National SAE Convention in Detroit. At that point, the AMX (American Motors Experimental) was nothing more than a fiberglass, non-operational shell, featuring a rumble seat.

The idea of the rumble seat was certainly clever, but in an age of Ralph Nader types it was just too risky a feature to see through production. However, in virtually every other aspect of its appearance, the AMX was a sensation. It effectively dispelled the image, in the words of an AMC official, ''that had slowly but solidly settled down on us, that of a company that turned out nice, dependable and economical cars, suitable for conservative adults and families.'' American Motors' recovery from this affliction gained momentum in June, 1966, when four ''Project IV'' showcars were displayed in cities across the nation. One of these was a fully driveable and roadable AMX with a steel body built by Vignale of Italy. Audience surveys indicated that the AMX was the most popular Project IV car by a margin of three to one. The appeal of the AMX plus the tremendous success of Lee Iacocca's Mustang suggested the obvious: market a four-seater pony car and a smaller two-passenger sports car, and not only would AMC grab a share of the former market but establish itself as a trend setter in the latter.

Journalists who had expected AMC to produce intact the original AMX with its mitered windshield, rectangular headlights and combined rocker panel-exhaust pipe exits were disappointed with what they saw in mid-March, 1968, when the AMX was introduced. Many of their criticisms were unjustified and unfair. Unlike Ford, which in 1963 had retro-created the Mustang II showcar out of the production Mustang, AMC had actually followed the path from dream car to production car. Most of the changes that took place along the way were necessary if the retail price of the AMX was to be kept within limits. In terms of overall dimensions

Below, 1968 AMX

the original AMX prototype was one inch shorter and four inches lower than the production model. Superficially, the AMX's 97 inch wheelbase was created by paring twelve inches away from the mid-portion of the Javelin chassis. This, however, suggests it was in the form of an afterthought. Actually, since the AMX and Javelin were developed for production concurrently, the body pressing was designed with dual use in mind.

Thanks to its smaller size, the AMX body at 755 pounds weighed 112 pounds less than the Javelin's. This lighter weight and more compact size gave the AMX better overall handling and less understeer than the Javelin.

American Motors experimental engineer, J. Kinemeth was responsible for the suspension design of the AMX. From the beginning, AMC planned to market the AMX as a limited production automobile intended for those who desired a high performance sports car. Thus, for its standard suspension the AMX was fitted with the Javelin handling option and was available with even stiffer springs and shocks. The standard AMX springs were rated at 120 and 130 lbs-in front and rear. Those of the optional handling package had corresponding ratings of 130 and 148 lbs-in. Rear trailing arms were also used to reduce axle hop. The handling of the AMX was further enhanced by the new wide-tread, fiberglass cord belted tires. These were supplied by Goodyear and put into production earlier than planned at AMC's request.

The standard AMX engine and transmission combination linked the 225 hp, 290 cid V-8 with a four-barrel carburetor and dual exhausts to a Warner T-10, close ratio, 4-speed transmission. The AMX was also the first AMC car to be available with its 315 hp, 390 cid V-8.

The ultimate high performance AMX was the super stock version, developed and assembled by Hurst Performance Research. Only 52 of these cars were produced, but with a horsepower rating beyond the 420 mark and a $5,994 price tag, they were super bargains as well as super performers.

Quarter-mile times of nearly 125 mph were easily within the realm of possibility for the Super Stock AMX.

American Motors first intended to race the AMX (group vice president Vic Raviolo once referred to it as "the Walter Mitty Ferrari") in SCCA Class A competition. Since its major adversaries would have been the 427 Stingray and Cobras this plan was quietly abandoned. Instead the AMX was handed over to Craig Breedlove who promptly set 106 speed records with it. Breedlove also prepared a special "AMX 600 Aerodynamx" kit for the AMX that included a revised fiberglass front end that reduced wind drag, a hood with NASA type ducts, a body pan to enclose the front suspension component and a rear air foil. In late 1968, under miserable conditions, Breedlove coaxed an AMX fitted with a sleeved-down version of the 401 cid engine displacing 373 cubic inches and sporting a GMC-Rootes type supercharger to a two-way, one mile average of 181.552 mph. Actually, the AMX did very well in SCCA competition. For example, Dwight Knapp raced an AMX prepared by a group of AMC engineers during the 1969 SCCA season in Class B production. Knapp won the SCCA's central division championship and placed a very close second in the Nationals to a well-driven Stingray.

After being virtually unchanged for the 1969 season, the AMX received a noselift for the 1970 year that incorporated twin, ram-air hood scoops and inboard-mounted parking lights. Its big 390 cid, 325 hp engine enabled it to finish the quarter-mile at just over 100 mph and reach 60 mph from rest in approximately 7 seconds.

After a three year production run of 19,134 cars, the two-seater AMX was dropped. It reappeared for 1971 as the Javelin AMX, the top of the line Javelin. While this change signaled the end of the AMX's individuality, it wasn't all bad. Mark Donohue was brought in to design its front and rear spoilers and, all in all, it was as much and maybe more

Above, 1968 AMX

of a sports car as before. In describing his role in the creation, Donohue remarked that, "I've done a street car, based on the Javelin . . . It's a design I felt was indicative of what a street car should be. The ride is harsh and the engine's pretty strong, but it's the kind of car I'd like to drive!" Coming from a man like Donohue, this was a strong endorsement of the character of the Javelin AMX.

Below, Top, 1969 AMX
Below, Bottom, 1970 AMX

Your father never told you there'd be Buicks like this.

'67 Buick GS-400. Engine: V-8. Bore & Stroke: 4.040 x 3.900. Horsepower: 340 @ 5000. Max. Torque: 440 lbs/ft @ 3200 rpm. Compression Ratio: 10.25:1. Carburetion: Single, 4bbl. Suspension: Front — Coil Spring and Ball Joint. Rear — Coil Springs. Steering: Recirculating Ball Nut. Wheels: 14-6.00 "JK". Tires: 7.75 x 14. Fuel Capacity: 20 gallons. Transmission type and final drive ratio: Manual 3-speed 3.36. Available are Manual 4-speed 3.36 and Automatic 2.93. Brakes: Duo-Servo. Available are Front Disc brakes. All GM safety features are standard.

BUICK MOTOR DIVISION

3. Buick

Buick's behavior in the performance car field was strongly affected both by its position in the General Motors automotive hierarchy and by a solid record of sales success. Placed just below Cadillac in prestige, Buick, when it built supercars, invariably priced them a good deal higher than Chevrolets or Fords offering as good or better performance. As a result, Buick never was a big seller among the supercars. However, while Buick had its marketing ups and downs, for the most part these setbacks were due to developments far afield from the supercar spectrum. After producing over 738,000 automobiles for the 1955 model year, Buick output fell into a tailspin, dropping under 280,000 in 1961. From that point, Buick gradually regained strength but not until 1973 was the old 1955 record broken.

Beginning in 1936 and lasting until 1942, Buick's prewar Centurys had enjoyed a justified reputation as quick automobiles and the 1941 version's dual carburetion system was a harbinger of things to come. There was little in the Buicks of the postwar forties that matched the old Century's get up and go, however. Instead, it seemed Buick's faithful old straight eight would just go on forever.

This was, of course, not to be the case since Buick, along with the rest of the GM stable, had been working on a V-8 engine for many years and when its Golden Anniversary arrived in 1953 the division was ready to commemorate the occasion with a new, 322 cid, ohv V-8. The output (in the Roadmaster series) was a respectable 188 hp, with a four-barrel carburetor and 8.5:1 compression ratio, which was then the highest of any American production automobile, but the matching of Buick's V-8 engine to the dated styling of its 1953 Supers and Roadmasters was an act akin to the putting of new wine into old goatskin. Clearly, it deserved better, and, in 1954, Buick came forth with both a new chassis and fresh, modern, revitalized styling. It was the proper time for Buick to resurrect not only the Century series but also its reputation for hot acceleration. Whereas the 1953 Roadmaster V-8 still moved in leisurely fashion from zero to 60 mph in 15.6 seconds, the 1954 Century needed only 12 seconds. Credit for this capability was shared by the Century's 200 hp, 322 cid V-8 and its relatively light, 122 inch wheelbase Special series body. The Century retailed for $250 more than an equivalent, 150 hp Special model but few potential customers balked at this cost. The Century was the fastest American car through the quarter-mile (17.9 seconds) tested by *MOTOR TREND* during 1954. *MECHANIX ILLUSTRATED* (July, 1954) reported that Tom McCahill, "not usually a Buick lover" found the Century "to be hot as a pistol."

By virtue of a 9.0:1 compression ratio and slightly enlarged (1.38 inch instead of 1.25 inch diameter) exhaust valves the 1955 Century with 236 hp broke through the then magical 10 second barrier for the zero to 60 mph run. Thanks to a longer duration cam and another boost in compression ratio, this time to 9.5:1, Buick's 1956 Century had 255 hp to push it to 60 mph in 9.6 seconds. One publication, *AUTO AGE*, reported a 9.1 second time. But the Century's image suffered at the hands of its new chassis and altered suspension which gave it an excessive amount of lean in the turns.

On the surface, Buick's position as a quick-motion

machine seemed secure for 1957. After all, new styling, an engine redesign and a new ball-joint front suspension offered a good deal to speculate about, but this time around the dream was better than the reality. Not the least of the Buick's problems that year was its new bodies whose old hat appearance nearly disguised the fact that they were new. The problem wasn't that they were terribly unattractive, rather that they looked like the 1954's with more bright work draped on them. This time around Harley Earl's gang had clearly been bested by the men at Chrysler.

Buick's 1957 V-8 was opened up to 364 cubic inches and fitted with larger, 1.88 inch intake and 1.44 inch exhaust valves. It was certainly willing enough and in the Century, Super and Roadmaster series it was rated at 300 hp. Unfortunately, most road testers found the 1957 Century a slower accelerating car than the earlier models. Zero to 60 mph in 10.1 seconds wasn't a disgrace but events were moving so rapidly in the performance field that even a slight regression was magnified into a major retreat.

This is not to say Buick's V-8 lacked potential. Far from it. On the West Coast, for example, Bill Murphy's Buick-powered Kurtis had no difficulty staying with and often finishing out front of the Ferraris. Buick itself offered an "export" cam kit consisting of a long-duration, high lift cam, solid lifters, special, heavy-duty, 11.0:1 compression ratio domed pistons, dual valve springs and big-port manifolds. This package boosted horsepower to a very healthy 330 at 4800 rpm. As Roger Huntington noted in *CAR LIFE* (December, 1962), "Buick's performance development in the '55-'57 period was relatively half hearted and the result was inevitable." Furthermore, the years immediately following were characterized by more of the same type of neglect.

There were a few bright spots. The use of finned, aluminum front brake drums on the 1958 models gave them the best set of brakes in the industry and the following year Buick's engine was enlarged again to a healthy 401 cubic inches. The 1960 Invicta, even with this 325 hp engine, was not a supercar by any stretch of the imagination, however: zero to 60 mph in 11.5 seconds meant nothing. Yet, early in 1960 at Daytona a team of Invictas averaged over 120 mph for 20,000 miles — good enough, if USAC of FIA representatives had been on hand, to have set numerous new records.

Any serious attempt by Buick to recapture some of its performance reputation was still several years away. In 1961, the big news from Buick was the new, 155 hp, 215 cid aluminum V-8 in the compact Special. When the nicely styled Skylark coupe joined the Special lineup later that year, its engine, thanks to a four-barrel carburetor and higher 10.25:1 compression ratio (instead of 8.8:1) developed a strong 185 hp. With "Dual-Path" automatic transmission, the Skylark's zero to 60 mph time was 10.9 seconds. The following year a jump in compression ratio to 11.0:1 moved its maximum horsepower up to 190, good enough to enable a 4-speed Skylark to break the ten second mark from zero to 60 mph.

"A top-handling performer that likes to GO in luxury" was *MOTOR TREND's* (August, 1962) opinion of Buick's, 1962½ Wildcat model. Back in 1953, the Wildcat had been

a Motorama dream car. In its production form, it was basically an Invicta hardtop with either a black or white fabric top with an all-vinyl interior sporting front bucket seats. The only engine available for the Wildcat was the 401 cid V-8 with a 10.25:1 compression ratio and rated at 325 hp with 445 lbs-ft. The identical V-8 was also available in Invicta and Electra models but the Wildcat did enjoy a lower 3.42:1 rear axle ratio. The Wildcat still wallowed in the bends but it did have those great aluminum drum front brakes and it could move from zero to 60 mph in just over 8 seconds. In 1963, the ten year old Buick engine was expanded to 425 cubic inches and in this size was offered in two optional forms for the Wildcat. With a single Carter four-barrel carburetor, 340 hp was developed at 4400 rpm. The Super Wildcat engine with dual four-barrels developed 360 hp, nearly twice as much as had the old, 1953 version.

A 360 hp, 4-speed Wildcat was both quick and agile.

With its 123 inch wheelbase it was a big machine, but as *MOTOR TREND* (June, 1964) reported, "In any type of corner the car *feels* as though it weighs about half as much as it really does." As to its quickness, the Wildcat's zero to 60 mph time of 7.7 seconds spoke for itself.

This Wildcat 360 hp engine was the standard powerplant for the GS (Gran Sport) version of the 1965 Riviera and moved that machine through the quarter-mile in 15.5 seconds, but neither Wildcats nor Rivieras put Buick into the performance mainstream of the mid-sixties. That task fell to the Skylark Gran Sport which debuted in late 1964. Edward D. Rollert, Buick's general manager, described the Gran Sport as "a completely engineered performance car . . . designed to appeal to sport car enthusiasts." Such

Above, 1962 Buick Skylark

16

a build up was hard for any car to fulfill and tended to magnify the first generation Gran Sport's short comings.

The Gran Sport was available in convertible, hardtop or thin-pillar coupe body styles, all of which were attached to a beefed-up Skylark convertible frame. Although the Gran Sport was not fitted with a rear sway bar, its road behavior was good, thanks to stiffer springs, specially valved shocks and larger 0.94 inch diameter front anti-roll bar. Its standard transmission was a Ford-built, all-synchromesh 3-speed unit with a floor shift. The Warner 4-speed with a 2.20 low was optional as was the 2-speed Super Turbine 300 automatic with an added disc installed in its clutch pack. The Gran Sport's engine was the veteran 401, which, in order to keep the GM shoguns happy, Buick was forced to label a 400 cid V-8 when used in the GS in spite of its actual 401.04 cubic inch displacement.

Unfortunately, Buick chose not to outfit the Gran Sport with its finned aluminum drums, deciding instead to go (or stop, as it were) with the far too weak, 9.5 inch x 2.5 inch drums used on run-of-the-mill Specials.

At the 1965 Winternationals, a GS Skylark did manage a highly respectable 13.42 sec., 104.66 mph run but the typical GS for the street suffered from the small valves of its "nailhead" V-8. It was the time for a new V-8 and after a 14 year production run Buick put the old unit out to pasture and replaced it with up-to-date 400 and 430 cid versions. Both had 10.25:1 compression ratios, very large, 3.25 inch main bearings and good sized 2.00 inch intake and 1.625 inch exhaust valves. The only significant difference between the two were their bore sizes; the 430's was 4.187 inches, the 400's, 4.04 inches. In terms of power these engines with a four-barrel Quadrajet carburetor developed 340 and 360 hp, respectively.

In 1966, the Gran Sport had still been part of the Skylark line. For 1967, it received separate GS400 status. More importantly, the new 400 cid V-8 was just what the Gran Sport needed. Now its good handling was linked to an engine that had good breathing characteristics and could rev up to 6000 rpm. *CAR LIFE* (January, 1967) described it as "the Dark Horse of the Year . . . Although it still has a 400 cubic inch engine in the intermediate sized chassis, the whole character of the car has undergone a transformation."

Now, with the Super Turbine automatic transmission, it turned the quarter-mile in 14.7 seconds and 97 mph, and reached 60 mph from rest in 6.0 seconds. Buick had also seen the need for better brakes and the GS400 had as standard equipment finned aluminum front drums with Delco Moraine front discs available as options.

The ultimate Gran Sport arrived in 1969, highlighted by a "Cool Air" induction system available for both the GS350 (introduced in 1968 as a 280 hp, 350 cid alternative to the 400 cid V-8) and the GS400 plus a Special Stage 1 option. Buick still rated the GS400 with Cool Air at 340 hp but reported that in tests conducted with an air temperature of 100 degrees the Cool Air package increased peak horsepower by 8%.

The principle elements of Stage 1 included a hotter cam, revised lubrication system, specially calibrated carburetor, fuel pump and exhaust system along with a heavy-duty cooling system. Also included was a 3.42:1 Positraction rear axle. In this form the GS engine was rated at 345 hp, but the following year, with GM abandoning its old 400 cid limit for its intermediates, Buick opened the gate on the GS455 Stage 1, a 360 hp, 455 cid creation that in street form ran the quarter-mile in 13.38 sec and 105.50 mph. Thanks to the 510 lbs-ft of torque at 2800 rpm, this Super-Buick needed only 5.5 seconds to travel from zero to 60 mph.

It was quite a way for Buick to end an era. After a slow start it hit its stride in high style and even as late as 1972, when low-lead, low-compression engines were dominant, a GS Stage 1 was still running 14 second quarter-miles. Buick had its share of rough times in the fifties and sixties but with a finish like that they were of little consequence. It is better to recall that when better performance cars were built, at least some had Buick nameplates attached to them.

Below, 1970 Buick GTS

Jewels by Van Cleef & Arpels

There are, of course, many obvious and excellent reasons for making the move to Cadillac. There is the car's beautiful styling, for instance, its magnificent performance, its marvelous luxury . . . and, of course, its great prestige. But there is also another important Cadillac characteristic which every motorist should keep in mind when he is considering the car—*its phenomenally long life*. A few years ago, a great tire manufacturer actually ran three Cadillacs in its test fleet close to a million miles each—and then sold them into private ownership where they are still in active service. And there are innumerable instances of Cadillacs as old as fifteen—and even twenty years of age — which are still driven with pride and satisfaction. Naturally, the man who takes possession of a new Cadillac does not anticipate owning the car for so long a time . . . or driving it over so many miles. But he finds it reassuring to know that the car is *capable* of such extraordinary service. For it means that he will enjoy the utmost in dependability through whatever period he elects to own the car . . . and that he can expect an unusually high return on his investment at the time of resale. Have you driven a 1953 Cadillac? If you haven't, you should visit your Cadillac dealer today. He'll be delighted to see you.

CADILLAC MOTOR CAR DIVISION ★ GENERAL MOTORS CORPORATION

4. Cadillac

In a very real sense, the renaissance of the American performance machine began in January, 1949, when Cadillac introduced its new 160hp, 331 cid overhead valve V-8. By the mid-fifties Cadillac was surpassed by both its lesser-light siblings and the performance oriented products from Ford and Chrysler. Yet, the significance of Cadillac as a standard for both brute power and straight line performance cannot be lightly dismissed. Both in the U.S. and in Europe, its ability to cover ground quickly was recognized and respected. The British publication, THE MOTOR (March 22, 1950), described its 1950 Cadillac test car as possessing a "performance which few makes can rival, even fewer surpass." Briggs Cunningham had loaned his Cadillac 62 Special to THE MOTOR for testing purposes and although it was not in the best state of tune it still attained a one-way speed of 101.1 mph, a feat which at that time only one other closed automobile, the Healey, had exceeded. Two years later, MOTOR TREND (September, 1952) awarded Cadillac its 1952 Engineering Achievement Award for "Outstanding Technical Achievement in Engine Performance, Handling Qualities, Safety Characteristics (and) Operational Economy." Moreover, Cadillacs were proving their mettle in open competition.

In the first (1950) Mexican Road Race, a Cadillac finished a close second to Hershel McGriff's Oldsmobile, and at LeMans that year a basically stock Cadillac Coupe de Ville finished tenth overall with a 81.54 mph average. By 1954, Chrysler's 235 hp V-8 was highly regarded for its acceleration but THE AUTOCAR (July 2, 1954) reported nearly identical performance figures for the Chrysler and the 230 hp Cadillac:

	Cadillac	Chrysler
0-30/mph	3.6/seconds	4.3/seconds
0-60/mph	11.4/seconds	11.1/seconds
Top speed	114.8/mph	114.6/mph

However, MOTOR TREND gave Cadillac the zero to 60 mph edge over Chrysler: 11.3 seconds to 12.3 seconds. Besides Chrysler, the only American sedan that could seriously challenge the Cadillac 62 in a zero to 60 mph drag race was the 200 hp Buick Century. Because of its ability, MOTOR TREND, (November, 1954), recognized the Cadillac as the hottest-performing car of 1954, describing it "as the fastest car under conditions where you want, or at least have, speed — from a traffic signal, at cruising speeds on the highway for passing and at the top end."

The following year the Cadillac 62 was still a tough car to beat on the street. AUTO AGE (January, 1956) regarded it as a car worthy of an "Index of Performance" award since it combined acceleration only slightly inferior to the Buick Century but better than the C-300's and with a top speed between them.

No doubt Cadillac could have fielded a worthy competitor to Chrysler's 300. Although the Eldorado Biarritz and Seville models of 1957 were more for show than go, they did have 365 cid "Q" engines with triple, two-barrel carburetors and a 355 hp rating. If Cadillac had chosen to climb into the ring with Chrysler, a very interesting hammer and tongs battle between two American super heavyweights would have ensued. Cadillac did not care to indulge in such adventurous behavior, however, resorting instead to a more dignified marketing of luxury motor cars. Still, as the manufacturer who was there first with a modern V-8, Cadillac's role in performance history, as short as it was, nevertheless was a significant one.

Below, 1954 Cadillac Series 62 Coupe

CHEVROLET IMPALA SUPER SPORT CONVERTIBLE

SPIRIT LIFTER

If you'd like to get away from it all, and who wouldn't, this Chevrolet will take you farther, fancier, than anything else we can think of. Take an Impala Convertible like the one shown, or, if a hard top is more to your taste, take an Impala Sport Coupe. Then add the optional-at-extra-cost Super Sport stuff: contoured bucket seats in front, special coil springs at all four wheels, distinctive wheel covers and special SS identification. If this isn't enough to make you want to take tomorrow off, there's more. Additional extra-cost options include a four-speed stick shift or floor-shift Powerglide, heavy-duty shocks for better handling, seat belts for safety, Positraction for better bite, an electric tachometer to help you keep an eye on the standard 195 horsepower V8 or optional V8's from 250 to 300, 340, 400 and up to 425 eager horses. Once your dealer has delivered your Chevy, with goodies on it, you'll never again have to put up with anybody else's wild tales about performance. You'll be driving a Chevrolet, old friend. That's the one they invented the word for!
Chevrolet Division of General Motors, Detroit 2, Michigan

The make more people depend on

20

5. Chevrolet

Prior to 1955, Chevrolet's most notable postwar performance achievement was a class victory in the 1953 Mexican Road Race. For car enthusiasts who appreciated the rigors posed by racing the length of Mexico and just finishing, let alone winning, this success reinforced Chevrolet's reputation as a tough automobile. It did not, however do very much to change its image as an automobile virtually devoid of features usually associated with performance. That had to wait until 1955 when Chevrolet's 162 horsepower, 265 cubic inch V-8 arrived. Even in this workaday form, attached to the reliable, but not exactly exciting, Powerglide transmission, it was strong enough to push a Chevy sedan from zero to 60 mph in 12.3 seconds. There were of course quicker cars on the market, but clearly the handwriting was on the wall; this engine came very close in reality to matching its advertised output, and once a dash of adrenalin arrived in the form of Chevy's version of the mid-fifties powerpack it did indeed become "The Hot One."

Shortly after Chevrolet's powerpack became available, *ROAD & TRACK* (February, 1955), proffered the opinion that "it certainly appears that a Chevrolet V-8 with optional 180 hp engine and 4.11 axle will out-accelerate any American car on the market today." Testing such a car with a 3-speed/overdrive transmission, *ROAD & TRACK* recorded a zero to 60 mph time of 9.7 seconds. At Daytona, the 180 hp Chevy with an 8:1 compression ratio, dual exhausts and four-barrel carburetor won its class championship with a "flying mile" speed of 112.877 mph, and defeated all opposition in the acceleration runs by virtue of a 78.158 mph speed. Only a 1955 Cadillac driven by Mexican Road Race veteran, Joe Littlejohn, achieved a higher speed in the acceleration runs.

Later in 1955, Chevrolet sedans appeared with the solid lifter, hot cam 195 hp version of the 265 V-8 used in some late model Corvettes. These were most certainly the fastest zero to 60 mph five-passenger cars built in the U.S.

Chevrolet started off the second year of its performance age with a top rating of 205 hp. This engine deceptively produced just 3% more torque at the same rpm as the powerpack equipped 1955 version but maintained a strong torque output throughout the power range, turning out, for example, 234 lbs-ft at 4600 rpm. Later in the season, the use of dual four-barrel carburetors increased the Chevy's output to 225 hp at 5200 rpm.

Like many new designs, Chevrolet's V-8 was not free from early valve and oil consumption problems, but these were soon corrected and some impressive examples of its durability, aside from its racing successes, were forthcoming. Shortly after its introduction in 1955, Chevrolet chief engineer Ed Cole reported that one Chevy V-8 successfully passed a 35 hour, 5500 rpm test. In the spring of 1956 a stock, 225 hp sedan averaged 101.58 mph for 24 hours at the 1.37 mile Darlington, South Carolina, track.

Having been firmly established as one of America's premier performance automobiles in 1955 and 1956, Chevrolet faced a severe challenge from both Ford and Plymouth in 1957. By creating the special Fury model,

Plymouth had scored a point over its competitors since it was, with all-new and very advanced styling, a very visible and very imposing automobile. Ford's styling was also all-new but, in contrast to Plymouth's, far more subdued. The use of a supercharger, however, helped Ford to maintain the performance momentum carried over from 1956. Against these forces what did Chevrolet pull out of the bag? Not much, really, just a fabulous restyling of a three year old body shell that was destined to become a postwar favorite. Not much really, just an ⅛ inch bore increase that transformed the 265 V-8 into a 283 engine destined to become a performance classic. Not much really, just a fuel-injection option that enabled Chevrolet to claim 283 hp or one horsepower per cubic inch. Not much, indeed!

Chevrolet not only received new bodies in 1958, but also a new engine. It seemed a good idea at the time to develop an engine that could serve equally well in either a truck or passenger car and thus a 348 cid V-8 debuted in 1958. From the start its attributes as a performance engine were suspect. *MOTOR LIFE* (June, 1958) observed, in regard to the 283 and 348 V-8s, ". . . The little one goes and the big one doesn't . . . Nobody seems able to make the big engine substantially out-perform the small one in top-end horsepower." Four years later, when the 348 was phased out, *CAR LIFE* (April, 1962) described the 327 cid version of the original 1955 V-8 as developing "more honest horsepower . . . than the larger 348 cid V-8 it replaces as the power option for 1962 Chevrolet passenger cars."

Obviously, the reputation of the W, or 348, engine wasn't helped by such unfavorable comparisons. Aside from its larger displacement, the 348 was 1.5 inches longer and 2.6 inches wider than the 283 and weighed approximately 110 pounds more. This greater bulk naturally reduced its versatility but the very respectable record it eventually chalked up suggests that the 348 was not quite the lump some critics considered it to be.

For 1958, Chevrolet offered the 348 either with 250 hp or 280 hp. The former version carried a 9.5:1 compression ratio and either a Carter or Rochester four-barrel carburetor. More interesting was the triple-two-barrel Rochester setup, identical to the Oldsmobile J-2 and Pontiac Tri-Power arrangements, that yielded the earlier mentioned 280 hp as well as 355 lbs-ft of torque.

A look at some of the statistics of the 1958 Chevrolet easily explains why a 280 hp, 1958 Chevrolet was markedly inferior to a 283 hp, 1957 model in performance. The newer model's wheelbase was 2½ inches longer, its overall length had grown by 9 inches and total weight had increased by 150 pounds. Unrelated to straight line performance, but still rather grim, was the reduction of the '58's brake lining area to 157 from 169 square inches. It's true all this shrinkage came at the rear where less stress was put upon the brakes, but it wasn't exactly the type of change welcomed by enthusiasts.

Midway through the 1958 model year the 348 began to shake off its slightly shoddy reputation when Chevrolet offered its "Law Enforcement" engine to anyone willing to hand over an additional $229 to his friendly local Chevrolet dealer. To put it bluntly, this option made the '58 Chevy one

Left, 1963 Chevrolet Impala Super Sport

of the hottest cars in America. The list of goodies that transformed the 348 from an ugly duckling into contender for King of the Road status began with the familiar triple deuces. Then were added the Duntov cam with solid lifters, a heavy-duty clutch and a close-ratio, 3-speed transmission borrowed from the Corvette. Rated at 315 horsepower, the Law Enforcement engine was equipped with heavy duty main and connecting rod bearings plus 11.0:1 compression ratio pistons and clearances for valve overlap. All Chevys equipped with this engine, which was also available with a single four-barrel and a 300 hp rating, had stronger than stock clutches, larger fuel tanks, stiffer suspension plus cerametallic brake linings.

After testing the 315 hp with a 4.56 rear axle and recording a zero to 60 mph time of 7.2 seconds, *SPORTS CAR ILLUSTRATED* (January, 1959), which liked the Chevy very much, concluded, "It sounds precisely like what it is: a legitimate racing engine." With a 3.36 rear axle its top speed was an imposing 135 mph.

Variations on this basic theme were developed for both the 1959 and 1960 Chevrolet. The 1960 lineup included three hot 348's, the mildest with a 11.0:1 compression ratio and 305 hp at 5600 rpm was available only with Power-glide. Both this engine and a 11.25:1 compression ratio, 320 hp version breathed through a single four-barrel carburetor. At the top was a 335 hp heavyweight with triple two-barrels available with four different transmissions: 3- or 4-speed manuals, (the 4-speed linked to a floorshifter), Powerglide or Turboglide. For less adventurous souls, the 348 was offered with either a single four-barrel and 250 hp as well as the triple carburetor version with 280 hp.

The increasing sophistication of the American supercar and the need for Chevrolet to remain competitive with its archrival from Dearborn made 1961 a year of action and advances at Chevrolet. Shortly after its slightly downsized and infinitely more attractive new models went on sale, Chevrolet let loose its Super Turbo-Thrust Special V-8. This name never won any plaudits from literary critics but it sufficed to identify an engine that delivered over 1 hp from each of its 348 cubic inches, for a total of 350 hp. This V-8 was a first class piece of machinery. Such components as valves, rocker arms, pushrods, pistons, connecting rods and crankshafts first received the regular product quality check and then were re-examined for dimensional accuracy, integrity of construction and proper surface finish. The close control Chevrolet exercised over the assembly of these engines assured their purchasers that they were nearly hand built.

Another important feature of this V-8 was its special cam and high speed valve system (it developed its peak power at 6000 rpm). The lifters were, not unexpectedly, mechanical and the valves were fitted with dual springs and aluminized faces. To handle the 364 lbs-ft of torque available at 3600 rpm, a clutch with a 370 lbs-ft capacity was used, with either a 3- or 4-speed manual transmission.

The rapid obsolescence of the Super Turbo-Thrust Special V-8 was a reflection both of how competitive the performance wars had become and how determined Chevrolet was to keep pace with its opponents.

In time for the 1961 NHRA Winternationals held at Pomona, California, Chevrolet unveiled a bored and stroked version of the 348, the memorable "409." The cam in the 409, described by *MOTOR TREND* (September, 1961) as "The most radical of any appearing in a Chevrolet product" provided more lift, 0.4396 inches to 0.4058 inches than the version used in the 350 hp, 348 cid V-8. A single Carter four-barrel with 1.62 inch primaries and 1.68 inch secondaries was another feature of the early 409. Chevrolet rated the 409 at a relatively conservative 360 hp at 5800 rpm, but at an impressive 409 lbs-ft of torque at 3600 rpm. To handle this additional power, a stronger clutch was also specified.

In its first competition appearance, the new Chevy emerged as the Super Stock champion at Pomona, clicking off a best run of 109.48 mph in 13.19 seconds. In street form, the same car was still very quick, running the quarter-mile in 13.9 seconds and crossing the finish line at 103 mph. Its zero to 60 mph time was 5.75 seconds.

Thus the stage was set for the introduction later in the year of the first Impala SS, identifiable by its SS medallion above the keyhole on the rear deck and similar ones on the rear fenders. The typical SS409 was not as fast as the race-tuned Super Stock Winternationals winner but it was still imposing. The factory required that all Super Sport Chevys with the 360 hp, 409 engine be equipped with a 3.36:1 rear axle, but dealers could replace it with a 4.56 ratio that made quarter-mile times of 14.02 seconds routine.

The definitive SS409 was equipped with RPO#1108, the police option chassis that included stiffer springs, heavy-duty shocks and larger stabilizer bars. Since the 409 engine weighed 660 pounds to the 530 pounds of the 327, these changes merely kept the Super Sport's handling within

Below, 1955 Chevrolet Bel Air

reasonable limits rather than moving it up a notch or two.

For 1962, the 348 engine was dropped from Chevrolet's passenger car powerplant lineup. Replacing it was a variation of the 409 with a single four-barrel carburetor and a 10.2:1 compression ratio achieved by using two head gaskets. Output was a healthy 380 hp. With dual Carter AFB four-barrel carburetors and a 11.15:1 compression ratio, horsepower rose to a claimed 409 at 6000 rpm. Such a cursory pass over of this engine hardly does it justice. Consider these comments made by *CAR LIFE:* ''This new 409 cu-in engine looks like the most potent of all the '400' engines . . . the 409 with optional 4-speed transmission is a well-brewed cup of tea. It is a car for the capable, responsible man who knows and appreciates finely designed and tuned machinery . . . It's just about as exciting an automobile as you can buy.''

The object of all this unbridled enthusiasm quite obviously had to be something special, and it was. The 409's cam with a 0.480 inch lift, valve springs of 340 lb. tension, instead of 320, and a new chrome alloy head with 2.19 inch diameter intake valves (the 1961 409 head provided for valves of 2.07 inch diameter) gave each cylinder an excellent breathing capacity. To reduce back pressure as much as possible, larger dual exhaust (2.5 inch diameter) and tailpipes (2.0 inch diameter) were also specified. And there was still more. Mandatory items included a fuel pump with nearly twice the output as the stock unit, a stronger clutch with coil springs instead of diaphragm action, and heavy-duty police springs and shocks front and rear. Among the recommended options were sintered-iron brake linings, 8.00 x 14 tires and wheels, and either the 4-speed, all synchromesh transmission or a heavy-duty 3-speed.

Chevrolet offered the 409 in either form in any body style except the station wagon and, regardless of what Chevy it powered, the 409 was a history maker and a record breaker. In June, 1962, Don Nicholson's Bel Air hardtop coupe set up for drag racing, but still a stock car as defined by the NHRA, turned a 12.22 second, 115 mph quarter-mile run. At the least, its engine developed 430 hp, allowing it to run

Above, 1957 Chevrolet Bel Air

from zero to 60 mph in four seconds; zero to 100 mph in 12.2 seconds. Even a 380 hp, 409 pulling a heavy, 3,500 pound convertible equipped with a 4-speed transmission and a 3.36:1 rear axle could make the zero to 60 mph dash in 7.6 seconds. With a 3.08:1 axle and no mufflers, *MOTOR TREND* (December, 1961) reported, it could reach a top speed of 150 mph.

It was also the 409 that ended a two-year-plus drought for Chevrolet on the NASCAR Grand National Circuit. Until the October 28, 1962, running of the Dixie 400 at Atlanta International Raceway, Chevrolet had not won a Grand National victory since Junior Johnson's on June 10, 1960, at Charlotte. At Atlanta the triumphant Chevrolet driver was Rex White who afterwards explained, ''We just haven't had the horsepower that Pontiac and Ford have been getting. We've tried a couple of new optional high-performance items during that time (1960-62), and the block has been steadily increased in displacement. But all we seemed to get for our efforts was one new headache after another.'' White's frustrations were not without substance for in each of the eight major Grand National races prior to the Dixie 400 either White or Ned Jarrett had blown their Chevy engines. Indeed, at Atlanta Jarrett had lasted just 12 laps before he drifted into his pit with a broken crankshaft.

Chevrolet offered a toned down version of the 409 in 1963 with a moderate cam, a single four-barrel, hydraulic lifters and a 10.0:1 compression ratio. Even with Power-glide (that in fairness was probably a better performing automatic transmission than it was usually given credit for), this engine was capable of very impressive performance: zero to 60 mph in 6.6 seconds, zero to 100 mph in 19.5. Other contemporary road tests didn't quite match these figures from *CAR LIFE* (March, 1963) but they still left no doubt that this engine and transmission made for a very livable, non-tempermental automobile with supercar capability. When mated to the 340 hp 409 engine, Powerglide was assembled with many heavy-duty components, having a 1.82:1 instead of 1.75:1 low ratio and upshifting at 5000 instead of the usual 4500 rpm.

The 380 hp and 409 hp engines were upgraded respectively for 1963 to 400 hp and 425 hp, certainly enough to keep the pot boiling but not as interesting as a mid-season Z-11 option offered with the proviso that, "Buyers require approval from the Central Sales Office before the order can be filled." They also had to be well-heeled since the Z-11 package, available only on the Impala 2-door hardtop, carried a price tag of $1,237.40. The heart of the Z-11 was the 409 engine given a larger 4.406 inch bore, yielding a total of 427 cubic inches and 430 hp. The usual performance paraphernalia of 4-speed transmission, heavy-duty suspension, Positraction, dual exhausts and metallic brake linings were also included. Thanks to its aluminum hood, front fenders and bumpers, the Z-11 also was a couple of hundred pounds lighter than earlier SS409 models. Led by the Z-11, Chevrolet did well at the 1963 Winternationals, winning ten classes including Z/Stock at 12.66 sec and 114.58 mph.

What happened next to Chevrolet gave new meaning to the opening line of Charles Dicken's *TALE OF TWO CITIES:* "It was the best of times and the worst of times." First, a look at the bad news. It was Monday, January 21, 1963, that the word was delivered from the 14th floor of the GM building in Detroit to all GM divisions outlawing performance activities. That kind of management edict was painfully bitter to swallow but it had to be at least publicly obeyed.

There was to be no more involvement in either racing or any other performance oriented activities by any GM automotive division. In a spirit of unfettered charity, the corporate demigods gave their subordinates until the end of February to comply with this edict. As virtually every automobile enthusiast knows, this requirement produced a bull market for white lies and subterfuge in the short run, but it torpedoed a season of rough, tough, no quarter asked or given, NASCAR racing between Ford, Chevrolet and Plymouth.

Coming into town for the Daytona 500 were five Chevys with engines that had just avoided the anti-racing meat-cleaver. The response from the motor press after they had a chance to strut their stuff was resounding, with *MOTOR TREND* probably saying it all: "The most powerful high performance engine at the 1963 Daytona 500 . . .," May, 1963 issue. "There's certainly never been anything like it in an American car. It's a pity that development of this fabu-

lous engine has to be dropped under the new GM anti-racing policy," October, 1963 issue.

Whether known as the Mark II 427, the porcupine V-8 or the mystery engine, this new Chevy creation, pumping out an estimated 575 hp at 6000 rpm enabled Junior Johnson, on the first day of qualifying runs, to set a new 163.681 mph, two-lap record. NASCAR never got the chance to enter it into the record books as John Rutherford soon exceeded it with a 165.183 mph average in a Smokey Yunick Chevrolet.

(During late 1962, a NASCAR Chevrolet had been extensively tested at GM's five mile track at Mesa, Arizona. Top speeds beyond 180 mph were recorded with numerous laps covered at speeds of over 178 mph. One 500 mile stretch was covered at 172-plus mph. An acceleration run in high gear from 90 mph to 150 mph was accomplished in 18 seconds. A similar test of a car powered by the older 427 required 31 seconds.)

Rutherford's car was the highest placed Chevy in the race but ninth place, behind a Ford romp of the first five places wasn't terribly noteworthy. The Mark II engine was just too new to expect a victory the first time out.

A victory did come to Chevy's new engine on June 30, 1963, at the Dixie 400. Junior Johnson, a loyal Chevrolet campaigner since 1955, was the winning driver. This success was not enough of an encouragement for Johnson and his chief mechanic, Ray Fox, to continue fighting against the numerically superior and far better equipped Ford forces. Johnson also won the Charlotte National 400 but that was the end. Fox called it "a last ditch effort that took every last part I had and some I had to borrow." Johnson drove a Mercury in 1964 and, looking back over his losses of 1963, he declared, "I don't know that we would've lost any of them if Chevrolet had stayed in racing and given us the help with parts we needed."

But Chevy was out of racing and for a time it looked as if its day of glory as a street machine was also part of the past. For 1965, the dual-quad carburetor option was dropped leaving a 400 hp version of the 409 as its top performance engine. This low ebb was the turning of the tide, however, and just after January 1, 1965, the son of Mark II, in 396

Below, 1958 Chevrolet Impala

cubic inch form, was in production, roughly coinciding with the introduction of the Caprice Custom Sedan. Initially the 396 was offered in three forms, 325 hp, 375 hp and 425 hp. The 375 hp version was reserved for use in the Chevelle and so won't be evaluated here. The 325/396 was a nice unfussy engine with hydraulic lifters, a moderate cam, single exhaust and either a single Rochester 4 MV Quadra Jet or Holley 4160 carburetor. It served as a smooth and reasonably quick propeller of the Caprice, which, since Chevy intended it to be a competitor to the LTD Ford, was anything but a rapid express machine. That task was handled quite nicely by the 425 hp engine, which, while sharing a common heritage with its lesser sibling, was in many ways a horse of a different color. For example, it carried a larger Holley 4150 four-barrel carburetor, with 1.686 inch barrels mounted on a big port aluminum manifold, larger 2.19 inch to 1.72 inch exhaust valves, special heat-treated connecting rods, molybdenum coated piston rings, four bolt main bearing caps (instead of two) and impact extrusion pistons in place of the casted ones used on the 325 engine. The price of the 325 horsepower engine was $161, and the 425 was $376, above that of Chevy's base V-8.

"The 1955 Chevrolet V-8 revised everyone's idea of what a production engine can do. Here we go again, Charlie — TURBO-JET 396 V-8." Thus read one of Chevrolet's famous performance ads, and that time, anyway, the copywriters weren't exaggerating. The 396 was as much of a clone of the Mark II as Chevrolet dared to manufacture while GM's anti-racing philosophy was in the driver's seat. The Chevrolet boys would have preferred to market this engine as a 427 cubic incher but Corporate policy prohibited an engine larger than 400 cubic inches in the A-bodied cars. Unless it wanted to leave the Chevelle out in the cold, Chevrolet had no choice but to put the Mark II on a dis-

placement reduction diet. None of this hurt the 396, of course. Its super sized valves, superb porting and excellent thermal efficiency were just a few of the characteristics prompting John R. Bond of *CAR LIFE* (March, 1965) to conclude, "It is, without a doubt, the most advanced V-8 design on the general market today."

Officially, Chevrolet was out of racing, but rumors were rife that some NASCAR campaigners were receiving Chevy engines ready to race from the factory. Jim Hall, the man behind the Chaparral, was running his car with a 396 Chevrolet engine even before it was announced to the public. It would have made for neat automotive history if Chevrolet had come on strong on the super tracks, swept both Ford and Plymouth into its dust and emerged as the champion of the Grand Nationals. Yes, it would have been nice, but it didn't turn out that way. The opposition was simply too strong, too entrenched and too committed for a clandestine factory effort to overcome. During the 1965 season, at Charlotte, at Atlanta, at Daytona, and in the World 600 the story was always the same. The Chevys were fast qualifiers and could run with the leaders in the early stages of the race but then their engines would blow and the threat they posed would evaporate into thin air. If Chevrolets were having it rough on the banks and straights, they were going from strength by building big, booming, super stocks that could match and usually outmatch anything the competition could come up with.

In 1966, the 396 became the 427 and in its detuned form turned out a healthy 390 hp at 5200 rpm. This engine with a moderate cam, and hydraulic lifters carried a sticker price of $313.68. As untempermental and quiet as an old shoe, it enabled a Turbo-Hydra Matic Caprice to break the 8 second barrier from zero to 60 mph. The Chevrolet Caprice has often been ridiculed as an automotive sybarite, but let's give credit where it's due. It was an awful lot of car for the money and for an additional $31.37 Chevrolet offered a suspension option of stiffer springs and shocks plus an

Above, 1961 Chevrolet Impala

additional rear stabilizer bar that tidied up its road manners quite nicely. The 427 was, at 683 pounds, no featherweight and no amount of chassis tuning could overcome the Chevrolet's front end weight bias. Yet for a mass produced, full-sized sedan, it was a tremendous performance bargain.

The loaded for bear solid lifter, RPO L72 engine was rated at 425 hp at 5600 rpm, the same as its 396 counterpart of 1965. However, Chevrolet without a great deal of fanfare also released a second data sheet showing it developing 450 hp at 6400. With a Delco K-66 transistor ignition it could rev up to 7000 rpm. A Chevrolet with this engine was both the B/S Stock champion and, on handicap, the Junior Stock Eliminator at the 1966 NHRA Winternationals. At this time, in spite of the poor harvest of gold being reaped on the NASCAR tracks, Chevrolet was a major force in drag racing, holding over 20 NHRA class records for either elapsed time or top speed.

From 1967 through 1969 there were only minimal changes made in Chevrolet's top power engine line up. The 1967 Chevrolets had all new bodies (except for their windshield and cowl sections) but both the 390 and 425 horsepower engines were dropped. This left the 385 hp 427 as the most potent engine for the SS or any full-sized Chevrolet. Incidentally, when this engine was used in the Corvette it had a 390 hp rating even though no changes were made.

By 1970, the performance age was on the wane. While the factors of higher fuel prices and restrictive government policies played their role in its demise, it's equally important to realize that, in a practical sense, Detroit was sending its high performance automobiles down a one-way street. There obviously was a limit as to just how big engines could get. For Chevrolet, it came in 1970 with the LS-4, a stroked version of the 427 displacing 454 cubic inches. With 450 hp it delivered the goods but it was ponderous, gas thirsty and woefully out of tune with the times. By contrast, in 1955 nothing was neater or more contemporary than a Two-Ten, 2-door coupe with a 180 hp V-8 and a 3-speed transmission with overdrive. It was easy to handle, easy to live with, and easy on the pocketbook. An LS-6 Chevrolet on the other hand had lost this fine balance of fun and function. Against such a backdrop, and in a changing social, political and economic climate, Chevrolet entered the seventies with the Vega in a starring role and its high performance autombiles little more than necessary nuisances awaiting their turn to be emasculated.

Above, 1965 Chevrolet Super Sport

6. Chevrolet Camaro

It's no secret that Chevrolet intended the Camaro to outshine the Mustang. Whether it did or didn't is probably more a matter of semantics and marque loyalty than the result of an objective judgment based on factual data. Since Chevrolet had the opportunity to go over Ford's finished product with a fine tooth comb, it's tempting to believe the Camaro was essentially a carbon copy of the Mustang. Obviously, they were similar in philosophy and basic engineering layout, but in terms of their performance characteristics they were distinct entities. When the Z/28 and Boss 302 were compared, important distinctions became quite apparent.

The corporate environment in which each car was developed and nurtured was partially responsible for their differences. The Ford men who wanted to fully exploit the Mustang's performance potential did their deeds out in the open, encouraged by the management lords. Their counterparts at Chevrolet enjoyed no such benign environment, having no choice but to become corporate guerrillas in order to keep their car in the running.

Yet, there were no Camaro fastbacks. And while Camaros did zip off the assembly line with 396 engines, and a few ZL-1 427 Camaros were built, there still was nothing to really compete with the big-engined Mustangs or the Shelby wonderments.

It is still a matter of record, however, that the Camaro had a fair share of the glory. It was the Trans Am champion in 1968 and 1969 and made forevermore "Z/28" synonymous with big performance from a small bore block.

When the Camaro climbed in the ring to square off against the Mustang its biggest and most powerful engine was a 350 cid, 295 hp V-8 with hydraulic lifters, four-barrel carburetor and a 10.25:1 compression ratio. This engine, initially exclusive to the Camaro, was essentially Chevrolet's 327 V-8 with its stroke increased from 3.25 inches to 3.48 inches.

An early objective for the Camaro was handling that approached the standards usually associated with European gran turismo automobiles. The early models, by no means milk toast machines in this regard, fell a little short of the mark. The primary culprits were the rear "Mono-Plate" single-leaf rear springs that permitted too much axle windup and jutter under maximum acceleration conditions. Customers who opted for the $210.65 Super Sport package (initially offered with only the 350 V-8) which included the RPO F-41 heavy-duty front and rear suspension got much more out of life in this department. As a separate option F-41 was well worth its $10.55 price.

Other excellent investments for the Camaro customer who anticipated putting some spirit into his driving were either the sintered metallic brake linings ($37.90) or the ventilated front disc brakes ($79). The standard brakes for Camaro coupes were 9.5 inch drums, identical to those used in Chevelle, Chevy II and Corvair. The heavier convertible did a little better in this department with 11 inch drums, but neither car was a distinguished performer with the standard brakes.

Powered by the 295 hp, 350 cid engine, the Camaro was obviously not a wishful thinker on the dragstrip, but with Ford offering its 335 hp, 390 cid V-8 in the Mustang for 1967, Chevrolet's offering of the L-35, 325 hp, 396 engine in late November, 1966, came as no surprise. In January, 1967, the 396 engine in its RPO L-78, 375 hp form also became a Camaro engine offering. These were, of course,

Below, 1967 Chevrolet Camaro Pace Car

great engines. In particular, the 375 hp version with 11.0:1 compression ratio and a Holley four-barrel was very strong, probably really delivering its horsepower rating. But its formidable straight line capability extracted a toll from the Camaro's handling. With the 396 engine, weight distribution became a miserable 59.3% in the front and 40.7% in the rear. And, if the severe understeer that resulted didn't jangle your sense of well-being, then all the rear axle jutter that took place when you put the pedal to the metal did. Camaros with any engine above the 210 hp baseline had a traction bar installed on the right side of their rear axles but the effects were overwhelmed by the might of the 396.

In spite of the less than happy marriage of the Camaro with the 396, two privateers offered versions of the Camaro powered by nothing less than Chevrolet's 427 powerhouse. Dana Chevrolet, of Southgate, California, built some 35 Camaros of this type. Their base price, $3995, was the same as that Carroll Shelby requested for one of his GT-350's. Dana began with the 425 hp version of the 427 fitted with a single four-barrel 850 cfm Holley carburetor. Other key items of the Dana package included special springs and shocks, tuned exhaust headers, 6 inch wide wheels, the close-ratio Muncie 4-speed, nylon Red-Stripe tires and a heavy-duty radiator. For another $150, a triple-carb setup, good for 435 hp, was also available. Dana also offered three additional suspension setups, increasing in competence to an all-out for racing, stage III version with a $2,000 price tag.

Obviously happiest when pointed in a straight line, the Dana Camaro with dragslicks on its rear wheels was capable of 12.75 second runs down the quarter-mile.

A very strong challenger to the Dana Camaro in what was a very low production race was offered by the combine of Chicago's Nickey Chevrolet and Bill Thomas, of Anaheim, California. This linkup brought together one of the nation's most proficient purveyors of high performance Chevys (Nickey) and an extremely talented constructor of super fast Chevys (Bill Thomas). The Nickey-Thomas 427 Camaro was, like the Dana versions available in a wide variety of power potency. Thomas began his re-creation work on a SS350 foundation since Camaros with those engines were equipped with heavy-duty engine mounts, F-41 suspension and axles. Thomas also installed the radiator and fans Chevrolet used on air-conditioned Camaros. At the front end, a large, 1 inch anti-roll bar was available to replace the standard, 0.6875 inch unit. To help control rear axle hop, Thomas devised a traction kit consisting of two arms that replaced the bottom spring plates.

In its fully optioned, most potent version, the Nickey-Thomas engine, judged by its 11.35 second, 127 mph quarters-mile runs with a 4.88:1 rear axle, was capable of turning out 550 hp. To achieve this level, Thomas installed a 310° duration, 0.565 inch lift cam, special lifters, chromemoly pushrods, 12.5:1 pistons, dual four-barrel Carter carburetors and tubular headers of his own design.

Camaros of this ilk were fine and dandy for the drag racing set but like the other big-engined pony cars they were really examples of automotive over-kill. These cars were happiest when pulled by a relatively light-weight, high revving, V-8 and in that regard the Z/28 Camaro was the standard by which all its competitors were graded.

Most applications of the adage, "Racing improves the Breed," are usually made regarding British and European automobiles. The Camaro not only bucked that trend quite nicely but also was a breed that improved racing as well. The reason for the Z/28's existence was of course to give Chevrolet a machine that would be a competitive factor in Trans Am racing, but that was just the beginning. Chevrolet quickly took notice of the sales potential a street-civilized Z/28 possessed and responded by producing over the 1967-70 time span a superb series of Z/28s that were the antithesis of the big engined supercar in every way but performance.

The Z/28 in model year 1967 was, to say the least, a rare commodity. Placed on sale, December 11, 1966, just 602 were sold. Four of these cars were purchased by Dana Chevrolet which prepared them for the 1967 Trans Am season. That wasn't the best competition year for the Camaros since they finished behind series champion Mustang and runner-up Cougar. Nonetheless, one of the Dana cars, by virtue of its win at St. Jovite, scored the Camaro's first Trans-Am victory.

In essence, the greatness of the Z/28, to quote CAR LIFE (August, 1969), was that it was "a race car that doesn't have to be raced." In other words it was a purebred performance machine, equally at home on the dragstrip or the crooked backroad, a well balanced, coordinated, poised and extremely competent road machine. If it had been built in Europe, thousands of so-called purists would have willingly paid twice the sticker price for a Z/28 with an Old World name. But a rose by any other name is still a rose and the Z/28 was one sweet machine.

The package of goodies that comprised the Z/28 carried a $400.25 price tag. Chevrolet extracted an additional $305 in exchange for front disc brakes plus the Muncie close-ratio 4-speed that were mandatory items.

To bring the Z/28's engine under the Trans-Am 305 cid limit was easily accomplished by using the crankshaft from the 283 engine in the 327 block. This combination provided a bore and stroke of 4 inches and 3 inches respectively. The Corvette L-79, big port head with provision for 2.0 inch intake and 1.6 inch exhaust valves was also used, along with solid lifters and a standard cam with a 346° duration. Other cams were offered but they were strictly state of the art racing items. Additional features of the Z/28 engine included 11.0:1 compression ratio pistons and a single, 800 cfm Holley four-barrel carburetor mounted on an aluminum "tuned runner" manifold.

Chevrolet rated the Z/28 at an inoffensive 290 hp. It would have been interesting to have had the parties involved testify under oath about its actual output. The whole truth and nothing but the truth was a minimum of 375 hp. CAR AND DRIVER (March, 1967) reported "it feels at least as strong as the 327 cu.in., 350 hp hydraulic lifter engine offered in the Corvette." When an engine was able to propell a Camaro through the quarter-mile in just 14.85 seconds it had to have a lot of energy. In order to bring out the best in the Z/28 engine, its 4-speed transmission got lots of use. The Z/28 was mighty unhappy at low revs but when it started to wind out it made life behind the wheel worth living. CAR AND DRIVER dubbed it "without a doubt the most responsive American car we've ever tested" and CAR LIFE after sampling a 1968 Z/28 called its engine "a jewel, an outstanding performer by any yardstick."

Its underalls were pretty fancy also. The F-41 suspension was installed with shot-peened ball studs along with the right side only rear radius rod. Helping the suspension keep its house in order, especially under racing conditions, was the optional $32.68 trunk spoiler. "The Z/28's ability to stick through turns," said CAR LIFE (September, 1968), "remains among its finest virtues; far superior among Chevrolets to anything but the Corvette."

For 1968, the standard Camaros in general and the Z/28

in particular were spruced up with an eye both towards better sales and increased racing competitiveness. Chevrolet's efforts in both areas were successful. Production increased from just under 221,000 to 235,151 for the 1968 model year. In Trans-Am competition, the Z/28 finished the season as champion with ten victories, eight of which were successful.

While certain elements of the 1967 Z/28 package, such as the steel tubing headers, became dealer installed options for 1968, other, more exotic items were added. Very late in the model run four-wheel disc brakes were offered, for $500.30, as a service option. This setup required a totally revised rear axle housing and was rarely seen. Also somewhat elusive outside of Camaro racing teams was the twin Holley four-barrel option. Like the four-wheel disc brakes, these carburetors didn't come cheap. To get a late sixties version of Mr. Goodwrench to install them required the reduction of the customer's bank account by approximately $500. Since their presence really wasn't felt below 3000 rpm, they proved of limited value on Z/28's for the street, but in racing they could give the Mustang's tail a pretty nasty tug. *CAR LIFE* (July, 1968) tested a dual-carb Z/28 and reported a zero to 60 time of 5.3 seconds with 13.77 seconds and 107.39 mph marks for the quarter-mile.

The overall excellence of the Z/28 prompted *CAR LIFE* to recognize it as one of its "10 Best Test Cars of 1968". "We must stress here," said *CAR LIFE,* "that the Camaro Z/28 isn't a car for everyone. We rate it most satisfying in its category, but that category is only for persons who put pure all-around performance ahead of pure transportation, tractability, a nice smooth idle and lots of automatic conveniences."

Camaro watchers quickly noticed the loss of front vent windows on the 1968 version but more important changes were made in the Camaro's rear suspension. By staggering the rear shocks fore and aft of the axle, engineers were able to cure its nasty hopping habit. For Camaros with the 350

and 396 cid V-8's or the 275 hp, 327 V-8 and 4-speed transmission new five-leaf rear springs were developed. The Z/28 also benefited both from this change plus the option of a 1.0625 inch diameter front anti-roll bar in place of the standard, 0.6875 inch unit.

A cold air "Super-Scoop" was available for all Camaros including the Z/28 for 1969 but more interesting were the fifty ZL-1 Camaros built by the factory expressly for drag racing. The price tag of these aluminum block 427 Camaros was a healthy $8,581 but Chevrolet had no difficulty finding customers.

When the second generation Camaro debuted as a 1970½ model, it received instant acclamation for its superb appearance. The development of this new Camaro not only made it possible for Chevrolet to improve upon the earlier model but also to revamp the Z/28. The result was another performance triumph. "The 1970 Z/28 Camaro is not a perfect car," conceded *CAR LIFE* (May, 1970). "It is merely great, improved to a degree that makes one hope for the eventual perfection of the automobile." From any and all angles the new Z/28 justified this extremely positive assertion. Its front suspension with better geometry, wider tread plus strong anti-roll bars at both ends maintained the Z/28's reputation for handling prowess and its engine, basically the 1969 LT-1 Corvette powerplant, rated at 360 hp was as strong as any 350 cid V-8 on the market. With a 4.10 rear axle and Turbo Hydramatic it moved the Z/28 from zero to 60 mph in 6.5 seconds.

The Camaros fell on hard times in the early seventies. The move toward lower compression ratios instituted by GM in 1971 signaled the beginning of the end for high powered Camaros. Then, the twin forces of a major UAW strike plus a sharply diminished market for pony cars almost sent the Camaro into oblivion. Happily the Camaro survived those bad times. But, to those whose motoring memories included magic moments behind the wheel of the earlier Z/28's, the post-1977 version, in spite of its excellent handling, just wasn't the same. Its name hadn't changed but a lot sure had under the Z/28's hood.

Below, 1974 Chevrolet Camaro

350-hp CHEVELLE by Chevrolet, the perfect squelch

That's a potent squelch to all those others who keep talking about lions, tigers and such.

A 350-hp squelch goes into any '65 Chevelle you specify. It's that big blue-jowled 327-cubic-inch V8 of song and story, fortified with an extra helping of brute in the form of 11.0:1 compression ratio, big 4-bbl. carb, dual exhausts and 360 ft.-lbs. of torque at 3600 rpm. With *hydraulic lifters*.

Then, too, you can order a 4-speed fully synchronized transmission. A beefier special front and rear suspension package. Sintered-metallic brakes. Positraction with 3.31:1 axle ratio. And an electric tach.

All this performance would go great in a heavyweight. Just run your imagination over what it does for the welterweight Chevelle. Not to mention the silencing effect on all those tigers and tamers.

But why rub it in? That's your privilege. Happy squelching.

Chevrolet Division of General Motors, Detroit, Michigan

MOTOR TREND/FEBRUARY 1965

7. Chevrolet Chevelle

Early 1964 showroom literature for the Chevelle concluded, after a brief review of its virtues, that "this first-time offering seems suited for everyone." There was ample justification for this claim with Chevelles being offered in various stages of trim and in every contemporary body style except as a four-door pillarless hardtop. Since Chevrolet was heavily into Super Sport models at this time, the availability of a Malibu Super Sport coupe came as no great surprise. Apparently General Motors' ban against any emphasis of performance didn't apply to color schemes for the Malibu SS was available in Daytona Blue! After all the years of chrome, glitter and geehaws that encrusted the outer surfaces of most American cars, some motoring journalists found the new Chevelle almost bland in appearance. Probably if it had emerged from Coventry or Stuttgart, the same critics would have lauded it for simplicity of line, good taste and so on, but you can't please everyone and to the unbiased eye the new Chevelle's styling was very refreshing.

From a performance perspective things weren't quite so promising. The SS was available with a 4-speed transmission but its top engine was a 220 hp, Turbo-Fire 283 V-8. This combination was good for a zero to 60 mph time of just under 10 seconds, but neither this nor a 17.4 second quarter-mile time were particularly viable attributes in the world of the supercar.

Chevrolet quickly remedied this condition once the Chevelle was established. Obviously, Chevrolet anticipated making the 327 V-8 an option for the Chevelle from the earliest point of its development. For early publicity purposes, an El Camino was the first "Chevelle" to be powered by a 327 V-8. Specifically, its powerplant was a 300 hp version which had found life in a pickup quite pleasant. Along with a 4-speed transmission and 3.36:1 rear axle, it made the El Camino a super truck. Top speed was just over 120 mph, zero to 60 mph needed less than 8 seconds and the quarter-mile was covered in 15.9 seconds with an end speed of 87 mph.

The 300 hp 327 was made available concurrently with 250 hp and 365 hp variations. In fact, the earlier mentioned El Camino had first been powered by the 365 hp version but all this power turned its lightly loaded rear axle into a jumping, twisting, metal eel whenever the throttle was opened wide.

The reason Chevrolet decided to offer an engine of this output in the Chevelle was, of course, the success of Pontiac's GTO. It appears that Chevrolet was caught off balance when Pete Estes put a 389 V-8 in a Pontiac Tempest, and once he had successfully ridden out the storm of consternation it created among the GM top brass, Chevrolet needed a GTO of its own — ergo, the 365 hp SS. Almost before this early Chevelle muscle car had a chance to show what it could do, it was pushed into the background. The first strike against its claim to fame was that there weren't many of them. The supply of 327 engines was short and this scarcity, plus the time needed to design a new exhaust manifold that would clear the Chevelle's front suspension, held up delivery of most 365 hp Chevelles until May. Almost at the same time, a small number of Chevelles with many fiberglass body panels and powered by the 427 cubic inch Z11 engine developing 450 hp with two Holley four-barrels started appearing on the nation's major drag-strips. Capable of quarter-mile runs in the 119-125 mph range, they were extremely potent spear carriers for the Chevrolet semi-clandestine performance program. Roger Huntington (*CAR LIFE*, October, 1964) speculated that they had been built in a private shop with factory sponsorship.

The hottest engine for the Malibu SS when the 1965 model year began was a 350 hp edition of the strong and durable 327. *MOTOR TREND* (December, 1964) saw it as ". . . competitive in the booming GTO market." No doubt it was, but the Chevelle needed more cubic inches under its hood to meet the GTO on even terms and early in 1965 they arrived in the form of the 396 V-8. The Z16 version of the 396, some 375 horsepower strong, was everyone's performance delight. *MOTOR TREND* (July, 1965) advised its readers to "expect to wait and expect to pay sticker price when yours arrives. It's the hottest of the hot intermediates. In fact, it's king of the road." Initially only 200 of these brutes were to be produced during the 1965 season but actually their total numbers exceeded this figure by a good deal.

Naturally, the heart of any American supercar was its engine and the Z16 engine shared many of the features of the 425 hp version used in the SS Impala. Thus, it had impact-extruded pistons, molybdenum-coated rings, special alloy connecting rods and 4-bolt main caps. It also was endowed with the big 1.72 inch exhaust and 2.09 inch intake valves first seen on the Mark II. It did have a hydraulic valve gear but its cam, with 342° duration intake and 356° exhaust made 6000-plus rpm runs no problem at all.

The Z16 package was expensive at $1,501.05, but, to Chevy's credit, the Malibu had been extensively re-engineered to cope with its potency. The end result was a fairly refined and very rapid automobile. Its front end carried a 1.06 inch diameter anti-roll bar, cast-steel wheel hubs and shot-peened ball studs. At the rear were four control arms: two short upper arms attached to the chassis near the differential plus two shorter ones positioned near the coil springs. To help keep the right rear wheel from lifting up under fierce acceleration, an anti-roll bar was also installed at the rear.

A real plus for the Z16 Chevelle was Chevrolet's decision to include in the package the large 11 inch brakes from the full-sized Chevrolets. These were not, of course, immune to fade but it was good to know that a car with a top speed in excess of 130 mph and with the ability to run from zero to 60 mph in 6.5 seconds had brakes that could haul it down safely and without fuss.

The external identification of the SS 396 was subdued and to the point. A "Malibu SS 396" name tag was placed on the trunk lid. Just ahead of the front wheel wells were "396 Turbo-Jet" logos and crossed Chevrolet and Checkered flags.

Like most of its contemporary big-engined counterparts, the SS396 carried a lot of weight on its front end. A weight distribution of 58% front, 42% rear made it "a trifle nose-heavy" said *HOT ROD* (February, 1966) in classic under-

statement. *CAR LIFE* (September, 1965) naturally praised the Z16 engined Chevelle for its straightline performance but viewed it as "only mediocre at covering curving roads at velocities more than 40% of its potential."

A strange thing happened to the SS396 in 1966: it got less super. As before, its base engine was the 325 hp 396 but the potent Z16 option was nowhere in sight. In its place was a 360 hp 396 and that didn't seem too bad until prospective Super Sport customers probed around in the spec book. There they found that the 360 hp engine was very similar to the 325 hp version. In other words, it had the small-port heads, a lower compression ratio, a milder hydraulic cam and no streamlined exhaust headers. Chevrolet couldn't do something mean like that and get away with it. A charitable soul might say the 1966 edition of the SS396 was slower than its 1965 version. If said soul was also truthful, he would say it was *a lot* slower. It had a hard time even with a 4-speed stick breaking the 8 second mark from zero to 60 mph and, in street form, traveled the quarter-mile in 15.5 undramatic seconds.

The one redeeming feature of this car was its cornering characteristics. Chevrolet described it as "more than just a straight-line machine," thanks to its 30% stiffer than stock springs and 15/16 inch diameter sway bar, but even this gain wasn't all it could have been because there no longer was a rear stabilizer bar! Furthermore, the SS396 had as standard equipment the same brakes as found on every other Chevelle!

A supercar with poor brakes, and a rev limit of about 5400 rpm didn't make many Chevrolet fans happy and they wanted to know where oh where their horsepower had gone! Their inquisitive incantations did not go unheeded. At midyear the Z16 engine was, in effect, reborn. This time around it had solid lifters and an improved exhaust manifold but for the most part it was a case of the good times rolling again. There they were, 375 horsepower at 5600 rpm, those heads with the great big valves, that hail and hardy big port aluminum intake manifold and of course everyone's favorite, the Holley 4150 four-barrel carburetor.

Looking at the 1967 SS396, it becomes awfully tempting to suspect that Chevrolet just couldn't leave well enough alone. It hustled the 375 engine off to never-never land, and down graded the 360 hp engine to 350 hp (although dealer installed options raised this to 375 hp). Thus the new SS396 was not as quick as either the 1965 and 1966 models. There was also regression in the handling area due primarily to a smaller front stabilizer bar, though, in fairness, the use of nylon, wide oval tires helped to mitigate the effects of this change.

The performance posture of the SS396 did not change significantly in either 1968 or 1969. After receiving front disc brakes the previous year, the Chevelle, along with the other GM mid-sized cars, received a new body. This was age when some sort of strange status symbol was imparted to any device on a car that could be hidden. Thus, the SS396 had hide-away windshield wipers as standard equipment. The L-34, 350 horsepower engine as well as the 325 hp standard SS396 engines remained unchanged both in 1968 and 1969, although a chambered exhaust system was featured on the 1969 model.

The SS396 was, in the late sixties, the best selling supercar and, in 1970, it entered into the ultimate form of its evolution as the SS454. Its engine (surprise!) was 454 cubic inches strong, and pumped out 450 rather husky horsepower. Its specifications were equally awesome. The 427 block with a longer stroke was its foundation and it boasted such delights as cast iron heads with large exhaust valves from the ZL-1 Corvette engine and an 800 cfm Holley carburetor. A cowl induction unit that picked up fresh air from a high pressure area at the base of the windshield plus a mechanical lifter cam with 0.500 inches of lift added to the impression of invincibility conveyed by this monster car.

From the pinnacle the fall was quick and irreversible, though. In a 1971 brochure, Chevrolet assured performance fans, "Don't panic. There's still a SS454." Thus mollified the reader soon discovered, however, its horsepower was down to 365. Sure enough, that was almost sufficient to yank the earth out of orbit but the times were changing and changing fast. The SS now was a "package" available on either the Malibu Sport Coupe or Convertible equipped with any V-8. Once that happened, the road to ruin (paved with decals and stripes that promised much but in reality signified nothing) was traveled by the SS Chevelle.

Above, 1968 Chevrolet Chevelle SS 396

8. Chevrolet Chevy II/Nova

The success of the Ford Falcon and the relatively poor showing of the Corvair in the original American compact car sales contest forced Chevrolet to make some rapid changes in its market strategy. The Corvair was given a dose of Monza cosmetics and quickly experienced a sales turnaround thanks to its virtually uncontested position as a low-priced American semi-sports car. This market repositioning might have saved the Corvair for a time but it still left Chevrolet without a product directively competitive to the Ford Falcon. The reasons for the Falcon's success were varied, but the base of its popular it was its straightforward, simple design. It was not without justification that many critics likened it to the 1928 Ford Model A. Realizing that Ford did, indeed, have a better idea, Chevrolet tailored the Chevy II in a similar pattern. Thus, it was a highly conventional, automobile that, since it was available with a 194 cid, four-cylinder engine, went back to basics to a greater degree even than the Falcon.

Still, in the two years separating the respective introduction of the Falcon and Chevy II much had changed. Economy was still a viable sales virtue for an automobile to possess but the spectre of the GTO was looming just over the horizon and big bore V-8's were proliferating. Thus it was that Chevrolet Engineering created a most interesting prototype vehicle known as No. H-333. Unless you looked closely, it appeared to be nothing more than a normal, friendly Chevy II, four-door sedan. This mundane exterior was, however, a mere facade, for H-333 was equipped with

Below, 1963 Chevrolet Chevy II Nova 400

a 327 cubic inch, 340 horsepower V-8 and a 4-speed transmission, both of which usually went about their business wrapped in fiberglass. In other words, they came from a Corvette. This experimental automobile also had stiffer springs, a 5/8 inch front stabilizer bar and Corvette torque links at the rear to help prevent spring wind-up. As would be expected, its performance was outstanding; zero to 60 mph in less than 7 seconds and a speed for the quarter-mile of 97 mph.

Chevrolet made it possible for Chevy II owners to experience this performance from their cars but only in a roundabout way. As a "dealer-installed option," any one of the four Corvette engines with horsepower ratings of 250, 300, 340 or 360 could power a Chevy II. Also available was the close-ratio Corvette, 4-speed transmission.

One Chevy II powered by the 360 horsepower, fuel-injected engine and equipped with the suspension components used on the H-333, plus metallic brake linings and the Corvette 4-speed left a vivid impression upon many English racing fans during the summer of 1962. The British were fond of "saloon" car racing which provided lots of competition in the smaller engined categories but was dominated almost totally by the Jaguar sedans in the top division. The 360 hp Chevy II was given a shakedown run amidst the Jaguars at the Silverstone course where it finished fifth overall. Two weeks later, though, at Brands Hatch it was driven by Chuck Kelsey to a victory over the Jaguars. The American car was inferior to the British champion in the turns but its tremendous power more than compensated for this deficiency on the straights. This particular Chevy II

with a 3.08:1 Positraction rear axle, had earlier been tested by *CAR LIFE* (June, 1962) which reported the following acceleration times:

0 - 30 mph — 3.9 sec.
0 - 60 mph — 7.3 sec.
0 - 100 mph — 16.8 sec.
S.S. 1/4-mile — 14.8 sec. at 94 mph.
Top speed — 131 mph.

In spite of an engine weight of nearly 600 pounds, or approximately 140 pounds more than the 120 hp six-cylinder engine usually used in the Chevy II's, *CAR LIFE* reported, "The car handles reasonably well, though it ultimately understeers if one takes a corner too fast."

When prepared for drag racing the 360 hp Chevy II needed no apologies. Don Nicholson campaigned a station wagon in the 1962 Winternationals. With a 4.55:1 axle his best run was 108.96 mph and 12.55 seconds.

The effect General Motors' anti-performance dictate had on Chevrolet has already been touched upon but in the case of the Chevy II its impact was especially harsh. Bill Thomas, the long time Chevrolet performance advocate, built at least three special Chevy II "study cars" for Chevrolet that were roughly analogous to the Falcon Challengers built by Holman and Moody. The most publicized Thomas-Chevy II was "Bad Bascom," as wild a Chevy II as there ever was. In case there are doubts about its virility consider this: In late 1963 the lap record at the Riverside Track in California of 1 minute 35 seconds was held by Roger Penske's Zerex Special (in effect a Formula I Cooper reskinned to qualify as a sports car). Skip Hudson, an accomplished, but by no means of Stirling Moss caliber, sports car driver, lapped in 1 minute, 39.8 seconds with Bad Bascom using a 5800 rpm red line.

Quite obviously Bad Bascom deserved a close look. Its engine, mounted eight inches further back from the normal position of the six-cylinder engine, was a bored-to-380-cubic-inches Corvette fuel-injected V-8 developing 412 hp at 6200 rpm. Thanks to Sting Ray independent rear sus-

pension, an awful lot of that power was put to good use. The front suspension used shortened Chevy II upper arms with the lower suspension arms reinforced with chrome-moly plates. Heavy-duty Chevrolet coil springs, cut to fit were used along with premium Monroe shock absorbers. Both front and rear brakes were fitted with sintered metallic linings. At the rear, Corvette units were used with the full-sized Chevrolet being the source of Bad Bascom's front brakes. Visually, Bad Bascom's appearance suggested that at least one of its parents was a Chevy II but upon close inspection the discovery was made that its hood, fenders, rear deck, doors and many inner panels were fiberglass. This change, along with plexiglass side windows, helped bring its weight down to 2310 pounds.

It could be argued that, because of the practical image of the Chevy II, Chevrolet was barking up the wrong tree by pursuing such a project. The earlier racing success of the Chevy II, however, plus its victory against factory entered Ford Falcons in the 1963 Shell 4000 Trans-Canada Rally one of five rallys counting for the World Rally Championship, and its strong sales suggest otherwise. But, like the competition career of the 427 V-8 of 1963, the Chevy II's reach for the gold was effectively short circuited by the GM brass.

Time does heal some wounds, though, and by 1965 hesitant steps were being taken to give the Novas at least a share of the performance action. That year, the 327 V-8 in 250 hp or 300 hp form became a factory installed option. In theory an L-79, 350 hp engine was also available but Bill Jenkins later writing in *HOT ROD* (February, 1968) claimed, "The optional L-79 (350 hp) engine had been listed for the II car in '65, but Chevy had never built the car."

They did, however, build the car in 1966 along with a 275 horsepower Nova Super Sport. This was a year of fairly substantial change for the Chevy II. All-new sheet metal took away much of its Plain Jane look and a zero to 60 mph time of 8.6 seconds by a 275 hp Nova Super Sport with Powerslide wasn't half bad for what was admittedly no

Above, 1965 Chevrolet Chevy II Nova Super Sport

34

exactly a supercar. That status was attained by the Nova Super Sports that got their get up and go from the 350 hp, 327 cid V-8. As would be expected from any V-8 developing over 1 hp per cubic inch of displacement, this engine was well endowed with classic high performance features. Carburetion was via a single Holley four-barrel with 1.561 inch barrels and its intake and exhaust valves measured a healthy 2.02 inches and 1.60 inches respectively. Some enthusiasts lamented the use of hydraulic lifters in this engine but they had a faster bleed-down rate than many other systems and did not seriously hamper its spirit.

The SS package included the usual stiffer springs along with a 0.87 inch front anti-roll bar and U.S. Royal Laredo tires. *CAR LIFE* (May, 1966) was pleased with the results, describing the Nova SS as a car whose ''level of handling was a cut above competitive,'' that ''could be cornered with a great deal of unconcern.'' Not so pleasing was the performance of the Super Sport's brakes. The logic that led Chevrolet to put the same 9.5 inch drums on a 350 hp Super Sport as were found on a 90 horse Nova 300, two-door sedan was hard to accept.

As a rapid accelerator, the 350 hp Super Sport received good grades. *CAR LIFE* (May, 1966) reported the following times attained by its test car equipped with a 4-speed with a 2.52 first gear:

> 0 - 30 mph — 2.6 sec.
> 0 - 60 mph — 7.2 sec.
> 0 - 100 mph — 18.2 sec.
> standing start 1/4-mile — 15.1 sec. — 93 mph
> top speed — 123 mph

At the 1966 Winternationals the 350 hp Novas weren't able to overpower the Mopar Street Hemis but Bill Jenkins' Nova did emerge as the A/stock NHRA Champion for 1966. Jenkins also was Middle Stock Eliminator at the AHRA Winternational the following year with a 11.70 second,

Below, 1966 Chevrolet Chevy II Nova Super Sport

120.20 mph run.

The availability of front disc brakes as an option plus a cleaner front end for the 1967 Chevy II were welcome changes, but sorely missed was the 350 hp option. The 275 hp engine was continued, available with either 3- or 4-speed manuals as well as Powerglide transmission but it lacked the verve to maintain the Chevy II's performance car status.

It might have seemed a bit novel, on the surface at least, for the 1968 Chevy II Nova (Chevrolet was starting to phase out the Chevy II name in favor of Nova at this time, thus the ''Chevy II Nova'' title) to be available with the Camaro's 350 cid V-8, but, in reality, both cars had been designed with component interchangeability in mind and there were many similarities between the two cars. For example, they used the same platform, floor and forward subframe as well as identical front and rear suspensions. Quite obviously the newly restyled Chevy II Nova had much more potential as a performance car than ever before. When the new Nova SS was introduced, its top engine was the L-48 350 V-8 rated at 295 hp. In quick succession a 325 hp variation of the familiar 327 V-8 was added with a price of $198.05 and before the dust had much of a chance to settle from that event along came the 396 cid V-8 in either 350 or 375 hp form.

Chevrolet offered the 396 engine in the Nova only in 1968 and 1969, reverting in 1970 to the 350 V-8, in 300 hp form, as the Nova's top engine. This was still enough to satisfy a lot of customers but in comparison to the 396 Chevy II brutes of '68 and '69 it was a pretty mild mannered automobile. From the point of view of what the 396 did to the Nova's handling, there was logic behind its deletion because it outweighed the 327 V-8 by over 200 pounds. Chevrolet did a lot of beefing up of the Nova's front end to try to cope with this increase but the end result was a poorly balanced machine with severe understeer and a very nasty tendency towards front end plowing in sharp turns. Ah, but how the beast could fly down the straight path! *HOT ROD* (July, 1969) reported a quarter-mile run of 13.87 seconds 105.14 mph with a 3.55:1 Positraction rear axle and Turbo-Hydra-Matic. Those indeed were the days, my friend.

YOU COULDN'T GET AN AUTOMATIC IF YOU TRIED —Which leaves you holding a stick shift. A happy fix to be in; Spyders respond best to brisk stirring motions with the right hand—either 3- or 4-speed* Synchro-Mesh. And no wonder, with a 150-hp Turbo-charged Six behind you and a 6,000-rpm tach before your eyes.

Some things the Spyder gives you that others don't: special brushed chrome instrument cluster with manifold pressure and cylinder head temperature gauges plus the tachometer. Special trim and interior appointments. Chromed accents in the engine compartment. And options* such as Positraction and wire wheels.

For those who just can't live without an automatic, Powerglide* can be had in the Monza, 700 and 500 series. Not the Spyder, though; that's strictly a case of stick with us and you'll go places. Chevrolet Division of General Motors, Detroit, Michigan.   *Optional at extra cost

CORVAIR MONZA SPYDER by CHEVROLET

9. Chevrolet Corvair

Once Ford uncorked its Mustang in early 1964, there was really no doubt about the Corvair's ultimate demise. Ralph Nader's article in *THE NATION*, "The Corvair Story," wasn't published until November, 1965, and while this plus *UNSAFE AT ANY SPEED* obviously dealt the Corvair a severe drubbing, its days were already numbered.

As a performance car, the Corvair was inherently at a disadvantage. There was just no way its aluminum rear engine could be pumped up to the necessary power level to enable the Corvair to equal any of the supercars in acceleration. That took a big V-8 and that simply wasn't part of the Corvair's format. Yet, viewed from another perspective, the Corvair was a successful failure, a predictor of what was yet to be, for in essence it was an early precursor of today's sporty sub-compact whose components come from a more mundane 4-door econo-box. The Corvair, of course, had its engine in the "wrong place" but a 180 hp Corsa fits into todays motoring world of soon-to-be $2.00 per gallon gasoline far more comfortably than a 426 Hemi for example.

The basic reason for the Corvair's existence was founded in the growing popularity both of the small imported automobile and the surprising success of the domestic compact Ramblers and Studebakers. Their success did not cause a Chevrolet commitment to the rear engine format: that was left to the credit of Ed Cole, then a G.M. vice president in charge of the Chevrolet division.

The Corvair was acclaimed as "a milestone in U.S. car design;" *MOTOR TREND'S* Car of the Year representing a "most significant engineering advancement" and a "profoundly revolutionary car," but, nowhere in this sea of superlatives and critical acclaim were any comments made in praise of the Corvair's performance. The reason was simple: there wasn't any to praise. A 140 cid, pancake six with tiny 1.340 inch intake and 1.240 inch exhaust valves delivering 80 hp had its hands full getting up the gumption to move the Corvair from zero to 60 mph in less than 18 seconds. But, with Zora Arkus-Duntov playing around with a special cam and modified cylinder heads for the Corvair plus the impending arrival of the Monza coupe and the not-too-surprising public interest in the racing ability of the compacts, the Corvair's evolution took a definite turn toward fun and games.

The Corvair's first racing appearance at Continental Divide Raceway, late in 1959, wasn't exactly a wine and roses performance. It was short on power and in sharp turns its outside rear tire would roll over in the manner that later was to bring it considerably notoriety.

The quality of competition confronting the Corvair in its second racing appearance, a compact car race preceding the Sebring 12-hour race, was rather formidable. Studebaker's Larks (see Chapter 32) and Jaguar's tough 3.4 liter Sedans, not to mention the Volvos, fulfilled that role very nicely. The Corvair couldn't keep company with the Jags and Larks but it did manage to stay ahead of several Volvos. The most severe shortcomings of the Corvair were its low top speed, 3-speed manual transmission and an annoying habit of flipping its accessory drive belt. Perfection doesn't come immediately or without effort, though, and the Corvair boys were trying hard. For Sebring, the Corvair's rear suspension was given 3° of negative camber, stiffer front and rear

shocks were used and a front anti-roll bar was installed. With an open exhaust, the Corvair's engine emitted sounds normally associated with racing and, with careful assembly, probably actually produced the rated 80 horsepower.

For the Daytona compact car races, four Corvairs were entered by Don Allen Chevrolet of New York and Miami which had earlier sponsored the Sebring venture. Thanks to the chassis mods that had been successfully sorted out at Sebring, the Corvairs were probably the best handling of the compacts around the Daytona course. In the tight corners they exhibited virtually no lean. *MOTOR LIFE* (May, 1960) described the Corvair's road adhesion as "phenomenal."

An Automobile Manufacturer's Association specification sheet for the Corvair dated December 1, 1959, detailed a "Special Camshaft" package that was eligible for use at Daytona. Along with the hotter, Duntov-developed cam and stronger, by approximately 15%, valves, this kit also included larger Rochester carburetors, a larger 2 inch (instead of 1½ inch) tail pipe and hotter Delco-Remy ignition. These changes boosted the Corvair's horsepower to 95 at 4800 rpm. There was no change in its 126 lbs-ft torque rating but it was now developed at 2800 rpm instead of 2400 rpm. Coinciding with the availability of the Special Camshaft feature, Chevrolet also offered a 4-speed manual transmission as a new Corvair option.

These changes gave the racing Corvairs considerably more zip, but the efforts of Jim Reed, Fireball Roberts and Pedro Rodriguez still couldn't pull the Corvairs up even with the Hyper-Pack Valiants. In practice, Rodriguez's best lap speeds were some 6 mph slower than the fastest Valiant's. Yet, with their hotter engines, tight suspension and sintered, metallic brake linings, the Corvair's 81 mph lap speeds were respectable. Surely they would have come closer to the Valiant's 86 mph mark, and further ahead of the Falcon's 76 mph, if a planned four carburetor system had been ready. But Duntov had to admit that time simply ran out on that project. Speculation that the Corvair *could* give the Valiants a harder time was fed by *MOTOR LIFE* which reported in its May, 1960, issue: "In a vine-covered garage near Detroit there resides a Corvair capable of 125 mph. It belongs to a Chevrolet official who shall for the time being be nameless."

In racing form, the 95 hp Corvair was capable of 12 second zero to 60 mph runs. Production models were several seconds slower but Chevrolet did credit them with a top speed "over 98 mph."

A slight engine bore increase (3.437 inches instead of 3.375 inches) gave the 1961 Corvair engine 145 cubic inches of displacement. This allowed the "Super Turbo-Air" engine to be boosted to 98 hp. Its peak torque moved to 132 lbs-ft at 2900 rpm from 128 lbs-ft at 2300 rpm. This engine carried a modest $26.90 price tag and, thanks to its fairly wild 352° duration cam, emitted some restless sounds at idle that helped enhance its budding reputation as a poor man's Porsche. Another big contributor to the Corvair's sporting personality was its 4-speed transmission, priced at $64. It "changes what would otherwise be a very dead, very dull car," said *CAR LIFE* (August, 1961), "into one with some sports-car-type characteristics; a car that is really fun to drive.''

Having successfully altered in mid-stream the Corvair's image from that of a strictly utilitarian vehicle to that of a spritely sports machine, Chevrolet took another giant step and numerous small ones in that direction for 1962.

The RPO 649 high-performance engine moved up to 102 hp (due to a change in compression ratio that had actually occurred in the spring of 1961 from 8.0:1 to 9.0:1) and the metallic brake linings earlier used at Daytona also became a Regular Production Option. Perhaps more interesting than either of these developments was the availability of a heavy-duty suspension option very closely related to the Don Allen Corvairs that raced at Daytona back in February, 1960. Stiffer front and rear springs were used that, since they were shorter than stock, provided the side benefit of lowering car height by approximately one inch. Along with the stronger springs were higher pressure Delco shocks and a front anti-roll bar positioned behind the suspension as on early, pre-production Corvairs. The rebound distance of the rear spring was reduced by 2 inches to approximately 2 - 5 inches by shorter suspension rebound straps.

The strong interest in boosting the stock Corvair engine's somewhat anemic horsepower output prompted several independent firms to see what they could do. Using a 1960 Monza with the 95 hp engine as a starting point, Barney Navarro, one of the true ''we were there at the start'' American hot rodders, created a *Powerglide* Corvair that ran from zero to 60 mph in 9.3 seconds! Navarro first bored and stroked the Corvair up to 165 cubic inches, installed Ford Falcon pistons and a special in-house crankshaft. The stock single-throat carburetors and manifold were replaced by a one-barrel, side-draft Carter YH unit. This in turn was joined to an AiResearch turbo-charger. The result was an estimated 135 hp at 4800 rpm and quarter-mile runs of 17.5 seconds and 81.5 mph.

Bill Thomas, of Pasadena, California, took a different route leading to more power for the Corvair. His 1960 coupe, first equipped with a 95 hp engine, was initially only slightly modified. Its heads were shaved providing a 9.0:1 compression ratio. Thomas also did a careful porting job, lightened the valve heads and altered the ignition timing. The biggest change was the adaptation of intake manifold carrying four stock carburetors. Whereas a 1961 Monza with the 98 hp engine delivered approximately 71 hp at the rear wheels, the Thomas car produced 102 hp. Its quarter-mile time and speed were 16 seconds and 86.8 mph.

This particular car went on to compile a sensational racing career. With 165 cubic inches, an Iskenderian cam, and Mitchell headers, it revved to 8000 rpm and in late 1962 it was hugging the 100 mph mark in the quarter-mile. In West Coast sedan racing, the Thomas Corvair with both fiberglass and aluminum body panels was quite successful, winning several major events.

During the same time span, when Thomas and Navarro were conducting their performance work on the Corvair, Chevrolet was also busy with its own high-output program. The fruits of this labor, the Corvair Monza Spyder, debuted as a 1962½ model, both in coupe or convertible form (the first Corvair convertible had been shown at the Chicago Auto Show in February, 1962). The Spyder remains today a visual delight with a minimum amount of extraneous trim and very tasteful special Spyder identification. But its main attraction, accounting for most of the RPO 690 Spyder pack's $317.45 price, was found in the engine department.

Chevrolet had decided, after considering a variety of alternatives, that turbo-charging was the most desirable way of increasing the Corvair's power. T.R.W. provided the turbo-charger whose maximum boost was 11 psi at 4000 rpm. Like Navarro, Chevrolet used a Carter YH carburetor. To cope with the Spyder's 150 hp and 210 lbs-ft torque, many internal changes were made. They included special connecting rods, high-alloy crankshaft, heavy-duty pistons, special heads, and heavy-duty bearing inserts. A stronger clutch was also used.

The changes made in the Corvair's personality by the Spyder option were startling. ''Turbo-supercharging,'' wrote *CAR LIFE* (August, 1962), ''comes off so well in the Corvair Spyder that we wonder if there isn't a large market around the corner for exhaust-driven blowers on the larger gasoline engines.''

The 4-speed Spyder, when considered as a small-engined supercar, delivered the goods. Zero to 60 mph required just 10.8 seconds and the Spyder ran through the quarter-mile in 18.5 seconds.

The reason for the existence of the Spyder was of course the popularity of the Monza models that by early 1962 were accounting for over half of all Corvair sales. Roger Huntington *CAR LIFE* (May, 1963) noted in this regard, ''This line has long ceased to have any utility car image — it's an out-and-out sports car today. Just one more sign of changing conditions in the American automotive market.'' To be sure, the Spyder's G/stock victory at the 1963 NHRA National Drag Championships with a 15.31 second, 89 mph run didn't hurt its image.

The impending 1965 arrival of the Corvair in its ultimate and finest performance form didn't detract from the importance of some key improvements in its 1964 version. The most notable changes were those made in the suspension system. An anti-roll bar became standard. At the rear, a single leaf spring was mounted transversely under the differential housing. By carrying 40% of the spring load, it allowed for softer coil springs and a significant reduction in the Corvair's tendency toward oversteer. This was an improvement long overdue in the Corvair's basic engineering, but, if Chevrolet was subject to criticism for waiting four years to accomplish them, it also deserved credit for applying posthaste the lessons learned from the Spyder to all the 1964 Corvair engines. Such features as the Spyder's chrome-alloy steel crankshaft, stellite-faced exhaust valves and stiffer valve springs were used across the board.

Nineteen sixty-five was the Corvair's time of glory. All new, hardtop and convertible styling, surely one of the best GM efforts of the decade, plus a totally revised rear suspension patterned after the Sting Ray's, clearly made this the most advanced and best Corvair of them all. Also welcomed as a positive step in the right direction were larger, 9.5 inch diameter drum brakes with 268.6 square inches of swept area. A boost in the turbocharger's pressure allowed Chevrolet to claim 180 hp for its blown engine. A notch below this level was a new 140 hp offering with four single carburetors.

Yet, the fate of this high quality, well designed, well styled and well engineered automobile was to be sealed in the marketplace by the Mustang. Once the 271 hp fastback Mustangs got out of the corral, it was the beginning of the end for the Corvair. Chevrolet belatedly began work on the Camaro and what was perhaps the most imaginative American car of its day stumbled on in an emasculated form until its final demise in 1968.

Right, 1963 Chevrolet Corvair Monza

The Corvair Sprint

Coinciding with the changes made by the factory in 1962 were the efforts of John Fitch to create what he felt was the proper sporting version of the Corvair. Fitch, one of great American sports car drivers of the fifties, first offered his Corvair Spring as a 1962 model based on the Monza coupe. The essence of Fitch's design philosophy was a simple one: By careful fine-tuning of the Corvair's suspension, along with some sensible, but by no means exotic, engine modifications, plus a tasteful restyling, the Corvair would become a grand touring car. Adding to its character were very strong overtones of Fitch's experience with European performance cars. Changes made in the Corvair rear suspension system included higher rate springs, a -2° negative camber plus stronger shocks. Along with softer front springs, these alterations advanced the road speed at which serious oversteer took place. A longer pitman arm reduced steering turns lock to lock to just 3.0. Fitch had first considered using a Paxton supercharger as the most desirable way of increasing the Corvair's power. He opted, however, for a four carburetor conversion plus a tuned exhaust system that yielded 144.5 hp (later revised to 130) for the production Sprints.

By early 1964, approximately 1,000 Sprints had been sold including a few of the turbo-charged Spyder variety. Fitch also offered a second generation of his Sprint based on the post-1965 Corvairs but the declining popularity of the Corvair during those years brought this program, plus a short-lived project to market the Phoenix, a rebodied Corvair with pseudo-classic styling overtones, to an end.

TIGER!

A Corvette is no tame kitten.

Sure, it can purr softly and gently as any household tabby, idling along in the sun. But even so, you catch a hint—a certain lithe competence in the way it moves, an undertone of raw power in the velvety exhaust.

For this one is a tiger! Under its sleek hood beats a savage heart—the steel-sheathed fury of 195 V8 horsepower. Its broad tread clings to the road with an incredible footsureness. And its 16-to-1 steering ratio, the taloned grip of its huge brakes, give it lightning-fast reflexes.

It is a tiger—but an obedient tiger. This fury of acceleration, these whiplash reflexes, are servant to the slightest nudge of your foot, the fractional pressure of your fingers. Your eye and your nerves command these steel muscles with an absoluteness you have never even dreamed.

True, this car can slip through the tangle of traffic with effortless serenity, its special Powerglide transmission metering out a faultless flow of power. In its foam-rubber seats, its deep floor-carpeting, its glove-soft upholstery, are the true marks of luxury.

But the tiger is always there . . . just under the surface. And, if there is fire in your blood . . . if your heart soars to the harsh music of excitement . . . this is the car that was meant for you. Corvette is its name. And *action* is its business. . . . Chevrolet Division of General Motors, Detroit 2, Michigan.

CHEVROLET CORVETTE

10. Chevrolet Corvette

Of all the great American performance cars, more has been written about the Corvette than any other marque. The reasons why aren't difficult to identify. No postwar American automobile can match the Corvette's decades-long output of performance milestones. None can equal its faithfulness to the philosophy of the two-seater sportscar and, over the years, no automobile built anywhere in the world has equalled the Corvette on a performance per dollar yardstick.

It was so fashionable for so many years to label the initial six-cylinder Corvettes as anemic performers that such a description assumed the stature of a Gospel Truth. This fundamental falsehood ignored the Corvette's capability compared not only to other, comparably priced two-seaters but to some of the fastest American sedans. The typical, run of the mill 1953 Corvette with its triple carb, 235 cid six-cylinder engine required 11 seconds to run from zero to 60 mph, a respectable time for any car of 1953-54 vintage with an automatic, 2-speed transmission and 150 horsepower. England's XK-120 Jaguar was quicker by about one second but it had the advantage of a modern, but long stroke, dual overhead cam engine and 4-speed transmission. Matched against such hot American machines as the 1954 Olds 88 and Buick Century, the Corvette also came away from a drag strip encounter in fine form. Both were zero-to-60-mph-in-approximately-12-seconds automobiles and, thus, the Corvette owner had no need to fear those modern, ohv V-8's.

However, sports cars were not, are not and never will be judged just on the basis of acceleration. They earn their stripes by cornering fast, braking quickly and staying together for long periods of racing. In that context, the Corvette of vintage 1953-54 found the going pretty rough. Simply put, it just didn't have the transmission and braking characteristics needed to match its far more seasoned adversaries.

In view of its future awesome performance capabilities, the progress towards that end taking place in the Corvette's early formative years was not dramatic, but it was there, nonetheless. Dick Thompson, looking back at his early impression of the Corvette, recollected for *CORVETTE NEWS* (Volume 4, Number 2), "We were running a driver's school prior to the races (at Andrews Air Force Base) and the local Chevrolet dealer brought a Corvette over for our opinion. The Corvette was a six-cylinder, Powerglide model with standard passenger car brakes and seat belts. But, surprisingly, when I drove it in practice the times were comparable to our Jaguar. Then the brakes heated and faded out. But I kept punishing the Corvette and by the end of the day I had blown the rear seal out of the transmission as well. Regardless of the damage I had inflicted on the car, I was impressed with its possibilities. The potential was there." In 1955, Chevrolet's superb 265 V-8, rated at 195 hp became a Corvette option that lowered its zero to 60 mph time to an impressive 8.7 seconds. The purists still pointed with distain to the Corvette's Powerglide transmission, but that became a meaningless gesture when, late in the model year, a few Corvettes with a 3-speed manual, all synchromesh transmissions left the St. Louis assembly plant.

A new fiberglass body, far more attractive and, with wind-up windows, certainly more functional than the 1953-55 version gave the 1956 Corvette a fresh new look. This visual vitality was matched by a very significant upgrading of the Corvette's performance capability. Zora Arkus-Duntov in the May, 1956, issue of *AUTO AGE* stated that one of his prime goals for the new Corvette was an upgrading of its high speed stability. Duntov, a man of substantial racing experience, noted that as a result "the driver of some ability could get really high performance safely." In effect, this was a codified message saying the 1956 Corvette was ready for serious road racing. To drive his point home, Duntov confidently added, "the car goes where it is pointed, and does so without hesitation. While pointed, it stays pointed, taking little notice of cross wind or any other disturbances."

Even with its base, 210 hp, 265 cid V-8, the Corvette could disturb a lot of preconceived notions about its athletic ability. The 225 hp version with dual, four-barrel Carter WCFB curburetors left no doubts whatsoever. Corvettes with this engine and the 3-speed manual transmission needed just 7.3 seconds for their zero to 60 mph sprint. Their top speed was nearly 130 mph. If more "go" was needed, Chevrolet offered on a "recommended for racing purposes only" basis the Duntov cam. Its price was a steep $188.30. The major advantage of the Duntov cam was its positive influence on the upper end of the Corvette's power curve. The normal 225 hp engine reached its peak power at 5200 rpm while the Duntov cam V-8 developed 240 hp at 5800 rpm.

In January, 1956, a month before the Daytona Speed Week, Duntov attained a one-way speed through the flying mile of 151.579 mph with a cobbled-up engineering prototype of the 1956 Corvette. His two-way average was 150.533 mph. For Speed Week, three Corvettes, all with the Duntov cam, were prepared for Duntov, John Fitch and Betty Skelton. Duntov's car was placed in the modified production sports car class due to its 255 hp engine equipped with experimental cylinder heads. As mentioned in Chapter 18, Chuck Daigh's Thunderbird outpaced Duntov's Corvette 92.14 mph to 89.75 mph in the standing start acceleration runs. Back in January, Duntov had managed a 91.69 mph run, which still fell shy of the T-Bird's mark. Both in the acceleration and flying mile runs for production sports cars, the Corvettes were more successful. In the former, Duntov led the field with a 88.77 mph average with Fitch putting it to the T-Birds by 145.54 mph to 134.40 mph through the flying mile.

Chevrolet, confident that the revamped Corvette could give a good account of itself in road racing, had to move in a hurry to get a four car team ready for the March 12-hour race at Sebring. John Fitch served as team manager and, almost as fast as his practice sessions indicated the need for revised components, as magnesium wheels, knock-off hubs, Al-fin brake drums, stronger shocks and sway bars, Chevrolet was making them available as Regular Production Options. Three of the Corvettes entered in the March 24th Sebring competed in Class C production. Thus, their performance was representative of Corvettes tuned to the teeth and equipped with SCCA approved racing options.

The fourth Corvette was an interesting hybrid. Its engine's bore and stroke were respectively 3.81 inches and 3.30 inches, providing a displacement of 307 cubic inches. With larger than stock valves and a 10.2:1 compression ratio it wasn't exactly your normal hot set-up Corvette. Also an uncommon sight in a Corvette was its 4-speed, German built ZF transmission.

The race's early laps gave Fitch lots of reasons to wonder if he really wanted to be a team manager. At the start, the sight of two Corvettes out front was a stirring, if short lived, spectacle since on lap two Fitch's 307 cid Corvette began to suffer from clutch slippage. This did not prove a terminal ailment but before the race was two hours out, two of the production class Corvettes were in the graveyard. At least

Below, 1953 Chevrolet Corvette

things didn't get any worse for Fitch, and at race end the Corvettes were placed 9th and 15th overall.

The Corvettes obviously hadn't put on the greatest sports car show on earth at Sebring but it wasn't long before advocates of the Jaguars and the Mercedes-Benz 300SL had to recognize the obvious: Corvette was their superior in SCCA competition. In fairness to its foreign opposition, and to other Corvettes running in class C prodution competition, the point has to be made that Dick Thompson's class winner was the best prepared Corvette on the circuit. In reality, it was a pseudo-official factory car, rebuilt, tested and prepared by General Motors before each race.

"Add fuel injection and get out of the way," served as an opener for *ROAD & TRACK'S* impression of the 1957 Corvette with fuel-injection and 4-speed transmission. Much has been made, and rightly so, of the landmark nature of the 1957 fuel-injected engine. Although Chrysler was there first with the 340 hp 300-B, Chevrolet's 1 hp per cubic inch output electrified the sports car world. *ROAD & TRACK* (August, 1957) said it as well as anyone: "The fuel-injection engine is an absolute jewel, quiet and remarkably docile when driven gently around town, yet instantly transformable into a roaring brute when pushed hard." In that latter stage, the fuel-injected Corvette with a 4.11:1 Positraction rear axle and the soon-to-be-a-legend Borg-Warner, all-synchromesh 4-speed compiled performance data unequalled, said *ROAD & TRACK*, "by any other production sports car." From zero to just-about-anything, the Corvette was unlike anything else available at its $3,909 price:

0 to 50 mph	4.7 seconds
0 to 60 mph	5.7 seconds
0 to 100 mph	16.8 seconds
standing start ¼-mile	14.3 seconds
top speed	132 mph

Above, 1956 Chevrolet Corvette

The fuel-injected engine with the Duntov cam and 10.5:1 compression ratio was priced at $481 and this probably accounted in part for the rarity of 1957 Corvettes with this engine. Of the 6,339 Corvettes built that year, only 240 were fuel-injected.

Some of them showed up at Daytona, but so did the very quick T-Birds, two of which were considerably faster than the Corvettes in the flying mile. However, Corvette was the class winner in the acceleration tests with a 93.047 mph finish.

One of several SR-2 Corvette specials was driven by Buck Baker in the modified class to a speed of 152.866 mph in the flying mile competition. This particular SR-2, which was the second one built, had revised bodywork to improve its aerodynamics. Its engine, rated at 310 hp, gained this extra power from a straight-through exhaust system.

Earlier, in November, 1956, Chevrolet had prepared two Corvettes to racing standards to serve as springboards for the 1957 competition campaign. Dick Thompson gave one of them a thrashing good time at Sebring. The lessons learned there and from racing both cars in the December, 1956, Nassau Speed Weeks helped Chevrolet develop the $725, Regular Production Option Number 684. Its components were all intended to upgrade Corvette handling and included stronger front springs, five instead of four rear leaf springs, a larger, 13/16 inch instead of 11/16 inch diameter front roll bar, stiffer shocks, quicker steering, cast iron finned brake drums with cerametalix linings and the Positraction limited-slip differential.

The intensity of Chevrolet's desire to make the Corvette a sports car respected the world over was exemplified by the SS Corvette. Its purpose was to better the best: in other words, beat the competition model Ferraris and Maseratis. This was far easier to desire than to achieve and when the SS arrived at Sebring for the 1957 Twelve Hours it was far from race ready and even further away from challenging the Europeans. Its early exit from the race after just 23 laps hardly served as a notice for the foreign factory teams to start shaking, but a closer look at its lap times, which, while slower than the Maserati 4.5 liter V-8, then the world's top performing racing car, suggest the SS could have developed into its near-equal. Before the race, both Stirling Moss and Juan Fangio put in some laps with the SS practice car and managed to come within 3 seconds of the big Maserati's 3 minute, 25.8 second lap mark. The greatest performance deficiency of the SS was in its relatively low 307 hp output. Obviously, Chevrolet could have improved on this and, since plans were well along on a desmodromic valve gear for the SS engine, it was prepared to do so. That is, until the June, 1957, ban by the American Manufacturers' Association on racing activities by its members.

This shortcircuit notwithstanding, Sebring '57 was an important event for the Corvette. Two standard Corvettes finished 12th and 15th, both many laps ahead of the nearest 300SL. Ed Cole, Chevrolet's Boss Man and unabashed Corvette advocate, saw that race as "the turn of the tide." As recounted by Karl Ludvigsen, Cole explained, "That was when the car started to attract attention in the areas where we had to have visibility. It began to take off and go, to confirm our original premise: that there was a demand for a product that recaptured the sport and fun of motoring." Underscoring Cole's statement was Dick Thompson's successful drive for the 1957 SCCA Class B Production Championship.

ROAD & TRACK featured the 1958 Corvette on its December, 1957, cover and aptly described it as "the subject of sundry improvements, as well as the corrosive influence of the "stylists." In terms of racing and performance options, the Corvette was an even more fearsome road machine. The top fuel injection engine now developed 290 hp at 6200 rpm and the various heavy-duty suspension options continued to do a creditable job of keeping things under control when the going got hot.

Less pleasing were the 1958 Corvette's phony hood louvers and meaningless twin chrome strips that cluttered its rear deck. Similarly, nine inches more overall length did little for the Corvette. Still, CORVETTE NEWS was well within the mark noting the Corvette, "has revitalized and nurtured a tradition of motoring sport, of driving just for the sheer fun of it."

The top-rated RPO579D engine was boosted up to 290 hp at 6200 rpm for 1958 and the RPO 684 competition suspension package now included functional air scoops positioned in the Corvette's small, side grilles. Since the 1956 turning point, the Corvette's weight had slowly been edging up and by 1958 it was pushing the 3,000 pound mark. No doubt this propensity toward obesity prompted Carroll Shelby's famous "hawg" reference to the Corvette, but in 1958 it was in "Purple People Eater" form, driven by Jim Jeffords, that Corvette once again was crowned the SCCA Class B Production Champion.

There were no engine changes for 1959 but Chevrolet suspension engineers added rear radius rods that helped combat the axle's tendency to wind up under full throttle stress. New shocks with nitrogen filled bags positioned between the shocks' cylinders and reservoirs gave the Corvette a smoother ride with less bottoming out.

ROAD & TRACK (January, 1959) concluded that the 1959 Corvette "probably has more performance per dollar than anything you could buy." This undoubtedly pleased Zora Arkus-Duntov, but Mr. Duntov would have preferred the Corvette with less bulk and weight. For a time in the late fifties, such a Corvette, based upon a proposed for 1960 production series of Q-cars, had a chance of becoming a

reality. The resultant "Q-Corvette" would have weighed approximately 2200 pounds, featured independent rear suspension, a rear mounted transmission and a 94 inch wheelbase. Its existence was dependent upon the success of the Q-sedans and when their development was abandoned so was that of the Q-Corvette. Its demise meant the Corvette was destined to continue in its basic form until 1963 and even then not become a light-weight sports car. It's interesting to speculate that if the Corvette had undergone this radical transformation in 1960, the AC Cobra's challenge to the Corvette's racing supremacy might not have been successful. On the other hand, the Q-Corvette would have been a very expensive car to produce and that could have had a detrimental impact on the Corvette's continuation during the not-so-rosy years of the seventies.

Looking back at the Corvette's evolution in the late fifties, Duntov told SPORTS CAR ILLUSTRATED (December, 1960), "Originally our plan was to develop the car along separate touring and racing lines, as Jaguar did with the XK series on one hand and the C-type and D-type on the other. With this in mind we first introduced racing options, then the SR2, finally the SS which was intended to be our 'prototype' competition car. When this project was cut off, we realized we had to approach the Corvette in some other way. Since we could no longer have two kinds of Corvettes with different characteristics, we decided to give the Corvette buyer as much of both worlds as we could — to use our racing experience to combine in one automobile the comfort of a tourer and the ability of a racer. A big order, yes, but an interesting and worthwhile one."

This restructuring of Corvette design philosophy still had to exist within the framework of a dated chassis and suspension (bolstered fortunately by one of the great American V-8's) and this was far more evolutionary than revolutionary in nature. The optional competition suspension was dropped while the stock suspension was used and a rear bar was added providing better road control. The spring rates for the front and rear suspension remained unchanged but another inch of rebound was provided at the rear. These changes made the 1960 Corvette more stable and less susceptible to roll in the turns.

Corvette's two top engines with fuel-injection reported in with 275 and 315 hp. Both were available with aluminum heads that reduced engine weight by 53 pounds. The larger (1.94 inch) intake valves and larger ports provided by these heads were, along with their light weights, points in their favor but their casting was a very precise operation and some that shouldn't have got past inspection, did. When that happened, the stage was set for trouble. The heads would overheat, warp and provide lots of woe to both Chevrolet and some mighty unhappy Corvette owners. Fortunately, Chevrolet moved quickly to blow the whistle on the production of these troublesome heads.

No such short-circuiting of the Corvette's racing career took place. Bob Johnson drove one to the SCCA B-production championship and, for the first time, Corvettes took part in the Le Mans Twenty-Four Hour Race. It wasn't exactly a rags to riches success story. Far more accurately it was a ragged run, limp to the finish line struggle. Both Briggs Cunningham and Luck Casner's Camoradi U.S.A. racing team entered Corvettes and both had their share of hard luck and heartbreak. The Cunningham entries, three strong, were beautifully prepared, having had the beneficient hands of Zora Arkus-Duntov and Alferd Momo laid upon them. In practice, the Corvette's 112.18 mph lap time compared favorably to the 113.62 mph speed of the quickest

250 GT Ferrari.

Fairly early in the race (lap 32), one of the Cunningham Corvettes, driven by Jim Kimberly, crashed in virtually zero visibility. Hours later, it was joined by the Dick Thompson-Fred Windridge Corvette which, after crashing into the same embankment as Kimberly had, struggled on until it was unable to complete the minimum 25 lap distance between stops for water and oil. This particular car had been the fastest Corvette in the race, having turned a lap at 113.13 mph with an all-out top speed recorded as 151 mph. The remaining Cunningham Corvette, running on seven cylinders and its engine receiving ice packs to ward off over-heating, clawed its way to an honorable 8th place finish. The single Camoradi Corvette also completed the twenty-four hours of racing but not within its minimum distance requirement to qualify as an official finisher.

SPORTS CAR ILLUSTRATED (December, 1960) grumbled about the 1961 Corvette's styling, which it viewed as having originated in "an era when design effort was concentrated on the simulation of devices and effects that were mechanical in appearance but not necessarily automotive or operational: phony louvers, scoops, jet pods here and there, dashboards that sought to confuse rather than clarify." At the same time they had to recognize the obvious: that the 1961 Corvette was "one of the most remarkable marriages of touring and violent performance we have ever enjoyed, especially at the price."

It was tempting to knock the Corvette's appearance and *SPORTS CAR ILLUSTRATED's* comments weren't exactly inappropriate but it wasn't alone among sports cars in being susceptible to criticism for its cluttered exterior (take a look sometime at a Daimler SP250 if you want to see really ugly fiberglass). Still, it remained alone as an American sports car, sold at a reasonable price, offering stirring, stunning and stupendous performance capable of overcoming all but a few very expensive, European automobiles. With the 315 hp, fuel injected V-8 fitted with

Below, 1964 Chevrolet Corvette

cast-iron versions of the ill-fated aluminum heads, the 4-speed Corvette tested by *CAR LIFE* (September, 1961) blasted from rest to 60 mph in 5.5 seconds and to 100 mph in 14.5 seconds. Its version of the zero-to-100-mph-to-zero time trial was accomplished in just 22 seconds. No wonder the Corvette had another great SCCA competition year.

Dick Thompson once again won the Class B Production title. Along with Don Yenko, he won more points than any other SCCA racer. No wonder *ROAD & TRACK* (January, 1961), wrote, "Continual refinements since 1954 have made the Corvette into a sports car for which no owner need make excuses. It goes, it stops, and it corners . . . The Corvette is absolutely unmatched for performance per dollar in terms of transportation machinery."

After six years as a 283 cubic incher, the Corvette V-8, by virtue of new bore and stroke measurement of 4.00 inches and 3.25 inches (the 283's respective dimensions were 3.88 and 3.0) grew to 327 cubes for 1962. This brought with it a boost in horsepower to 360 at 6000 rpm and equally important, a dramatic change in its torque curve. The older engine hadn't been particularly strong in this department, with only 295 lbs-ft at 4700 rpm. The 327 delivered a respectable 352 lbs-ft at only 4000 rpm. Armed with this engine, the Corvettes captured both the SCCA's Class A and B production national championships.

After ten years of production and development the Corvette entered its second decade in a wholly new form that in the early eighties was still serving as its basis. Although much of the credit (or blame) for this design longevity is due to the changes wrought upon the industry by profound shifts in consumer expectations, economic and environmental concerns, it also speaks well for the basic excellence of the 1963 Sting Ray. Compared to the 1962 model, its wheelbase was, at 98 inches, four inches shorter, its height reduced by 2.4 inches, and its weight almost identical to the older model! This latter point didn't make Duntov happy but on a lot of other details he had good reason to be pleased. After all, "For the first time," he said, "I now have a Corvette I can be proud to drive in Europe." Its styling,

closely patterned after Bill Mitchell's racing Sting Ray of 1959-60, while still a bit too much for sensitive European critics, was visually very exciting. Its independent rear suspension was derived from the basic geometry of the CERV-1 rear-engined research automobile and for power there was the great 360 hp, 327 fuel injected V-8.

CORVETTE NEWS reported that "The word 'American' keynoted all of our preliminary planning discussions. The new Corvette was to be a broad-shouldered masculine American sports car." It was that and more. A 150 mph top speed under favorable conditions was possible with the 360 hp Sting Ray coupe, and, with its traditional zero to 60 mph runs under 6 seconds, the Corvette's straight line performance was as American as Apple Pie. Now, however, with its new rear suspension, and reduced unsprung weight, the Corvette cornered with the best of them. No longer did Carroll Shelby's comment that if "You learn to handle that hawg . . . you can handle anything" apply. Now the Corvette's new level of sophistication made every one of its drivers reach new levels of competence.

With its excellent 49% — 51% front-rear weight distribution and RPO Z06 competition package, the new Sting Ray looked like a sure bet to continue the Corvette's reign as the top SCCA production sports car. Then, old Carroll Shelby suddenly took a liking to snakes and before long Cobras were winners and Corvettes were also-rans.

Duntov was not willing to accept this setback, coming as it did when the Corvette was finally coming of age as a true, international class sports car. By late 1962, a lightweight Corvette was being tested at Sebring and, until the January 21, 1963, General Motors' decree that all its divisions stop their racing programs, all signals were green for this Gran Sport Corvette to debut at Sebring and then cross the Atlantic for a shot at winning the Le Mans race. If they had been given a chance to mature to full greatness, these GS Corvettes would have made the all-out Corvette-Cobra confrontations into road-racing legends. With a race weight of under 1900 pounds and 377 cid V-8's (with aluminum heads and blocks) pumping out close to 500 hp there was no way it could have been any different.

Chevrolet was able to spirit several GS models into the proper hands where they aptly demonstrated their potential. Racing journalist Bernard Cahier was given the opportunity by John Mecom to spend some time with a GS during the 1964 Nassau races. Writing in *SPORTS CAR GRAPHICS* (March, 1964), Cahier reported, "It is a very large car but quite easy to drive, immensely powerful but very controllable, and having general performance and handling which put it well ahead of the Ferrari GTO and Ford Cobra." Cahier went on to record zero to 100 mph runs in 9 seconds and standing start quarter-miles in under 12 seconds with the Gran Sport. With a direct, above-board racing program prohibited, though, the Corvette's corporate supporters did the next best thing, improve what was already a very fine automobile, smooth out its rough spots, sharpen its fine performance points and continually upgrade the Corvette's street capabilities.

In 1964, work began (which continued through 1967) to clean up the Sting Ray's exterior body lines. A great start was to trash its split rear window. Ironically, this one-year only distinction of the '63 coupe has made it a great collectible, but, in terms of a contemporary change, the move to a larger, one-piece window made good sense. The top-level engine for 1964 was boosted to 375 hp and used a new high-lift cam in place of the old, but memorable, Duntov Mark I cam that originated back in 1956. Enhancing its

handling were new, front and rear variable rate springs that were derived from the old SS and CERV-1 programs and recalibrated shock absorbers.

Nineteen fifty-five brought both four-wheel disc brakes and, after January 1, 1965, Chevrolet's 396 cid-425 hp Turbo-Jet V-8 to the Corvette. The excitement this development aroused had scarcely settled down when the 427 cid version with either 390 hp or 425 hp came on line for the 1966 Corvettes. This amount of power made availability of the fuel-injection Corvette engine redundant, and Chevrolet dropped it from the 1966 Corvette option line-up.

Experts have described the use of the big 396/426 cid engine in the Corvette as a watershed "in that it marked a distinct change in Chevrolet in its interpretation of the sports car." Actually, Chevrolet was just making certain that the two-seater Corvette wouldn't suffer humiliation at the hands of any four-seater domestic supercar. By 1967, the 427 V-8 was available in five different versions for the Corvette, ranging in horsepower from 390 to 435. The two top Corvette 427's had identical, 435 hp ratings. Both were suspiciously low. The RPO-L-71 engine with triple carburetors and mechanical lifters probably was a true 460 hp unit and the elusive and expensive ($805.75) RPO-L-89 with its big exhaust valves and aluminum heads was capable of turning out 500 horsepower.

By 1969, the Corvette, having received a new fiberglass suit the previous year, was unlike any other sports car in the world. The L-88 engine with its giant four-barrel, aluminum intake manifold, cylinder heads and special 12:1 pistons was hiding its ability under a bushel labeled 430 hp. If this engine wasn't enough to cause a rapid pulse there was ZL-1. Its all aluminum block brought the ZL-1's weight down from the L-88's by one hundred pounds. Just about all the bits and pieces associated with *extreme* performance were found in this engine. It had strength where it was needed, in its connecting rods for example, and size where it did the most good, again, to cite just one illustration, in its valves and ports. It had no difficulty in recording quarter-miles of 12.1 seconds at 116 mph. With 585 hp at 6600 rpm, its top speed cast a shadow over the 200 mph mark.

After 1970, all Corvette engines were designed to run on either low lead or leaded regular fuel with research octane number of 91 or higher. The highest compression ratio of any Corvette engine was 9.0:1 and, in general, both horsepower and torque output was down approximately 10-12%. *CORVETTE NEWS* conceded there was drop off in performance but maintained, "Normal street performance is off very little. Of course, the top end is down somewhat . . ." Once the floodgates were opened, push came to shove and the Corvette was on its way towards performance never-never land.

In this regard, it was fitting and proper that in its last year (1970) of unadulterated performance ability, the Corvette was available in a potent, small block form as the 350 cid LT-1. Its single four-barrel Holley, lightweight intake manifold, high-lift cam and 11.0:1 compression ratio provided a conservative 370 hp rating and concrete quarter-mile speeds of 102 mph. Nowadays, a tour behind the wheel of a 1970 LT-1 is an experience owners of newer model Corvettes should avoid—unless they want to find out what they've been missing.

Right, Top, 1968 Chevrolet Corvette
Right, Middle, 1974 Chevrolet Corvette
Right, Bottom, 1980 Chevrolet Corvette

The Car That "Swept the Field" at Daytona...

CHRYSLER 300

It's the most breathtaking car to drive you've ever known! You'll be off and away in this brilliant new low-slung beauty to the throaty roar of 300 hp — the greatest, *safest* power in any American car. You'll feel the same thrill that today's most avid sports-car enthusiasts enjoy . . . the same light-handed, light-footed control and ground-gripping security.

In a Chrysler 300 *you* can enjoy *the same flashing performance that won 1st and 2nd places in the 1955* NASCAR

Daytona Beach "Flying Mile," at speeds over 130 mph—plus the safe maneuverability and endurance that swept 1st and 2nd places in the 160-mile Grand National stock car race. For the sleek and stunning new CHRYSLER 300 . . . in regular, though limited production . . . has the same road-hugging *look, feel, and safety* that have made the Chrysler name famous in the world's greatest road races.

Arrange for a drive today . . . your Chrysler Dealer is the man to see!

AMERICA'S MOST POWERFUL STOCK CAR

Brake HP: 300 @ 5200 rpm . . . Comp. Ratio: 8.5 to 1 . . . Two 4-barrel carburetors . . . Special suspension for maximum cornering, road-hugging performance and control . . . PowerFlite Automatic Transmission . . . Power Brakes . . . Dual exhaust system . . . Wheelbase: 126 inches . . . Over-all length: 219 inches . . . Height: 58.6 inches.

See Your Chrysler-Plymouth Dealer

11. Chrysler

In 1950, the most powerful Chrysler one could buy possessed a straight eight engine developing 135 hp. A year later the situation was somewhat different. Chrysler had, with the introduction of its "Fire Power" V-8, leapfrogged over its arch rivals at General Motors and Ford and had become the leader in the horsepower race then rapidly gaining momentum in America.

The use of hemispherical combustion chambers in Chrysler's 331 cubic inch, 180 hp V-8 was in itself hardly new. In 1923, one of the patron saints of engine design, Sir Harry Ricardo, had referred to them in his book, *THE INTERNAL COMBUSTION ENGINE,* as being "almost ideal on theromodynamic grounds." Yet, as events unfolded their espousal by Chrysler was to have a far reaching impact upon Chrysler's role in the supercar era.

Upon its introduction, Chrysler stated several reasons for the use of "hemi-heads" on its new Fire Power V-8. This design, noted Chrysler clearly with an eye on the future, with its large valve area and excellent manifolding was more than just a highly competitive engine for the present. If the need arose, far more power via larger valves, increased displacement and a much higher compression ratio was on tap.

In a sense the Fire Power V-8 was a blend of European and American design preferences. Its V-8 layout, and nearly equal 3 3/16 inch bore and 3 5/8 inch stroke were clearly reflections of modern day American thinking. Its valve train, with its 60° inclined valves and the centrally located spark plug were more European in structure.

In terms of horsepower rating, the new Chrysler engine exceeded Cadillac's top figure of 160 by a comfortable 20 horsepower margin. It's also worth noting that Chrysler's 180 hp rating was taken from an engine with its fan, water pump, air cleaner and generator installed. No other American car then in production exceed its 0.544 hp per cubic inch of displacement ratio.

The response to the new Chrysler by the nation's motoring press was, as expected, highly favorable. *ROAD AND TRACK* (November, 1951) called it "the leading contender for the Mexican Road Race, America's fastest production car." *MOTOR TREND* considered the Chrysler to be the best U.S. production car it tested during 1951. While *MOTOR TREND* had not evaluated DeSoto, Chevrolet or Plymouth models for 1951, it's not likely any of those would have offered anything to cause for change of opinion.

Chrysler had built a car that combines "safety, economy and outstanding performance," wrote Griff Borgeson for *MOTOR TREND.* "It is not perfect," he continued, "yet it is closer to the goal than any other family automobile currently produced in America. It cost the Chrysler Corporation a lot of money to build the new V-8: it took a lot of courage to flout tradition and experiment with design. The Award winner is, in concept, a major step ahead in American automotive design."

England's Christopher Jennings, then editor of *THE MOTOR,* offered similar sentiments that, if anything, emphasized further the historical importance of Chrysler's new engine. "If ten years ago one had read of a car fitted with a V-8 inclined-valve-head engine giving 180 hp, hydraulic transmission, disc brakes and power steering, one would have concluded almost certainly that it was the product of one of the smaller European makers . . . It is sobering to realize that this specification today pertains to an American vehicle designed for production not at the rate of hundreds per year, but in terms of thousands per week . . ." wrote Jennings.

Undoubtedly with an ear to the ground and his eye to the future, the technical editor of *THE MOTOR,* Laurence Pomeroy, observed (*THE MOTOR,* February 28, 1951) that "the design is clearly capable of considerable development . . . A potential output of some 250 hp can thus be envisaged and even up to 300 hp might well be possible by suitable changes in inlet and exhaust pipe design. The influence of such a modified engine on the American position in sports car racing will not escape the eye of the European observer."

The eyes of Chrysler engineering, after the basic Fire Power design had been finalized and production was underway, were directed toward the objective of assuring that in future years Chrysler's position of supremacy over its competitors would be maintained. Towards this end several exotic versions of the hemi-head were developed. One particularly sophisticated version illustrated just how far the basic design could be developed. Beginning with a stock Fire Power V-8, engineers raised its compression ratio from 7.5:1 to 12.6:1. Its intake valve diameters were increased by 1/8 inch, the diameter of the exhaust valves by 1/4 inch. Replacing the production cam which had an intake duration of 252° and a 30° valve overlap was a special unit with respective specifications of 280° and 60°. Dual exhaust headers plus exhaust ports that were considerably more efficient than production counterparts were also used. Topping off these modifications was an intake manifold equipped with four single throat carburetors. The result of tests using a special fuel consisting of 100 octane gas with 1.3 cc lead added per gallon, known as ISO-Octane, were startling. A maximum horsepower rating of 353 was attained as was a peak torque output of 383 lbs-ft at 5200 rpm. James Zeder, Chrysler's Engineering Vice-President whose late brother Fred was one of the principle designers of the original Chrysler high compression engine of 1924, related some of the details of this aspect of the Fire Power's development in a paper delivered to the Society of Automotive Engineers in March, 1952. Even when regular premium grade fuel was used and the compression ratio lowered back to 7.5:1 the output was an impressive 309 hp.

A similar engine with an 8.1:1 compression ratio and developing in excess of 310 hp was given extensive publicity as an engine for which Chrysler's experimental K-310 was designed.

In 1951, the American Automobile Association announced that henceforth engines based on non-racing, production designs would be allowed to run at Indianapolis provided their displacement did not exceed 335.5 cubic inches. With the Chrysler V-8 well within this limit, the development of an engine for possible competition use at Indy by Chrysler engineers was not exactly a surprise. In effect, the end result was a logical extension of the work

Left, 1955 Chrysler C-300

done earlier by Chrysler engineers to extract 353 hp from the 331 cid V-8. For Indianapolis, a Hilborn-Travers fuel injection system replaced the four carburetor set-up used earlier. A Vertex Scintilla magneto system was also installed as a battery based electrical system was not needed for Indianapolis. Other modifications included a wilder camshaft, mechanical tappets and domed pistons. These changes brought the engine's output up to 404 bhp at 5200 rpm with a maximum torque rating of 442 lbs.-ft. A subsequent change of heart by the A.A.A. which placed the limit of 271 cid on a stock block entries wrote *finis* to this project but in late 1952 the possibility was very strong that with Corporate blessing Chrysler-powered Indy cars would have been at least in the running for starting berths for the 1953 Indianapolis 500.

Results of two separate test sessions conducted at the Indianapolis Motor Speedway in late 1952 reflected the Chrysler's potency. Joe Jostillio driving a Chrysler-powered Indy car averaged 135 mph for 140 miles and compiled a total of 900 miles so trouble free that the plugs never needed changing. Later, a Kurtis roadster with a Hemi V-8 was used at Indianapolis for tire testing by Firestone. Over a two week period, Joe James completed 200 laps at an average speed of 134.35 mph. Fifty-six consecutive laps were run at 135.02 mph. In total, 356 laps, or 890 miles, were compiled by the Chrysler-Kurtis on the same set of Champion NA-19 spark plugs.

The significance of this interlude upon the subsequent evolution of the C-300 cannot be ignored. *CAR AND DRIVER* (August, 1961) reported a Chrysler engineer's belief that "The Indianapolis project's contribution to our knowledge of performance was immeasurable. Without such experimental race engines, we couldn't have been successful with the Chrysler 300 package. As to ram induction, this is where we learned to do it!"

Indianapolis was not, however, the only racing avenue explored by Chrysler Corporation at this time. In the 1950 LeMans 24-Hour Endurance Race, Briggs Cunningham had entered a team of two Cadillacs. Both had originally been Model 61 Coupes, but one had been rebodied with a special "streamlined" body known and "LeMonstre." Its engine was fitted with five twin-throat Carter carburetors. The second entry retained its stock appearance but had a slightly modified engine. The two cars finished 10th and 11th overall with the coupe leading its more radical teammate to the finish line.

Upon his return to the United States, an advance look at Chrysler's upcoming new V-8 was enough to convince Cunningham that this was the engine he wanted to use for his next, considerably more ambitious LeMans venture. Although far too bulky and, at 3400 pounds, much heavier than the competition, the Chrysler-powered Cunningham was a far better performer in the 1951 LeMans race than its 18th place finish seemed to suggest. Until it suffered a combination of valve and bearing ills, most likely stemming from the poor quality of gasoline used that year, the C-2 Cunningham ran with the leaders. Two of the three Cunninghams entered went out early in the race due to damages resulting from off-road excursions and bouts with an immovable retaining wall. However, until its engine began to rebel against the forced consumption of low octane fuel the remaining C-2 did extremely well. At one time it held second place and at the race's mid-point its average was a respectable 88 mph, with a best lap of 98.9 mph. On the Mulsanne straight it was credited with a maximum speed of 152 mph.

In the 1951 Carrera Panamericana, Carl Kiekhaefer's two 1951 Chryslers driven by Tony Bettenhausen and John Fitch turned in performances that, like those of the Cunninghams at LeMans, appeared on the surface to be rather dismal. Fitch had gotten off to a super start passing all the cars that had started before him except one until, due to a malfunction of his engine's oil presure relief valve, its mainbearings burned out. Bettenhausen had a miserable time in the early mountain sections, ending the first day of racing in 66th position. Gradually, however, as the terrain flattened out the Chrysler picked up the pace, at times exceeding 140 mph and coming on strong for a 16th place finish. Up ahead of Bettenhausen, another Chrysler, driven by Bill Sterling had done even better, finishing third behind the two leading Ferraris. The following year, the Kiekhaefer Chrysler, driven by Roger McFee, finished fifth, its average speed only 1.8 mph slower than the Lincoln which won the stock American car class.

A witness to the race was Bob Rodger, chief engineer at Chrysler, who played a major role in the development of Chrysler's "Heavy-Duty" engine-suspension option for 1953. This package included a dual-four-barrel carburetor manifold, a higher compression ratio, roller tappets, longer duration cam, front and rear anti-roll bars, air-lift suspension stiffeners and disc brakes (which the Imperial had used in 1951). A total of 15 of these "super" Chrysler New Yorkers were built in 1953-54. Chrysler rated these engines at 235 hp, the same as that of the 1954 Chrysler New Yorker DeLuxe. In actuality they were 300-plus h engines. On February 21, 1954, Lee Petty drove one to

Above, 1952 Chrysler K-310

victory in the l60 mile Daytona Beach Grand National race. Another Chrysler victory was scored by Tony Bettenhausen in an A.A.A. l50 mile race at Milwaukee's State fair Park on July ll.

When Chrysler opened its new 4,000 acre proving grounds at Chelsea, Michigan, the activities included a twenty-four hour run with a l954 Chrysler New Yorker DeLuxe. Drivers including Tony Bettenhausen averaged ll8.184 for the twenty-four hours. Their maximum speed exceeded l25 mph and many lap averages were above l24 mph. Another twenty-four run conducted at Indianapolis Motor Speedway was successfully completed at an average of 89.76 mph.

The prowess the Chrysler hemi-V-8 had exhibited since its introduction in l95l clearly marked it as the most advanced production model engine available in any automobile. Yet, Chrysler Corporation, even with the introduction of a 276.l cid, l60 bhp hemi V-8 in the DeSoto in l952 (Dodge received a 241.3 cid "Red Ram" V-8 with hemi-heads the following year), was not keeping pace with Ford and General Motors in the sales race:

Production

	1951	1952
General Motors	2,255,500	1,801,500
Chrysler Corporation	1,233,300	952,600
Ford Motor Company	1,165,000	1,004,800

	1953	1954
General Motors	2,799,600	2,874,300
Chrysler Corporation	1,296,600	723,300
Ford Motor Company	1,546,500	1,687,200

Chrysler was clearly in trouble. In l953, all Chrysler Corporation cars had received new styling. "Bigger on the inside, shorter on the outside" was how Chrysler touted its new models but in l954 even price cuts of up to $274 failed to move them off Chrysler dealers' lots. Chrysler's share of the market fell below 13%. Its Plymouth had dropped to fifth place in sales behind Chevrolet, Ford, Buick and Oldsmobile. Help was on the way, though, in the form of Virgil Exner's new styling proposals for l955. The price tag was high; Chrysler described its l955 offerings as the cars with the "Hundred Million Dollar Look," but at last Chrysler's great hemi V-8 would be available in an automobile whose appearance visually matched its dazzling performance. Nonetheless, there was still another element missing from Chrysler Corporation's projected lineup for l955 that by its absence tended to accentuate Chrysler's growing reputation as something less than a full-time competitor to Ford and General Motors. In the early fifties, Chrysler had easily matched its adversaries' dream cars with such handsome projects as the K-3l0, C-200 and d'Elegance. But Chevrolet had clearly gotten the jump on its opposition with the 1953 Corvette. The impact of the "First of the Dream Cars to Come True" was not lost on Ford and for l955 its Thunderbird was ready and by most standards it was superior to the Corvette. With no sports car of its own, Chrysler apparently was out in the cold in what was shaping up as strictly a two-way contest. For years, Chrysler men such as Bob Rodger had worked to make Chrysler America's top performing car and now it seemed that Chrysler, financially strapped as it was, was going to take it

in the chin once again. Chevrolet and Ford would pick up all the marbles and Chrysler, still hamstrung by the ghost of the Airflow, would be left without representation in what promised to be a prestigious, if small, segment of the marketplace.

In the fall of 1954, Rodger made his move. Chrysler could not meet the opposition head-on but it could outflank them. The early Corvette with its side curtains and so-so weather protection hadn't exactly set sales records and Ford, eager to outdo Chevrolet at every opportunity, had avoided making a similar mistake with the Thunderbird. It was weather-tight, possessed roll up windows and in general was more in tune with American motoring tastes than the early Corvette. Chrysler, Rodger maintained, could go a step further and build a full size sedan with the comfort and size Americans were accustomed to but also endowed with performance second to none. Chrysler possessed the bits and pieces needed to make such an automobile; all that was needed was the corporate desire to put them together. Rodger got E. C. Quinn, Chrysler division manager to approve his proposal and the C-300 was just months away from becoming a reality.

Key figures in the styling aspect of the C-300's development were Cliff Voss, Chrysler-Imperial design boss, and of course Virgil Exner. The end product of their efforts was a blend of the best elements of Chrysler's Forward Look for l955. The C-300's appearance was dominated by the bold, divided grille of the Imperial that, in concert with the smooth, relatively chrome-free body from the New Yorker, gave it an appearance perhaps best described as purposeful. The C-300's underpinnings consisted of the front suspension and brakes from the Imperial, to which were added heavy duty springs and shock absorbers. The expression "heavy-duty" when applied to the suspension components of the C-300 was, if anything, an understatement. The front coil springs of a stock New Yorker had a defection rate of 480 pounds per inch. The C-300, by contrast, was fitted with units with an 800 per inch rating. At the rear, seven leaf springs were used. Here, too, the l60 pounds-per-inch spring rates for the C-300 were substantially greater than the New Yorker's l00 pounds-per-inch. Goodyear 8.00 x 15 Super Cushion Nylon Special tires were used on the C-300 and were available with either the standard steel wheels or the optional wire wheels (actually left-over Imperial units). Not since the days of the great Duesenberg J had a large American automobile been built like the first C-300. Like that earlier masterpiece, the new Chrysler could lay claim to being America's Most Powerful Automobile at 300 hp via the use of dual four-barrel carburetors and a cam with 60° overlap was the claimed output of the C-300's 331.l cubic inch V-8.

Due to the late starting date of the C-300's development, the first production models did not begin leaving the Jefferson Avenue Imperial assembly line until January, l955. It didn't take long, however, for the word to get spread around that production of the C-300 marked the beginning of an automotive legend. The racing heritage of the C-300 certainly was not something Chrysler sought to down play when it introduced the C-300 to the press. "Powered by a 300 horsepower modified Chrysler Fire Power V-8 and fitted with special suspension, the ground-hugging hardtop," Chrysler said "was designed to the specifications of motor sport enthusiasts who, since the introduction of the Fire Power engine in l951, have been asking Chrysler to build an automobile with many sports car characteristics."

"Among the things they asked for were a modified Fire Power engine like those used at LeMans and Watkins Glenroad races, a simple unadorned exterior, the roadhugging look and feel of a sports car and a practical, durable leather interior which will take hard wear. This car incorporates these qualities."

Within three days of its press presentation Chrysler had received over 1000 orders for the C-300. In late February, not long after its January 17, 1955, public announcement, the C-300 (an awkward term almost universally ignored by the motoring press which favored calling this new automobile the Chrysler 300) was turned out in force for the 1955 NASCAR Speed Week. In the American Stock Car Flying Mile competition, Warren Koechling drove a 300 at 127.580 mph, just ahead of a second Chrysler 300 at 126.542. The highest placed 1955 Cadillac stood third behind the two leading Chryslers with a speed of 120.478. The fastest Chrysler New Yorker registered a maximum speed of 114.631 mph, the Buick Century, 116.345 mph. The big 300's with Chrysler's 2-speed PowerFlite transmission standard didn't do as well in the standing start one mile acceleration competition. In that category, the best Koechling could attain with his 300 was fifth place with a speed of 76.840 mph. Ahead of him was a 1955 Cadillac (80.428 mph), two Chevrolets (78.158 mph and 77.519 mph) and a Buick Century (77.436 mph). This relatively poor showing, however, merely emphasized the true character of the C-300. From zero to 60 mph it was quick, usually reaching 60 mph in roughly 10 seconds, but there were many American sedans that could match or exceed that mark. Where the 4,300 pound C-300 excelled was in its ability to reach 60 mph in short order and then keep on going up to nearly 130 mph in safety. The great stability of the C-300 was demonstrated by one driver conducting a road test of the C-300 for *AUTO AGE* magazine. Traveling across an expansive parking area at 55 mph he suddenly cut the wheel to the right and hung on for dear life (the Chrysler's slippery leather interior didn't do much for this kind of maneuvering). The 300 went into a controlled drift, kept its composure and displayed not a trace of bad handling manners.

Tom McCahill tested Warren Koechling's 127 mph 300 after his record run and found it an automobile very much to his liking. In his report published in *MECHANIX ILLUSTRATED*, (May, 1955), he described the 300 as "hard-boiled magnificent piece of semi-competition transportation, built for the real automotive connoisseur." The 300's suspension, which came as a shock to some owners who expected the same silkiness of more mundane Chrysler sedans, was seen by McCahill as "severe as a New Hampshire winter . . . To hand-rock one of these cars when parked," noted McCahill, "is similar to playing ping-pong with an anvil." During the 1955 racing season, the combination of Carl Kiekhaefer and the C-300 became the dominant force both in NASCAR Champion for 1955. In AAA races. Frank Mundy's eight first place finishes earned him the AAA racing title.

The C-300's successor, the 300-B, began the letter car tradition at Chrysler. Like the earlier model the second 300 was introduced after the rest of the 1956 Chrysler line had been unveiled in late 1955. For 1956, Chrysler designers blended the Imperial grille with the C-71 Windsor body in which specially located holes were drilled to accomodate the 300's special trim. If anything, the 300-B was a more attractive car than the D-300. The redesigned rear fender line, which, of course, suggested the fins of '57, gave the 300-B a profile somewhat sleeker than the C-300 whose rear tail light arrangement seemed almost dowdy by comparison. Useful, both in terms of appearance and function, were the 300's larger 3 inch exhaust pipes and 9 inch wide wheels.

For the first time since its debut in 1951, the Chrysler engine was given a boost in displacement. With a larger 3.94 inch bore, up from 3.81; it now stood at 354 cubic inches. This plus a higher 9.0:1 compression ratio, rather than 8.5:1, resulted in a rating of 340 hp at 5200 rpm. The optional 10.0:1 compression ratio heads increased this figure up to 355 hp. New connecting rods, tri-metal bearings and a forged and hardened crankshaft were also new engine features for 1956. Suspension changes were limited to the replacement of the "export" shocks used in 1955 with modified heavy duty Oriflow units. These were somewhat softer and slightly improved the 300's ride at low speeds. Center-plane-type "Power Smooth" brakes were adopted *en masse* for all 1956 Chryslers. Several interesting changes were made in the transmission area, one being the availability of the small 3-speed manual transmission as used on the Chrysler Windsor. Since the Windsor still used the 331 cid hemi developing only 225 hp, the desirability of the linking of this engine with the far more robust 300-B engine was debatable although it was mated to a special 11 inch clutch not used in any other Chrysler Corporation automobile. In any case, only 31 of the 1,050 300-B's manufactured were so equipped. More interesting and useful was the switch over, late in the model run, to Chrysler's new 3-speed Torqueflite automatic transmission. A total of fourteen rear axle ratios were available for the 300-B ranging from 3.07 to 6.17. Most of these higher ratios were for Kiekhaefer's use in stock car competition.

With a wheelbase of 126 inches and an overall length of 222.7 inches, the 300-B was hardly a sports car. Rather it was as *SPORTS CARS ILLUSTRATED* concluded, "a luxury Gran Tourismo within the American tradition."

The improved low speed performance of the Chrysler 300 in its 1956 form was, along with its continued status as the fastest American sedan, amply demonstrated by its performance in the 1956 Daytona Beach Speed Week. In the one mile standing start acceleration competition for the *MECHANIX ILLUSTRATED* Acceleration Trophy, a Dodge 500-D just edged Brewster Shaw's 300-B, 81.786 mph to 81.762 mph. Across the beach in the Flying Mile competition, it was Tim Flock's 300-B however that set a new 139.373 mph record. Vicki Wood also used this "Beast," as it was called by Carl Kiekhaefer, to set a mark of 136.081 mph, which the highest speed set by a woman driver at Daytona in 1956. The previous year, with Brewster Shaw's 300, she had also been the fastest female on the beach having been timed at 125.838 mph. Flock also had things his way in the 160 mile Grand National race where he led the field with a 90.836 mph average.

In spite of strong efforts by the official factory teams from Ford and Chevrolet, the Kiekhaefer 300-B's emerged as the NASCAR Grand National Champions for the second consecutive year. Out of 56 NASCAR Grand National races held, Kiekhaefer cars contested 51 and attained 30 victories.

Whereas the 1955-56 300's had used a checkered flag medallion, the 1957 300-C carried a new insignia consisting of a circle with red, white and blue horizontal stripes in whose center "300-C" were placed. This new design, Chrysler explained, was "intended to remind people that this is truly an American car. We use the circle because

what makes a car different from a boat or plane is the circle or wheel." But in the case of the 300-C, it was an automobile far different not only from its predecessors but its peers as well. The year 1957 was one of tremendous change for Chrysler Corporation and, while history has not in general dealt kindly with Mopar products of that vintage, the reputation of the 300-C as one of the greatest of all the supercars has remained intact. This is not to say the 300-C was totally exempt from the overall poor quality of assembly that plagued Chrysler products that year. However, since 300-C production didn't commence until December of 1956, at least some of the early problems confronting other Chrysler products did not affect the 300. Also placing the 300-C several notches above its corporate cousins was its limited production status which assured that extra care was taken in its assembly. Chrysler's new torsion bar front suspension endowed the 300-C not only with handling superior to earlier models but also provided the dividend of a far smoother ride. One Chrysler engineer noted that the 1957 Chryslers possessed such inherently good handling qualities that "we didn't have to firm up suspensions nearly as much in the 300-C to get the controllability we wanted." Yet, while the rear leaf springs of the 300-C were rated at 135 pounds per inch as compared to the 160 pounds used on the 300-B, they were still 30% stiffer than those of the 1957 Chrysler New Yorker. The front torsion bars were correspondingly larger than their New Yorker counterparts, resulting in a twisting resistance some 40% greater than that of the stock units. The new chassis and body design for 1957 lowered the 300's profile approximately 5 inches. This reduction, plus the high Chrysler fins, gave the 300-C a very strong "don't tread on me" type of demeanor. At the front, a hood-grille design adopted virtually "as is" from a Chrysler experimental car, known simply as Number 613, enhanced the impression of the 300-C, either in hardtop form or in the new-for-1957 convertible body style, as a car not intended for the faint of heart. A look under the hood confirmed that impression as 392 cubic inches of hemi-head V-8 greeted the beholder. With a compression ratio of 9.25:1 (10.0:1 was also available) and with dual four-barrel Carter WCFB carburetors the 300-C engine developed 375 hp at 5200 rpm. The same cam as used on the earlier 1955 and 1956 models, with a 60° overlap and 280° intake and

Above, 1957 Chrysler 300-C

270° exhaust duration was also standard on the 300-C.

As part of an "Optional Chassis Package" an even more powerful, 390 horsepower engine was available. Chrysler cautioned prospective purchasers that "this optional engine is not recommended for the average 300-C customer as the longer duration high speed camshaft increases idle roughness and reduces low speed performance." This wild and woolly high lift cam had a 300° duration for both intake and exhaust valves and an overlap of 95°! A compression ratio of 10.0:1 was also part of this package. A low pressure exhaust system using Dodge truck manifolds and 2½ inch diameter exhaust and tail pipes was also included. Emphasizing the specialized nature of this package was its mandatory manual transmission, limited slip differential, and non-power brakes and steering. The total number of 300-C's equipped with the 390 engine was very small since only between 20 and 50 such units were constructed.

A total of 13 rear axle ratios ranging from 2.92:1 to 6.17:1 were available for 1957. This allowed 300-C owners to tailor their cars for highly specialized use if they desired.

The 300-C in 390 horsepower form was the fastest stock American sedan on the beach at the 1957 Daytona Speed Weeks. However, Red Byron's mark of 134.128 mph fell short of Tim Flock's 300-B run of 139.373 mph of 1956. Gil Cunningham, in the Spring, 1976, issue of *THE MILESTONE CAR*, places the blame for this relatively poor showing on the 300-C's greater wind resistance and the use of too low a rear axle ratio. Since Chrysler had clocked the 300-C on its Chelsea track at 145.7 mph, there is little reason to doubt the 300-C was the fastest 300 to date. Furthermore, this top speed ability was tied to excellent acceleration. *MOTOR LIFE* reported in its May, 1957, issue that in their tests of a 300-C the slowest time recorded in a series of zero to 60 mph runs was 7.8 seconds. The 300-C was the most popular Chrysler letter car built to date with sales reaching 2,188 (1,718 coupes, 474 convertibles).

In contrast, Chrysler produced only 809 units of its successor, the 300-D. Style-wise, the 300-D was almost identical to the 300-C except for its new "complex curve" windshield, an altered wheel cover design and the removal of the small lip above the windshield. In addition, due to repositioning of its bumpers, the 300-D's length grew by one inch. There were minor interior and exterior trim changes. The hemi V-8 remained at 392 cubic inches but its output was slightly upgraded to 380 hp at 5200 rpm.

However, since a new standard cam with less lift and overlap, down from 60° to 55°, was used, it seems probable that the 300's engine was perhaps slightly less potent for 1958. No longer available was the Optional Chassis Package with its super high-lift cam. Supposedly replacing that cam and the 390 hp engine of which it was an essential element, was the "Bendix Electrojector," an electronic fuel injection system. A pre-production fuel injected engine was installed in a 300-C that appeared at Daytona in 1957. The only time the outside world got a chance to put a clock on its runs its clutch, having seen better days, gave up the ghost at 120 mph. Out of the 809 300-D's manufactured, less than 20 were equipped with this overly complicated feature that was, for all its fuss, bother and cost ($400) worth only 10 horsepower. While electronic fuel injection enjoyed a revival in the 1970's, it was for entirely different reasons. Back in 1958, it was, like the Edsel, the answer to a question no one had asked. Likewise, the availability of Chrysler's Autopilot on the 300-D was more a concession to what was thought to be the appeal of gimmickry than a contribution to the 300's overall refinement. This device was operated by two controls, a dial and pushbutton that were installed on the 300's steering column. The dial's indicator could be placed at any number of markings indicating speeds from just under 30 mph to over 90 mph. When the automobile reached the speed selected, the pressure against the accelerator became substantial. Thus the Autopilot in this form acted as a form of speed regulator. If the driver, however, set his speed dial and then pushed the pushbutton the car would maintain the indicated speed until the brakes were applied.

The 300-D was still an excellent automobile. *ROAD & TRACK* (April, 1958) in spite of having some strong reservations about its size nonetheless gave the Devil his due, noting that, "It is an American prestige car, whose sportscar-derived features and characteristics make it outstanding." With only 13.65 pounds for each of its claimed 380 horses to tote around, the big Chrysler, which weighed nearly 5000 pounds ready for the road, could still accelerate from zero to 60 in just 8.4 seconds, and cover the quarter-mile in 16.1 seconds. It should be noted that the 300-D did not have the forged and hardened crankshaft used on earlier models; rather the drop-forged crank was adopted. If the deletion of the Optional Chassis Package and the arrival of the Autopilot as a 300-D accessory was seen by some enthusiasts as signs that Chrysler was tampering with a good thing, their fears were confirmed the following year.

From the outside, the 300-E, with a simpler grille design, altered side trim and restyled tail lights, maintained the good lines of the C and D models. The interior of the 300-E was highlighted by the first use on an American production automobile of swivel front seats. As installed on the 300-E, they swung outward to a 60° angle when a lever located at the base of the seat was operated. But a look at its mechanical innards sent more than one 300 fan into depression. Under the hood, the Hemi was gone! In its place was a new 413 cid V-8 with a bore and stroke of 4.18 inches x 3.75 inches, wedge-shaped combustion chambers and, horror of horrors, for the first time in Chrysler 300 history, hydraulic valve lifters! The cam used in the 300-E engine had a duration of 260° and an overlap of just 42°, the mildest ever used by Chrysler in the 300 series. The ensuing debate over the relative merits of this Golden Lion V-8 engined 300-E compared to its older counterparts probably never will be resolved. Clearly, if measured by its sales, the E was the runt of the litter since only 647 were sold. Yet, the

300-D hadn't done that much better and since the E matched the D's 380 hp and offered more torque, 450 vs 435 lbs-ft, Chrysler's claim that the 300-E was superior in acceleration to the 300-D was credible. Specifically, Chrysler claimed a zero to 60 mph time of 8.3 seconds for the 300-E. *MOTOR TREND* (March, 1959) actually bettered this with a 8.2 second figure and *SPORTS CARS ILLUSTRATED* wasn't that far off the mark with its 8.7 second reading. From Chrysler's viewpoint, the abandonment of the Hemi made good economic sense since it was a costly engine to manufacture. The complaints of 300 enthusiasts about its demise have to be matched against the opinions of professional motoring journalists with familiarity with all the 300 letter cars. *SPORTS CARS ILLUSTRATED* (August, 1959) saw the 300-E as "a Porsche Carrera with an overactive thyroid." In comparison with its adversaries both foreign and domestic, *S.C.I.* concluded that "there's nothing as fast, as comfortable and as civilized in the world."

Certainly the same words aptly described the 300-F of 1960. Along with the rest of the Chrysler line the 300 received an all-new unitized body, marking the third major body revision in its short history. For the first time, the Chrysler 300 was fitted with bucket seats both front and rear. The swiveling front seats were carried over from 1959. As a point of interest, when this feature was installed on other Chryslers it was electrically operated. On the 300-F it remained manually controlled.

The 300-F scored a victory in the NASCAR Flying Mile Championship (Unlimited Stock Car Class) competition with a two-way average of 143.0 mph. Another 300-F topped all entries in the NASCAR Standing Mile Acceleration Championship with a mark of 90.7 mph. More interesting, however, were the changes wrought for 1960 in the 300-F's engine. Chrysler may have gotten a bit carried away when it called ram induction "the greatest advance since the Supercharger," but certainly its use on the 300-F as standard equipment was not a trifling move. The theory behind the use of ram induction tubes, with a length of 30 inches on the 300-F, was simple; its performance impact was substantial. When the intake valve of an engine closes, a consequence in the manifold is the creation of high speed compression waves. Obviously, if the length of the manifold tube is adjusted so that these waves reach its end at the same time the valve reopens the effect is not unlike that of a supercharger: namely, the fuel-air mixture is drawn into the cylinder at a very fast rate of speed. In its standard form, the 300-F engine developed 375 horsepower, five less than the E engine. However its torque, 495 lbs-ft at 2800 rpm, was substantially better than the 450 lbs-ft at 3600 rpm developed by the 300-E engine. Perhaps they should have labeled it the Chrysler 400 since a 400 hp engine with larger exhaust valves (1.74 inch diameter instead of 1.60), hotter cam and solid lifters was also available in the 300-F. This engine, which was matched to a 4-speed Pont-a-Mousson manual transmission, was inferior in low speed operation to the standard engine. However, whereas the 30 inch induction tubes of the 375 horsepower engine hampered its performance above 4000 rpm, the optional engine with shorter, 15 inch tubes was in its true element above that point.

At Daytona Beach in 1960, a batch of 400 hp Chrysler 300-F's demonstrated their virility with speeds through the Flying Mile ranging from a low of 141.509 mph up to 144.927 mph! Not only was the 300-F the fastest American sedan for 1960, but in acceleration its ability to reach 60 mph from rest in just over 7 seconds also placed it in the category of being one of the fastest accelerating automobiles in the world. Chrysler historians differ as to the actual number of 400 hp 4-speed 300-F's built. Current estimates place the number of such Chryslers between seven and fifteen.

The 300-G carried over the F's engines for 1961, although the Pont-a-Mousson transmission was replaced by a heavy-duty 3-speed, non-synchronized first gear, Chrysler-built unit. Styling changes included the elimination of the phony tire cover from the 300 rear deck, a revised and less pleasing taillight assembly and new front end with diagonally positioned dual headlights that blended rather nicely with the simple new grillework introduced on the 300-F.

Joe Granatelli, whose supercharged 300-F set a new Class B Supercharged Coupe and Sedan record of 165.981 mph at Bonneville in 1960, had, as would be expected, high praise for the Chrysler 300. It had, said Granatelli, ''all the qualities of America's best passenger cars and the handling, maneuverability and performance of foreign cars, without losing any of the advantages of passenger car comfort.'' These features of the 300, so often overlooked and over-shadowed by its shattering straight-line performance, were also given their due by sports car racing champion, Bob Grossman, who concluded after driving a 300-G that it had ''more handling quality than any car of the same weight.''

In 1962, seven years after the first 300 had grown out of the existing stockpile of Chrysler corporation's parts bin, the circle turned back on itself. The 300 name became the successor to ''Windsor'' as the label for a line of sedans and hardtops and was bracketed by the more expensive New Yorker series and the lower priced Newport series automobiles. The 300 tradition did continue in the guise of the 300-H, but Chrysler, by diluting the integrity of the 300 nomenclature, committed an unpardonable sin in the eyes of many. Somehow, the blending of a four-door sedan body with a 383 cid, 305 hp V-8 with the 300 nameplate seemed to be automotive opportunism at its worst. Yet, there was a certain irony in all this for it just so happens that the 300's could be equipped to qualify as early examples of the no-frill supercar concept later developed to its height by the Plymouth Road Runner. Furthermore, the 300-H might just have been a better all-around performer than the earlier letter cars.

For one thing, the 300-H, since it was built on the shorter, 122 inch Newport chassis, was a trimmer (by 4½ inches) and lighter (by 300 pounds) automobile than its immediate predecessor. Some of the advantages of this down-sizing were lost by a further softening of the 300's suspension, but the end product was still worthy of praise for its excellent handling. TODAY'S MOTOR SPORT in its March, 1962, issue interviewed several of the world's top sports car drivers competing in the 1961 Nassau Speed Weeks program after they had the opportunity to drive a 300-H around the racing circuit. Dan Gurney had high praise for the 300-H, noting that ''it handles like a small car — almost like a racing car.'' Graham Hill was equally enthusiastic, saying, ''I was sure on going around some of the corners that the car had independent rear suspension'' Stirling Moss' assessment was, ''This 300-H is an excellent handling car — very firm suspension, fine quick steering and excellent brakes.''

Even in heavy convertible body form, the 300-H, with its standard 380 hp engine and solid valve lifters, could turn zero to 60 mph times of 7.7 seconds. Top speed of a 300-H in good, but by no means full race, tuning was beyond the 130 mph figure.

Seldom seen but available nonetheless for 1962 was a ram inducted version of this engine with 15 inches induction tubes, an 11:1 compression ratio, a 284° duration cam, special cylinder heads with superior breathing qualities and the same dual four-barrel Carter AFB carburetors as used on the 380 hp engine. This piece of machinery, which was optional both in the 300 and 300-H, carried a rating of 405 hp at 5400 rpm. A third engine, a 426 cid ''wedge'' rated at 421 hp at 5400 rpm, was also available as an ''over the counter'' package. Ray Brock reported in HOT ROD for February, 1962, that a 300 hardtop equipped with the 405 engine, Torque Flite, and a 4.56:1 Sure-Grip rear axle could run the quarter-mile in 14.28 seconds with a speed of 100.11 mph. Brock was running this car with, in addition to 9.00 x 14 tires at the rear, open exhausts, advanced timing and a disconnected power steering pump.

Even in ''Power Pak'' form, which meant a 340 hp rating via a four-barrel carburetor, the 300 so often maligned by critics was nearly the equal of the older, 1961 300-G. The following figures from the February, 1962, issue of CAR LIFE illustrate just how similar the two cars were in performance.

	300-H	300-G
0-30 mph	2.9 sec	3.2 sec
0-40	4.6	4.6
0-50	6.5	6.1
0-60	8.7	8.4
0-70	11.1	10.6
0-80	14.5	13.8
0-100	23.0	21.2
Standing ¼-mile	16.7	16.2
Speed at end	83.0	87.4

Where the 300 revealed its inferiority to any letter car, and to the 300-H in particular, was in its handling. Whereas the 300 became increasingly uncomfortable to drive at speeds above 80 mph due to its soft suspension, the 300-H was true to its tradition, keeping the situation well under control.

Chrysler skipped over the letter ''I'' as the designation for the ninth version of the 300 letter car, feeling that it might be more a source of confusion than identification. Instead a 300-J in hardtop form only appeared in 1963, still on a 122 inch wheelbase but featuring styling that seemed to fit the 300's performance image quite well. Only one engine was available for the 300-J, a 390 hp, 413 cid unit that mated the 15 inch Ram Induction pipes with the mildest cam, 260°, 40° overlap ever used in a 300 letter car. The 300-J remained a potent straight line performer in the best 300 tradition and its new Bendix duo-servo brakes were a long overdue improvement. Yet, that great 300 strong point, roadability, took a turn for the worse that symbolized more than any other quality of the 300-J that the great age of the 300 was just about at its end.

Chrysler builk K and L versions of the 300 in 1964 and 65 (some with 4-speed transmissions) but by that time the term ''high performance'' implied something that the Chrysler 300's no longer represented. In 1955, the first 300 had been an innovator, a path breaker in the very best sense of the term. Ten years later, Plymouth and Dodge were Chrysler Corporation's front line combatants in drag strip and NASCAR competition. The 300-L with its single four-barrel carburetor and hydraulic lifters was a car of a totally different character. Indeed, at Chrysler the torch of performance had been passed on.

Announcing the exciting new

345 h.p. DE SOTO Adventurer

When you drive the new 345 hp De Soto Adventurer, people sit up and take notice! You own the very last word in luxury, beauty, and appointments. You have absolute mastery of the road. You enjoy effortless driving and the world's smoothest ride—De Soto's road-leveling Torsion-Aire. Command the ultimate in automobiles. See your neighborhood De Soto-Plymouth dealer today!

most exciting *and glamorous* car in the world today!

Interior of gold and white vinahide with tan tweed fabric and lustrous jewel-case instrument panel. De Soto Division, Chrysler Corporation.

12. DeSoto

DeSoto joined the V-8 ranks in 1952 just one year after Chrysler had unveiled its potent 180 hp V-8. Like the Chrysler FirePower, V-8, DeSoto's new engine used laterally opposed valves and hemispherical combustion chambers. In essence, the 160 hp FireDome was a scaled-down version of Big Brother, Chrysler's pride and joy.

To call the 1952 DeSoto stodgy is charitable. It was reliable and trustworthy but also homely, old fashioned in many ways, and not terribly exciting to ride in or drive. It was for good cause that Griff Borgeson (MOTOR TREND, July, 1952) described the FireDome V-8 as "an engine ten years ahead of the rest of the car . . ." Although it was a willing performer, the new V-8's potential was almost drowned by DeSoto's Fluid Drive transmission which restricted the 1952 DeSoto to a zero to 60 mph acceleration time of 15.7 seconds.

DeSoto's new look and new outlook of 1955 removed most of these self-imposed inhibitions. It wasn't the quickest accelerator, although its 12.5 second, zero to 60 mph time was certainly respectable. Now with 291 cubic inches, up from 273, thanks to a larger bore, DeSoto's V-8 developed 200 hp in its 4-barrel, 7.5:1 compression ratio "Fireflite" form. At Daytona, a DeSoto Fireflite won the class C flying mile championship for cars with engines of 250 to 299 cubic inches with a two-way average of 112.295 mph. By comparison a Chevrolet V-8 averaged 112.877 mph and a Buick Century reached a speed of 116.345 mph.

The following year the Fireflite grew to 330 cubic inches, developed a respectable 255 hp and needed just 9.3 seconds for the zero to 60 mph grind.

After making a tremendous impression with its original C-300, Chrysler continued to make waves in the motoring world by creating special high performance versions of Plymouth, Dodge and DeSoto. In its standard Fireflite form, the 1956 DeSoto was no slouch. As the Adventurer it was one of America's fastest automobiles. Due to a larger 3.78 bore, up from 3.72, the Adventurer V-8 displaced 341 cubic inches. This in itself provided more power but when the influences of dual four-barrel carburetors, a high-lift cam, stronger valve springs, revised timing and a 9.25:1 compression ratio were added, the result was a healthy 320 hp output. Along with these changes were a number of chassis modifications including heavy-duty Oriflow shocks and stiffer springs. At Daytona in 1956, the Adventurer with its distinctive gold colored body trim left no doubt, thanks to its two-way 137.273 mph average through the flying mile, that it possessed plenty of muscle.

It's interesting in light of all the excitement surrounding

Left, 1957 De Soto Adventurer

Chevrolet's now legendary one hp per cubic inch achievement in 1957, that more wasn't made about the Adventurer's similar status, especially since it possessed 345 cubic inches and thus 345 hp. The 1957 version of the Adventurer was a very smooth appearing automobile. Lacking the brute force overtones built into the 300-C, it stands out in retrospect as the perfect blend of Chrysler's Forward Look styling and strong engine and chassis engineering. Like the 300-C, the Adventurer wasn't at its best in 0 to 60 mph situations. Instead it was tuned for long runs hovering on the far side of the century mark.

But the close performance proximity to Chrysler's 300 was also the Adventurer's greatest liability. Like the entire DeSoto line it really didn't have a strong grip on any particular niche in the marketplace.

Thus, as DeSoto's fortunes started to slip, the Adventurer began, what was an irreversible slip towards oblivion. In 1958 the use of the Chrysler "B" type, wedge engine took away some of the Adventurer's glamor although rated horsepower remained unchanged at 345 at 5000 rpm. At least a few Adventurers were produced with the Bendix electronic fuel-injection system which DeSoto claimed increased horsepower to 355.

Both in 1959 and 1960 Adventurers were powered by assorted versions of the "B" engine in its 383 cid form. For 1959 it delivered, with dual four-barrels and hot cam, 350 hp. The following year, Adventurer customers could chose from either an "Adventurer Mark I" engine with a single four-barrel carburetor and 325 hp or the 330 hp ram inducted, "Ram Charge", V-8.

But, unfortunately for DeSoto, there weren't many prospective Adventurer purchasers and in fact not very many Americans who wanted any kind of a DeSoto. The end came quickly. Amidst rumors that the 1961 DeSoto would be a luxury compact it appeared as full-sized as ever, but sporting a singularly unattractive grille. Only two body styles, two-door or four-door hardtops were offered. There were no series designations, only the DeSoto name and just one engine, a 361 cid V-8.

This somewhat dismal show of life was followed by Chrysler's announcement of November 18, 1960, that DeSoto production had come to an end.

Although they suffered from the horrors of Chrysler's late fifties misassembly ills, the high performance DeSotos still possessed the basic elements of greatness. But when stabled too close to Chrysler's Big Brute and unable to match the quickness of the less expensive hot Dodges and Plymouths, the Adventurer was doomed to a one way trip to extinction.

Jim Thornton and Herman Mozer (979) coming off the line in S/SA class.

Some days you win

Mozer and Al Eckstrand in final run for Top Stock Eliminator title.

Some days you lose

The fortunes on the straight and narrow warpath change as quickly as the gears in the go-box! Today you tear 'em up. Tomorrow is another day. Your machine has got to be mean . . . you've got to be good . . . and you've got to come out of the hole with more togetherness than Amos and Andy! That's the drama of the drag strip, man and machine.

That's why more than 100,000 buffs bulged the track at Indy for the NHRA's big showdown—the world championships.

And what a showdown! On Saturday, Jim Thornton in a '63 Dodge downed his Ramcharger teammate, Herman Mozer, on his way to royalty in the Super Stock Automatic Class. Next day, running for the meet's most coveted honor—Top Stock Eliminator —Mozer turned the tables and gave Thornton the thumb. But the event was far from over. Mozer still had to face the present "Mr. Eliminator," Al Eckstrand in Lawman, another specially equipped '63 Dodge. And another winner is defeated. Mozer edged him by 1/100th of a second with an e.t. of 12.22.

Some days you win. Some days you lose. That's what keeps the quarter-mile jaunt so interesting. But have you noticed? When a Dodge loses these days . . . it's to another Dodge.

DODGE DIVISION ◆ **CHRYSLER**
MOTORS CORPORATION

13. Dodge

The role played by Dodge in the supercar era reflected much of the basic character of the age. It began with the introduction of a modern overhead valve V-8, picked up momentum in the mid-fifties with the availability of "power packs" and reached maturity a decade later with the creation of a true racing engine, the famous 426 Hemi, and specially bodied Dodges for both drag racing and NASCAR stockcar competition. After this glorious segment of the Golden Age came the period of decline. Insurance rates and pollution/emission regulations dealt a heavy blow. But the manufacturers, with Dodge being no exception, also contributed to the supercars' demise by producing cars with higher price tags, chassis not equal to their engine's weight and potential, and such a profusion of body styles and forms that the supercar lost much of its originally unique stature.

The factor of boredom must also be listed as a contributor to the supercar's decline. Sooner or later it became a tiresome chore to fire up a gas hungry, rough idling, 400 hp machine every time it was called into service as a mere transportation device. As difficult as it is to conceive after the fact, cars with high-strung temperaments eventually bored their owners who, while not relinquishing their romance with the automobile, were ready in the early seventies to look for a new way to express their affection.

Dodge was a long way from having to deal with these changes in 1953 when its new Red Ram V-8 was introduced. Like that of the entire Chrysler line, the Dodge's styling was definitely on the stodgy side. However, with the present day emphasis upon trim size and space efficiency, the "smaller on the outside, bigger on the inside" 1953 Dodge warrants some recognition as an early effort at a space efficient automobile.

If Chrysler erred by styling its new models according to the small box on top of a larger box philosophy it was guilty of no sins in the designing of Dodge's new Red Ram V-8. In essence, this 241.1 cubic inch engine was a scaled-down version of Chrysler's Fire Power V-8. Thus, it possessed such features as hemispherical combustion chambers, a relatively short (3½ inch) stroke and a large (3 7/10 inch) bore that allowed fairly large valves to be used.

Like the Chrysler V-8, the Dodge engine was fairly heavy (610 pounds), but its stiff crankshaft and five main bearings promised long, trouble free service. With a modest 7.1:1 compression ratio the Dodge V-8 developed 140 hp at 4400 rpm and 220 lbs-ft. of torque at 2000 rpm.

The new Dodge engine was correctly perceived as one of the best in the early period of the high performance age. Tom McCahill (*MECHANIX ILLUSTRATED*, April, 1953) declared that Dodge's V-8 "makes it a wildcat on wheels," claiming that when tied to the newly available manually controlled overdrive, "it will stay with the hottest cars on the road and will top 100 miles per hour."

Chrysler still was marking time in 1953 as far as a fully automatic transmission was concerned and insisted instead in spending money on such devices as the new-for-1953 Gyro-Torque transmission. Basically, this was a torque converter tied to a 4-speed, dual range transmission. A clutch had to be used only when the car moved away from a standing start; from that point on it was not needed. With Gyro-Torque, the Dodge V-8 accelerated from zero to 60 mph in a respectable 15 seconds.

The Red Ram's muscles were flexed at Bonneville in September, 1953, where under AAA supervision a four-door, 1954 Dodge V-8 set numerous records for automobiles with engine displacements of 183 to 305 cubic inches. Among its achievements was a 48 hour run at 101-plus mph. The Dodge was also clocked at 108.36 mph for ten miles. A year earlier a 1953 Dodge had set a 10 mile mark of 102.62 mph.

During the 1953 NASCAR season the ability of its V-8's to score several victories in minor events encouraged Dodge to offer a competition kit for 1954. The basic Dodge V-8 was unchanged from 1953 except for a compression ratios boost to 7.5:1 which increased its output to 150 hp at 4400 rpm. The factory modifications for racing included a dual carburetor intake manifold, special high lift cam, stiffer valve springs and stronger axles, hubs, wheels, shocks and springs.

Dodge made a strong showing in the 1954 Mexican Road Race, capturing the top four places of the small American stockcar class. Of the ten Dodges in the race, all but one finished and its retirement was due to a crash and not from a mechanical failure. The class-winning Dodge was placed 23rd overall and its average speed of 84.36 mph compared favorably with the top Lincoln's 92.22 mph.

The Red Ram V-8 grew to 270 cubic inches in 1955 and, with a power-pack, dual exhausts and a four-barrel carburetor, it was rated at 193 hp. A Dodge did win one NASCAR Grand national race that year but the greatest single factor in its sales resurgence was undoubtedly its "Flair-Fashion" styling.

The performance virtues of the Dodge Hemi-Head were also matched by high production costs and it was for this reason that the basic Dodge V-8 of 1956 used a simpler and less costly cylinder head with polyspherical combustion chambers and single rocker arms. However, this economy move was also accompanied by the creation of the first of the true high performance Dodges, the D500 and its "for racing only" version, the 500-1. Dodge had earlier used the "500" label on a small number of replicas of the Dodge convertible that had paced the 1953 Indianapolis 500, but the name was really the only similarity between the two cars. The 1954 Dodge Royal 500, of which 701 were built by the factory, featured Kelsey-Hayes chrome wire wheels, a continental tire kit and special "500" trim items. Some of these pace car replicas were sold with dealer installed Offenhauser intake manifolds and four-barrel carburetors.

The D500 package, with a price tag of approximately $175, was available on any Dodge model. The only external hint that a Dodge with the D500 treatment was not your ordinary run-of-the-mill, "Forward Looking" Mopar were not-so-discreet crossed-checkered flags placed on its hood and trunk lids. Once the D500 was given its head there was no doubt, at least among the knowledgeable, about its identity. "There are few cars in the world that you can't run away from in a D500," wrote Racer Brown in *HOT ROD* (May, 1956). "For the sake of your necks and your driver's licenses, take it from me, the D500 will turn in excess of 125 mph," Brown assured his readers.

With machined hemispherical combustion chambers, double-rocker arms, solid valve lifters and a semi-race cam with 250° duration the D500 engine was one tough engine. A single four-barrel Carter WCFB carburetor, 1¾ inch dual exhausts, a dual breaker distributor a 9.25:1 compression ratio, and domed pistons contributed to the D500's 260 hp at 4800 rpm.

Most of the Chrysler Corporation high performance cars had beefed up suspension systems and the D500 was no exception to this rule. At the rear were six, thick, leaf springs with the axle mounted forward of their mid-point to limit axle hop. These springs were also flatter than stock and, as a result, a D500 Dodge was approximately two inches lower than a normal 1956 Dodge. At the front were shortened coil springs of ¾ inch diameter steel with a 581 pound per inch compression rate. Oriflow shock absorbers with the same valving as specified for Dodge police cars were fitted front and rear along with a 13/16 inch front anti-roll bar.

Chrysler's excellent center-plane brakes with two leading shoes at the front were specified for the D500. Their healthy, 12 inch x 2½ inch dimensions gave 256 square inches of braking surface and encouraged *SPORTS CAR ILLUSTRATED* (August, 1956) to suggest, "Chrysler deserves some sort of citation for giving their hot cars stopping power proportional to the going power."

The D500-1, a more powerful version of the D500, was available for NASCAR stock car racing. A hotter, 280° duration cam, dual Carter four-barrel carburetors plus better porting and larger valves boosted its horsepower to 275. The D500-1 chassis also had stiffer springs than those used in the D500.

Although their reputation was seriously damaged by the poor assembly and workmanship found in so many Chrysler Corporation cars in 1957, the high performance versions of the new Dodge were not only excellent accelerators but possessed handling comparable to that of many foreign sports cars. "We feel in fact," wrote Karl Ludvigsen (*SPORTS CAR ILLUSTRATED*, June, 1957), in reference to the D500, "that this is probably the most advanced and best all-around conventional chassis in the world today." The object of Ludvigsen's enthusiasm, the front torsion bar-rear leaf springs arrangement common to all 1957 Chrysler-built automobiles, was beefed up in its D500 form to cope with the 285 hp of the D500 engine. The $113.65 D500 package as before was available on any Dodge model. Unfortunately, while it was increasing the power and improving the roadability of its supercar, Dodge took a step backward in the braking category. With smaller, 11 inch drums, the D500 now had only 207 square inches of braking area. "This special Dodge," concluded *SPORTS CAR ILLUSTRATED* (June, 1957), "is suspended and powered, but not braked for fast driving on U.S. highways . . ."

A few D500 Specials with dual four-barrel carburetors and 310 hp at 4800 rpm were built, to quote Dodge, "for NASCAR racing and to special order." More elusive than this Dodge with its 325 cubic inch engine was the D501. Apparently never raced, this mystery car was equipped with the Chrysler 354 cid, Hemi V-8 fitted with a cam from the C-300. One D501 with a large bulge on its hood made an appearance at Daytona Beach in 1957. Because of poor surface conditions no serious speed runs were made with it.

For 1958, the D500 package was continued in both D500 and Super D500 versions. Dodge altered their nomenclature form, referring to them as the D-500 and Super D-500 engines. More important than the semantic switch was the replacement of the Hemi V-8 with a new 361 cid V-8 with wedge-shaped combustion chambers. A similar move had been made in the Chrysler 300-D but Dodge's lower performance profile was no doubt responsible for the relative silence that greeted this change in the D-500. The "normal" D-500 developed 305 hp but, in its Super form with twin four-barrels, it developed a very healthy 320 hp at 4800 rpm with TorqueFlite. This made for a zero to 60 mph time of 8.2 seconds, a quarter-mile speed of 94 mph and a maximum velocity of over 121 mph. The D-500's power, in union with a tight suspension, "gives it," noted *SPEED AGE* (April, 1958), "the impression of being a car designed for high speeds, not a sedan forced to go faster."

Historically, the 1959 D-500 and Super D-500 are remembered as the first Dodges equipped with the workhorse of the performance age, the 383 V-8. With its single four-barrel, the 383 D-500 peaked at 320 hp at 4600 rpm, while the dual carburetored Super D-500 developed 345 hp at 4500 rpm.

Dodge sales had rebounded in 1959 to 192,798 from the poor 114,206 mark of 1958. In order to maintain this revival and increase its spread in the marketplace, Dodge introduced not only new styling for 1960 but also the Dart series. The Dart with a shorter, 118 inch (to the Dodge's 122 inch) wheelbase competed in the low price field against Ford and Chevrolet as well as Plymouth. This broader sales horizon for Dodge was also matched with a fresh approach to the technical character of a high performance engine. Chrysler had been experimenting for nearly ten years with various forms of induction systems in attempting to exploit the ram effect of gas flow into a combustion chamber. As outlined in Chapter 12, Chrysler engineers had concluded that induction pipes with a 30 inch length provided the best performance for non-competition purposes.

Early in the model year, the D-500 version of the Dart used the 361 cid V-8 with ram-induction, a 10.0:1 compression ratio and dual four-barrels. Unlike previous years, this 310 hp engine was available only in the top-of-the-line Dart Phoenix models. Its price, which included the mandatory purchase of TorqueFlite, was $413. Although these Darts were very quick (zero to 60 mph in 8 seconds), Dodge later changed its mind and not only made the D-500 available in any Dart but also offered the regular D-500 package (used in the larger Dodge) to the Dart series, as well. This switch made the D-500 Dart, now with 340 hp and 460 lbs-ft of torque, one of America's fastest accelerating sedans. With only 11.7 pounds per horsepower, the Dart needed only 7.8 seconds to get to 60 mph. Dodge's standard 3-speed transmission, which wasn't very desirable as a performance gearbox anyway, was not available in Darts or Dodges with the ram-inducted engine. Both the Dart and the Dodge could be equipped with heavy-duty, "export" suspensions that were more in keeping with the potential of a ram-tuned 383 V-8 than the standard setup.

Early in 1960, Valiants with ram-piped slant sixes ran roughshod over the "high performance" Corvairs and Falcons at the Daytona speed weeks. After Dodge received a slightly restyled version of the Valiant known as the Lancer, it was almost a foregone conclusion that a high performance Lancer would soon follow. Thus the April, 1961, introduction of the Hyper-Pack as a $403.30 dealer installed option for the Lancer caught no one off guard.

The Chrysler slant six, which had replaced an L-head six used since 1932, was available in both 170 or 225 cubic inch form. The only distinction between the two was a larger bore for the 225. Aside from its ram induction and Carter AFB four-barrel carburetor, the Hyper-Pack included

tubular pushrods, both lighter and stiffer than stock, a cam with 276° intake duration (stock was 232°), stronger valve springs, and a free-flowing exhaust manifold and exhaust system. The influence of the Hyper-Pack upon the slant six was startling:

Engine	Horsepower	Horsepower with Hyper-Pack
170 six	101	148
225 six	148	196

No wonder *CAR LIFE* (April, 1961) concluded, ''With Hyper-Pack installed the Lancer becomes a car for the connoisseur . . . The Hyper-Pack Lancer is every bit as fussy about how it is driven as is the most sophisticated high-performance sports car.'' A few Lancers were sold with aluminum block, 225 cubic inch engines that weighed 66 pounds less than their cast iron counterparts. The exceptional road manners of such a Lancer prompted *HOT ROD* (January, 1961) to declare, ''This scaled down Chrysler is the best handling American stock car on the road regardless of size.'' Unfortunately, the high performance life of the Lancer was very short. The Hyper-Pack was quietly dropped during 1961 and two years later the Lancer also faded from the Dodge line-up, replaced by an all-new, compact Dart for 1963.

Even when the excitement stirred up by the Hyper-Pack Lancer is included, 1961 was not a particularly happy year for Dodge. New styling that used a concave theme as the dominant shape for both its front end and rear fins was not a

Above, 1956 Dodge D-500

success and Dodge production fell from 356,572 to 225,945. This dismal showing was matched by a lack of success on the NASCAR racing circuit against Pontiac. The bright spot for Dodge was on the dragstrip where it was consistently a strong competitor and often a winner in the Super Stock Automatic class. The ram-tuned 383 V-8 was unchanged from 1960 although its horsepower rating was now 330 at 4800 rpm. The factory would also prepare, on a special order only basis, a 383 V-8 with mechanical lifters, modified ram tubes, adjustable rocker arms and a higher lift cam. This racing engine had the same horsepower and torque ratings as the ''normal'' ram-tuned Dodge but they were now attained at higher engine revs of 5200 rpm and 3600 rpm, respectively.

Dodge enthusiasts had a choice of two excellent transmissions to carry the 383's power to the rear wheels. A new 3-speed manual gearbox that was the first designed specifically for use with high-output engines had, claimed Chrysler, larger, wider and stronger gears than any other manual transmission available in an American car. Chrysler also beefed up its TorqueFlite by installing a heavier pressure regulator spring for greater oil pressure, different governor weight plus a stronger reverse planet pinion carrier. The durability of the heavy-duty TorqueFlite was demonstrated all over the nation's dragstrips but the most convincing show took place in Los Angeles where a number of newspaper sports writers put a TorqueFlite ram-tuned Dodge through over 200 quarter-mile dragstrip runs at speeds ranging from 91 to 95 mph. At day's end the Dodge was running just as strong as ever and was little the less for the wear and tear it had experienced.

When the 1962 Dodge models debuted in September, 1961, devotees of the marque with a lust for quick quarter-mile times and lots of healthy all-American cubic inches and horsepower were stunned. The reason for their confusion was simple: the most powerful Dodge engine available was the veteran 361 V-8 with "only" 305 horsepower. This engine downsize was matched by the full-sized Dodge's shorter, 116 inch wheelbase. These weren't necessarily bad moves. The 305 hp, trim-sized Dodge was a nicely balanced automobile, but no match for a Tri-Power, 421 cid V-8 Pontiac. Furthermore, with DeSoto's demise in 1961, Chrysler didn't have a really competitive, "full-sized" car in the then strong, medium priced field. Chrysler Corporation, to its credit, quickly moved to rectify this situation. The Dodge Custom 880 series appeared as a mid-year model. These automobiles were a blend of the 1961 Dodge front end with the 122 inch wheelbase, 1962 Chrysler body. Quick as a flash Dodge, was again a strong competitor in a lucrative segment of the market, although not because the 880 was a potent machine. That gap in the line-up was filled the day the 383 V-8 returned as an option in the 116 inch wheelbase Dodges.

At this point, just a word on usage of the Dodge nomenclature in 1962 seems in order. All 116 inch wheelbase models were identified as Dodge Darts except for the three Polara models that carried only the Dodge name. Either as Polaras or Darts, the smaller Dodges were the basis of its high performance offerings for 1962.

In its 1962 form, the ram-tuned 383 was still rated at 330 hp and 460 lbs-ft, but in the lighter 1962 body it easily outperformed its 1961 version. Moreover, Dodge's hot options for the 383 were far more abundant and easier to obtain than ever before. Short, 16 inch ram tubes joined the older Sonoramic versions and boosted the 383's horsepower to 340 at 5000 rpm. A runner-type manifold for the 383's dual four-barrels was also offered with a 330 hp rating at 5200 rpm. The hot 383 setup in any of these stages of tune was further enhanced by mechanical valve lifters and a 268° cam, or, if the short tubes were used, a 284° duration cam. Dodge also recommended the purchase of the Hurst floor shifter if the manual 3-speed transmission was used with the 383. Topping off this list of delectables was Dodge's willingness to sell performance fans the same 383 engine normally reserved for its two-door, Police Pursuit Special model. This package had as standard equipment heavy duty alternator, battery, brakes and the usual stiffer springs and shocks.

Dodge was on the move and that meant Dodges were moving machines. A 340 hp short-tube 383 with a 4.10:1 rear axle stormed through the quarter-mile in just 14.88 seconds and at 96.77 mph. Even better performance became possible when Chrysler, obviously getting Dodge fever, added Chrysler 300 heads with their space for large valves, and domed-topped, Forged True, 12:1 compression ratio pistons to the Dodge performance option list.

But there were even more and bigger things in store for Dodge. "These two powerplants make the 1962 Dart the hottest automobile Chrysler Corporation has ever offered the public," was CAR LIFE magazine's verdict of the performance impact of the 410 and 420 horsepower versions of the 1962 Dodge Dart. The NHRA regulation calling for cars running in stock classes to be factory equipped models prompted Dodge, after January 1, 1962, to make the 413 engine available in any Dart body.

During 1960 and 1961, the 413 engine had been available as a special option but the quantity produced was very limited and for all practical purposes the 383 had been Dodge's high performance standard bearer. This posed no problem, at least as far as drag racing was concerned, since a 383 cid Dodge with short ram tubes won the A/Stock class at the 1961 NHRA Championships.

Dodge's opening shot with the 413 offered either a 385 hp, dual four-barrel version or the thundering 410 hp unit with dealer installed ram-induction. A variety of hot cams with durations of 276°, 284°, 292°, or 308° were also offered with mechanical lifters and stronger valve springs as dealer options. A 385 hp Dart with manual, 3-speed transmission was capable of zero to 60 mph in 7.4 seconds but it also was an instant antique after the 385 hp version was scrapped in favor of the direct-from-the-factory 410 and 420 hp engines.

Both engines had the familiar twin AFB Carter four-barrels but they now were tied into a new, and far less bulky 15 inch ram induction system. This new aluminum manifold delivered maximum resonance effect above 4000 rpm. Chrysler also provided new heads for the 410 and 420 hp engines with approximately 25% more port area, and new 2.08 inch intake and 1.88 inch exhaust valves. Both engines used a 292° duration cam. Whereas the 410 hp engine had a compression ratio of 11.0:1, that of the 420 hp version was 13.5:1. This engine was strictly for drag racing. "Owners must be cautioned," Dodge instructed its dealers, "to limit w.o.t. bursts to 15 second duration with the 13.5:1 ratio."

With a close-ratio Warner T-85, 3-speed transmission and Hurst linkage (heavy-duty TorqueFlite was also available) the 410 hp package initially carried a price tag of $504.60; the 420 hp version was an additional $62.50. However, Dodge soon lowered the price tag of the Ramcharger 413 package to $374.40. In either form, the 413 Dodge made its presence known at the drag strip. With 410 hp it moved from zero to 60 mph in 5.3 seconds and chalked up figures of 13.75 seconds and 106.75 mph for the quarter-mile.

The origin of the 413, which for 1963 was expanded to 426 cubic inches by virtue of a larger, 4.25 inch to 4.190 inch bore, dated back to 1958 and through the years saw use in 350 and 361 cubic inch versions in addition to its 383, 413 and 426 forms. For 1963, in high performance Ramcharger form, the 426 was offered with 415 hp and a single four-barrel carburetor. In its Ramcharger form, with two four-barrels, a 13.5:1 compression ratio and a high rise manifold (Dodge continued the Ramcharger label but dropped ram-induction after 1962) the 426 was rated at 425 hp and 480 lbs-ft of torque. The potency of the Ramcharger was demonstrated at innumerable drag strips during 1963 but nowhere more impressively than at the 1963 Winternationals. There a '63 Dodge prepared by the Ramcharger Club of Detroit emerged the overall stock eliminator champion with a best run of 12.44 seconds and 115.08 mph. This performance was particularly impressive since it was achieved without benefit of the light weight front end sheet metal offered by both Dodge and Plymouth early in 1963. The NHRA did require that all cars running in the Super Stock category had to have a minimum shipping weight of 7.50 pounds per cubic inch of engine displacement or 3200 pounds. This still left room for Dodge to pare off some excess weight from its racing car by offering front fenders, hood, splash shields, and front bumpers of aluminum.

Dodge celebrated its 50th anniversary in 1964 by offering a special Anniversary Gold exterior paint and interior trim package and continuing to promote its performance campaign. The 426R (for Racing) with 11.0:1 compression ratio and mechanical lifters was rated at 415 hp at 5000 rpm. Although its compression ratio was dropped a point to 12.5:1, the top 426's horsepower remained at 425. As was common to most racing engines of the day, actual output was considerably higher. Depending on the type of racing contemplated, the 426R engines were fitted with either dual AFB carburetors or a single four-barrel Holley with 1 9/16 inch throats. Joining the "TorqueFlite Eight" heavy-duty automatic transmission as an option for the 426 engines, was a new 4-speed manual transmission designed by Chrysler Central Engineering. Dodge also cited a new, wider by 2.1 inches rear track and longer rear springs as examples of the benefits accruing to its production cars from racing.

As a road car, a Dodge powered by the 365 hp 426S engine was a potent yet surprisingly docile automobile. With a relatively mild, 260° duration cam it idled in a civilized fashion while still possessing sufficient power when the occasion arose for spectacular acceleration. Even in the heavy, 4,370 pound convertible form *CAR LIFE* magazine found the 426S Dodge able to move from zero to 60 mph in 7.2 seconds. Chrysler required the installation of its largest, 11 inch diameter, 380 square inch brakes on 426S Dodges. Although *CAR LIFE* could manage only one such run, these brakes contributed to a zero to 100 mph to zero time of 25.7 seconds which bettered Aston Martin's highly touted 26.2 second mark with its very expensive DB4 model.

With 1964 its Golden Anniversary, it was appropriate for Dodge to win the July 4, 1964, Daytona Firecracker 400. This victory, by A.J. Foyt, was Dodge's first major stock car victory. Foyt, who was originally scheduled to race a Ford in this race, later explained that he decided to switch because he had not had particularly good luck with Ford and felt their relatively poor aerodynamics would inhibit them at Daytona. The real reason, however, was found under the hood of the top Dodge (and Plymouth) cars. In short, Chrysler had reached back to the roots of its modern experience with high performance V-8's and had beckoned from the past the Hemi-head V-8. Both Plymouth and Dodge offered the same 426 Hemi with Dodge's known as the Hemi-Charger 426. This engine, which was available in three versions, shared only the same 4.25 inch bore and 3.75 stroke with the older 426. All of its major parts were different and considerably stronger. For drag racing, the Hemi was fitted with an aluminum, ram-tuned manifold with dual four-barrel Carter AFB carburetors. Either a 11.0:1 compression ratio, 415 hp version, or one with a 12.5:1 ratio rated at 425 hp was available. For stock car racing, the large Holley four-barrel mentioned earlier rested on a high riser aluminum intake manifold. This engine was also credited with a 12.5:1 compression ratio and 400 hp. True horsepower of all these engines was well beyond the 500 hp mark.

The new Hemi weighed about 80 pounds more than the older wedge-head version and, prior to Foyt's July 4th victory, set a new NHRA A/FX records on April 26, 1964. Driven by Jim Thornton of the Ramcharger team, it recorded a 11.17 second, 125.17 mph run at the Detroit Dragstrip. At Daytona, Foyt set a new record for the Firecracker 400, averaging 151.451 mph.

Two years later, in 1966, Dodge offered the Hemi in detuned form for the street with dual four-barrels and a relatively mild, 275°/276° cam. With TorqueFlite, a Street Hemi Coronet ran from zero to 60 mph in a thundering 5.5 seconds. The larger Polara models were offered with a 440 cubic inch, bored-out version of the 413 engine which was no longer available. This was not a performance engine in its 1966 form, but in future years it was developed into a lower priced performance alternative to the Hemi.

The rebirth of the Hemi seemed to act as a catalyst upon Dodge's approach to the creation of high performance automobiles. Throughout the final years of the sixties, the Hemi was the crown jewel of fast Dodges but it was also joined by a bevy of exciting road machines, not all of which relied upon brute horsepower for their vitality.

In 1964, Dodge had offered a new, smaller, 273 cid V-8 for its compact Dart series. Originally rated at 180 hp, by 1966 it was available with a four-barrel carburetor that boosted this figure up to 235 hp. In this form, the 273 V-8 was a fairly strong competitor in the smaller V-8 classes in NHRA drag racing. Early in 1966, Dodge gave this healthy piece of V-8 engineering a new "D/Dart" form with the specific intention of making it the scourge of both the D/Stock and D/Stock Automatic classes. The D/Dart was an extremely well balanced, factory high output package that included a heavy-duty suspension system, a rear axle from the larger Dodges with a 4.86:1 ratio and the Sure-Grip differential. Its automatic transmission was of course heavy-duty TorqueFlite and its 4-speed manual transmission ran through a Weber racing clutch. Its engine with a single Holley four-barrel carburetor, Edelbrook aluminum manifold and a solid-lifter, 284° duration cam turned out 275 strong horsepower.

A rough counterpart of the D/Dart in the big engine league was the 1967 Coronet R/T which had its suspension beefed up with a swaybar, special shocks and high performance nylon cord tires. To help prevent rear axle torque windup, its right rear spring was given an extra leaf. As its standard engine the R/T used a high output version of the 440 cid V-8 known as the 440 Magnum. With a single Carter AFB four-barrel and 268°-284° cam, 375 hp was available at 4800 rpm. For those R/T customers who wanted even more, the King Kong 426 Hemi was also offered.

The R/T with the 440 Magnum needed only 6.3 seconds to run from zero to 60 mph and was, aside from its rapid road manners, easily distinguished from lesser Dodges by its grille which was inspired by the design of Dodge's Charger fastback model.

The first Charger's styling, which was derived from the Charger II show car of 1965, never was particularly well received. In 1968, though, when it was given a new, fresh look, the Charger and its high performance version the Charger R/T became one of the best styled American sedans on the market. Dodge had first planned to produce only 35,000, but early sales, some 437% higher than that of the older Charger, shot that schedule to pieces and by year's end some 85,000 Chargers and R/T Chargers had been sold. During the entire 1967 model run, this figure represented 15.5% of all Dodge sales.

During the remaining years of the sixties, Dodge continued to use its strong 383's, 440's, and Hemis as the basis for a wide variety of "Scat Pact," "Dodge Fever" and "Scat City" high performance cars. In 1969, the limited production Charger 500 with its aerodynamic front end and high mounted rear wing represented the ultimate Golden Era Dodge.

In 1970 Dodge offered Charger, Swinger 340's, Super Bees, Challengers and R/T's with engines that ranged from 340 to 426 cubic inches. This was the peak year for Dodge's high performance cars. For a time they continued on but cars intended to run on low lead and regular octane fuel, forced to conform to emission and safety mandates, gradually became shadows of their earlier greatness.

SLEEPER!

To the old carnival guessing game of "Which shell is the pea under?" you can add another—"Which Galaxie is hiding the new six-barrel?"

You can get a very precise answer, it's true, when one of these sleepers suddenly goes "zzz-z-z-ZOW!" and vanishes. But that leaves you sitting foolishly in the middle of a lot of empty landscape.

Better to know beforehand. But how? You'd think 405 horsepower, header exhausts, six-barrel carbs, 406 cubic inches and 11.4 compression couldn't be hidden. But Ford's V-8 magicians have brewed up a real street machine—no wild 2000 r.p.m. idle, no dragster noises, no battle to fire it up. Girls drive these things down to the supermarket and never suspect they are a half-throttle away from escape velocity.

Of course, you do get a clue watching one straighten out a corner. They handle! Because this engine (and the 4-barrel version) come only as a package with Heavy Duty shocks, springs, driveshaft, U-joints, brakes —plus 15-inch wheels and nylon tires. That's what makes the tab of $379.70* so fantastic—and why there are so many Galaxie sleepers around to embarrass you. But why be dominated? Get your own 406 and you won't need to guess which Galaxie has the six-barrel.

A PRODUCT OF (Ford) MOTOR COMPANY

*Manufacturer's suggested list price for extra equipment

FORD V-8

14. Ford

Ford, in a technical sense, entered the modern performance age in 1954 with its 239 cid, overhead valve, V-8. With the same compression ratio (7.2:1) and displacement as the legendary flathead Ford V-8, this new engine's power ratings of 130 hp and 214 lbs-ft of torque were not exactly awesome. Linked to Fordomatic, it performed, as its specifications implied, rather modestly. Zero to 60 mph took place in a leisurely 17.2 seconds and when the Ford reached 90 mph it was close to its maximum speed.

Some of the early production ohv V-8's line experienced premature (which Ford repaired free of charge) cam lobe wear but, overall, Ford's new generation V-8 slipped quite nicely into the automotive mainstream. It soon became apparent, though, that just a slight movement forward in performance by Ford wouldn't be enough. Nineteen fifty-four slipped away and suddenly it was 1955 and sedate old Chevrolet, the automotive embodiment of American conservatism, was breaking away not only from its own past but, thanks to its new V-8, from just about everyone else at traffic lights all across the land.

On paper, the '55 Ford in power-pack form should have at least been the equal of Chevrolet's 180 hp bombshell. After all, 182 hp, 8.5:1 cylinder heads, a big four-barrel carburetor and dual exhausts made for some pretty interesting reading and the anticipation of "good times." However, Ford fans, more often than not, were soon taking lumps instead of trophies when they squared off against the energetic Chevys.

The first few months of 1956 brought more of the same to Ford. Its top engine, with 292 cubic inches was rated at 202 hp but relative to the hot Chevys was bog-slow from zero to 60. For example, a 170 hp Chevrolet with Powerglide could easily reach 60 from a standing start in 11.9 seconds. The 202 hp Ford with Fordomatic was less than ½ second faster.

The apparently over optimistic power claim for the "Thunderbird V-8" and Chevrolet's highly successful "The Hot One is Even Hotter" advertising campaign forced Ford to review its racing and performance posture. The conclusion was easily reached that changes were called for and in late 1955 Ford Division general manager Robert McNamara decided to provide technical and financial support for a Ford racing program. The entire operation was a function outside of the formal Ford umbrella but it eventually included Peter DePaolo as its manager with Curtis Turner, Joe Weatherly, and Fireball Roberts in its drivers' line-up. Not everything ran smoothly but towards season's end there were clear signals that the Ford team was getting its act together.

In late August, Ford made available for racing purposes a "205 horsepower, 292 cubic inch high output engine." To complement the performance of this engine, which was far more potent than the aforementioned 202 hp Thunderbird engine, Ford also offered options including heavy-duty front and rear springs, stiffer shocks, a larger diameter front stabilizer bar, a 4.27:1 rear axle from the Ford station wagon and a radiator with extra cooling capacity.

In the 1955 Southern 500 at Darlington, South Carolina, two Fords with these new engines were entered and Joe Weatherly's was headed for sure victory when a tire blowout, just 50 miles from the finish, put him on the sidelines.

However, for a 300-mile race at the Memphis-Ark Speedway, Ford mounted a major effort with cars for Joe Weatherly, Curtis Turner, Johnny Mantz and Chuck Stevenson. Ironically, it was Speed Thompson in a '56 Ford entered by Carl Kiekhaefer that took the checkered flag, leading the nearest Chevrolet, back in third place, by ten miles.

ROAD & TRACK reported on its test of a 205 hp Ford in its February, 1956, issue. To put it mildly, the sports car gang from Glendale were suitable impressed. The husky Ford hustled from zero to 30 mph in 3.5 seconds, reached the 60 mph mark in 8.8 and ran the standing start quarter-mile in 16.4 seconds. Its top speed was a respectable 111 mph.

In November, 1956, the Ford racing team made two excursions on courses usually reserved for sports car racing. The first venture at Paramount Ranch northwest of Los Angeles ended with Troy Ruttman falling from the lead after his car started flipping its fan belts. Just five days later, on November 11, at the Willow Springs track the Fords had far better luck, being led by Marvin Panch to a 1-2-3 finish.

After having been ridiculed for years by the sports car set as an ill-handling beast, the American automobile, when set up for racing, had become a force to be reckoned with. During 1956, the fastest Ferrari at Willow Springs had lapped in one minute, 47 seconds, Panch's Ford cut a one minute, 54 seconds lap in practice and during the race lowered this down to one minute, 51 seconds.

Historically, 1957 is remembered by most automobile enthusiasts as the year of Chevrolet's sensational fuel-injected "283" and the awesome Chrysler 300-C. Yet, a strong argument can be made that Ford produced a car that year equal to both these milestones in performance.

That car was the supercharged Ford, an elusive, almost will-o'-the-wisp type machine that had its performance life cut short by a NASCAR edict that banned fuel-injection, superchargers and dual carburetors from Grand National competition.

While it was legal, the blower Ford did just about everything right. It was not, as many still believe, simply a move by Ford to produce just a few, special factory cars to grab all the performance headlines. Ford, by contracting with McCulloch to take all their "VR" supercharger production, fully intended it to be available on a fairly wide basis. As sold to the general public, the supercharged Ford carried a conservative 300 hp at 4800 rpm rating. The pure, racing NASCAR versions with a hotter cam and 6 pounds of boost (stock supercharged Fords had 256° cams and their blowers delivered 5 pounds pressure from 3000 rpm on up) had no difficulty in turning out 340 hp at 5300 rpm.

In September, 1956, a supercharged Ford set numerous new AAA records at Bonneville reaching speeds up to 131 mph. The following spring at Daytona they were in abundance and ran through the two-way measured mile at 131 mph. Ford then took its hot number to the Indianapolis Motor Speedway where it lapped at 117 mph. On the dragstrips the Ford was equally impressive, scoring quarter-mile times in the high 14's and terminal speeds near the 100 mph mark.

One of the meaningless yet interesting speed contests of the fifties involved Ford and Chevrolet cars streaking from coast to coast attempting to set new records for crossing the continent. In 1956, a Chevrolet driven by Betty Skelton and Caroline Russ set a new speed mark of 51.14 mph. When they approached the California state line they bided their time in a motel, fearful that too high an average speed might result in adverse publicity. Danny Eames and Chuck Daigh, driving the same Ford that had earlier set numerous endurance and speed records at Bonneville, didn't let such fears slow them down at all. They covered the 2,913 miles between New York and Los Angeles in just 47 hours, 37 minutes, averaging 61.18 mph, easily eclipsing Chevrolet's record.

All such fun and games plus the more serious (and legitimate) forms of automobile competition officially became off-limits to virtually all the U.S. car manufacturers when the Angel of Death, in the form of the AMA's performance ban, became effective early in 1957. This action of the Automobile Manufacturer's Association was spearheaded by General Motors' President Harlow Curtice. The irony of this situation was incredible. To have the AMA sponsor a ban on factory involvement in racing and the advertising of engine power output and performance was a personal crusade of Curtice. Yet, Chevrolet managed quite nicely to continue operating a pipeline of performance parts and technical know-how to its operatives in racing. Over in Dearborn, compliance was far more complete although Jacque Passino, then in charge of special events, and Lee Iacocca, Ford Division car marketing manager, kept Ford's basic racing program at least intact even if it was nearly moribund.

The winding down of Ford's active commitment to racing didn't happen immediately. Even as late in the year as the running of the Pikes Peak hillclimb the supercharged Ford was still a winner. Victory in the stock car class that year went to Jerry Unser who made the climb in his Ford in 15 minutes, 39.2 seconds.

During the next two years the best that can be said of Ford's performance status was that it regressed. The worst that could be said was that it was terrible, and the truth lies somewhere in the middle.

Ford's top engine both in 1958 and 1959 was a 352 cid 300 hp V-8 that was closely related to the 361 cid Edsel engine. During those two dismal performance years for Ford, its customers who pitted their cars against arch rival Chevrolet's finest usually ended up second best.

Ford's performance inferiority existed at a time in automotive history when American stock car racing was on the verge of a dramatic step forward. The event that signaled the start of a new racing era was the inaugural race at Daytona International Speedway in February, 1959. The following year, tracks at Charlotte and Atlanta opened and a new era of ultra-high speed racing on super speedways was in full swing. The growth into maturity and respectability of drag racing under the direction of the National Hot Rod Association (NHRA) was virtually equal to these events in alerting the public to the really hot cars currently in production. By continuing to offer mediocrity in place of real performance, it was obvious that Ford would soon be an also-ran, that is if anyone who took their racing seriously would be foolish enough to run Fords.

Fortunately, this sad state of affairs didn't come to pass. Just as it had in 1955, the pendulum at Ford started swinging back towards participation in racing and marketing of true high performance autos. This time around, this mentality was not going to be diluted into nothingness by the whims of a General Motors president. This time around it would grow, expand and mature into a tremendous committment and involvement in automobile competition.

Ford's decision not only directly contributed towards the creation of some memorable American high performance machines but also influenced the most innovative and significant automobile of the 1960's, the Ford Mustang.

In 1959, which marked the end of the Dark Ages for Ford performance, Don Frey, executive engineer of Ford Division product planning, conspired with various other personalities and factions within the company to get Ford back in the ballgame. One of the engineers working with Frey was Dave Evans, a key figure in the creation of the Ford Interceptor Package which became available after December 1, 1959. As we shall see, the Interceptor wasn't the

Above, 1955 Ford Fairlane

complete remedy to the ills afflicting Ford's performance image but it was a mighty step forward. Most importantly, it represented the first really significant development leading to Ford's Total Performance program. Instead of 300 somewhat anemic horsepower that behaved on the dragstrip as if they suffered from tired blood, the Interceptor engine developed 360 very healthy horsepower at 6000 rpm. Ford accomplished this impressive transformation with considerable ease. In its basic form, the Interceptor V-8 wasn't all that different from the run of the mill 352 cid engine, but, where it mattered, there were some interesting changes made. The early 300 hp engines of 1958 had used solid lifters and these, plus the cam that accompanied them, were resurrected for the Interceptor. Lightweight pushrods from the Falcon engine were also adopted. Sizewise, the Interceptor intake and exhaust valves were now of drop-forged, rather than cast, construction and wider valve clearances were used to accommodate the much hotter cam. A reshaping of the combustion chamber pushed up the Ford's compression ratio a full point to 10.6:1. A new aluminum intake manifold weighing 40 pounds less than the earlier version carried a single 540 cfm Holley four-barrel carburetor. Ford also made available as dealer installed options many suspension and brake modifications that were appropriate for a car of this potential.

In the late autumn of 1959, an Interceptor-engined Ford was shipped to Daytona where both Ford and the Firestone tire company conducted an exhaustive test program with it. Cotton Owens held the Ford to a forty lap average of 142 mph and then ran five final laps at 145.4 mph. Four days later this car lapped Ford's 5-mile track at Romeo, Michigan, at 152.2 mph. Prior to both runs its engine had logged 450 hours on the dynamometer under full load at 5800 rpm. On the dragstrip the Interceptor was equally impressive. Without the benefit of super-fine tuning it was capable of zero to 60 mph runs in the seven second range. Quarter-mile times hovered around the 15 second mark with corresponding speeds in excess of 92 mph. At least one super hot 360 hp exceeded 105 mph in a quarter-mile run. No wonder *MOTOR LIFE* (June, 1960) could state with confidence that ''Ford has accomplished more than a come-

Below, 1956 Ford Fairlane

back, it has reversed its performance trend. Until this year, the make has actually been slower every year since 1957.''

Unfortunately for Ford and its supporters, the Interceptor's career wasn't without its rough spots. Soon after it went on sale, gripes about its lack of durability and its inability to perform on the dragstrip, as its specifications promised, prompted Ford to do some hasty re-engineering work. As a result, all Interceptors built after February, 1960, carried a K series distributor that helped push their rev limit up to 6800 rpm from 5800 rpm. The valve float that often took place at approximately 5500 rpm was cured by the use of stronger valve springs and retainers.

The full-size Fords with new sheet metal below the beltline were both shorter and narrower in 1961. This change was accompanied by an overall reduction of horsepower for all of Ford's ''normal'' V-8's.

Happily, Ford's high performance engines were exempt from such happenings. By expanding the bore of the 352 V-8 from 4 inches to 4.05 inches and increasing its bore from 3.5 inches to 3.78 inches, Ford was able to market a 390 cid V-8 for 1961. This engine was offered in two performance forms. The first, the 390 Police Special with 330 hp was not terribly exciting. However, with a 10.6:1 compression ratio, large 600 cfm Holley Carb, big-port aluminum intake manifold and solid lifters the 390 pumped out 375 hp at 6000 rpm. Since Ford expended considerable effort to assure the precise construction of these engines, their true horsepower was close to 400.

With large main bearing webs and special, beefed up engine blocks, these Fords were seen as real threats to Pontiac at the 1961 Daytona 500. This belief was certainly substantiated by the 390 cid Ford's ability to lap the Romeo track at 158.8 mph. At Daytona, Ford was the only car beside Pontiac to average over 150 mph around the course, but the Fords simply didn't have the stamina to hang tough with the Pontiacs for 500 miles. One by one they fell by the wayside, one with water pump failure, another with overheating brought on by a newspaper clogged grille. Finally, only Banjo Mathew's Ford was up with the leaders but his car couldn't stay together either and with just fifty miles left, while running in second position, his engine blew and Marvin Panch's Pontiac went on to a unchallenged victory.

Just in time for the 1961 NHRA Winternationals held at

Pomona, California, Ford introduced a 401 hp version of its 390 V-8. Except for triple carburetors and a new aluminum intake manifold, this engine was identical to the 375 hp version. Initially, this new performance option was dealer installed but it soon became a regular production option.

In terms of its horsepower to engine weight and horsepower per cubic inch the 401 hp Ford was the king of American engines.

Late in the model year Ford offered the Warner 4-speed transmission as a $188 option. This gearbox was identical, except for gear ratios, to the 4-speed used by Chevrolet, Pontiac, Buick and Studebaker. A 3-speed with overdrive transmission was also available for $108.

At the Winternationals, the triple carburetor Fords were quick but the Chevrolet 409's still held an edge over them, though not by much. Don Nicholson's Chevrolet emerged as the Super-Stock Champion, just edging out a 401 Ford prepared by Les Ritchey for the gold. Their respective quarter-mile speeds were 105.88 mph and 105.50 mph. The source of the advantage enjoyed by Chevrolet was not found under its hood or for that matter beneath the Ford's. It was simply a matter of physics. The Chevys running in Super Stock drag competition consistently weighed anywhere from one to two hundred pounds less than their Ford counterparts and in drag racing that made all the difference between winning and losing. Losing, however, was something that Ford would soon be doing far less of.

On the surface it would seem that the really big performance news from Ford in 1962 was its new 406 cid engine. Although it was a derivative of the old 332 cid V-8, which, in turn, had begat the 352 and 390 V-8's, the new Ford powerhouse had a block casting that increased the thickness of the engine cylinder walls and which also would serve as the basis of the legendary 427.

With triple Holley carburetors, the 406 Ford developed 405 hp; with a single four-barrel, its rating stood at 385 hp. The 405 engine carried a $379.70 price beyond that of a normal 292-V-8 powered model. Included in this price were many mandatory heavy-duty chassis, suspension and brake options. The reason Ford required these items to accompany the purchase of cars equipped with high-output engines was explained by George Merwin of its sales department. "If all the buyers of this engine understood the full performance potential and respected the stress levels, there would be no need to add the cost of special chassis equipment," he remarked, "but we have to allow for the careless, youngster who jumps into this car, with no break-in, and flogs in unmercifully on the street and dragstrip without maintenance or tuning. This guy can get in trouble if we don't make special provisions."

When it came time for the 1962 Winternationals, held that year at Indianapolis Raceway Park, the chief competitors for the Mr. Stock Eliminator title were the 406 Ford, 409 Chevrolet, 413 Mopars and the 421 Pontiac. Over in the experimental class, Fords showed up with fiberglass body panels and aluminum bumpers that dropped their race-ready weight down to 3,355 pounds. But, in Super Stock competition, it was another year as an also-ran for Ford. As *MOTOR TREND* (December, 1962) reported, the "Ford threat never materialized, as top-flight drivers like Gas Ronda went down early before quicker '409's, '413's, '421's." One Ford did make it to the semi-final stage, but, when it was over, Mr. Stock Eliminator was Hayden Proffitt whose stick-shift 409 Chevrolet turned in a winning 12.83 second, 113.94 mph performance.

Seen in its entirety, Ford's 1962 performance record was similar to its showing in the Winternationals, respectable but not all-conquering. Its best showing had been in stock car races of over 250 miles duration where it won more races than other competitors, including Pontiac, but in the final 1962 NASCAR standings Ford was not terribly impressive. Pontiac won 22 of 53 NASCAR Races, Chevrolet was victorious in 14, Plymouth in 11. Ford trailed with only 6 victories. In the race for the NASCAR Drivers Championship only Rex White among the Ford campaigners made it into the top five and his 19,424 points put him far behind champion Joe Weatherly whose Pontiac helped him gather 30,836 points.

In mid-summer, just after he had been reelected president of the Automobile Manufacturer's Association, Henry Ford, II, by announcing that the Ford Motor Company would no longer abide by the 1957 anti-performance ban, made it crystal clear that Ford was ready to begin a drive for domination of auto racing. In part, Ford explained his company's decision by noting, "Today we feel the resolution has has come to have neither purpose nor effect."

That Ford was not mounting its offensive for just the sport of it was obvious from the beginning. The first issue of *THE AMERICAN ROAD*, a newsletter for Ford salaried employees, made that point clear by telling its readers, "An estimated 32 million fans yearly attend automobile races. They come to cheer performance and, on the drag stip or asphalt oval, performance is spelled *winner*. And away from the track, winner translates in *sales*."

Thus, the stage was set for Ford's Total Performance program which was kicked off with the strong mid-year introduction of its 1963½ models, participation in European rallies and the arrival of its long awaited 427 cubic inch V-8. The stock car equivalent of the Battle of Armageddon was about to begin.

Ford's initial high performance lineup for 1963 was unchanged from 1962. A new 390 cid engine option mating the triple carburetor and big-sport aluminum manifold from the 406 engine with hydraulic lifters and the standard heads and exhaust manifold was added, however. Cruise-O-Matic was available with this engine, which developed 340 hp at 5000 rpm.

The long expected Thunderbird 427 High Performance V-8, along with Ford's 1963½ fastback Falcon and Galaxie models, made their debut in January amidst a promotional fanfare conveying the message that "Ford" and "Total Performance" were synonymous. Ford defined Total Performance as "the ability of a vehicle to fully accomplish its intended function." There was little doubt what accomplishment Ford had in mind for the 427 Galaxie. The simple act of abandoning its old Thunderbird-inspired squared-off roof line and replacing it with a far smoother one boosted the Ford's top speed by several mph, and its larger engine assured Ford top speed parity on any NASCAR supertrack. For NASCAR competition, the 427, rated at 410 hp, was equipped with a single four-barrel carburetor. For street use or drag racing, the familiar dual carburetor set up raised this to 425. Actually, the most interesting feature of the 427 was not its carburetion or horsepower rating, but the cross bolting of its main bearing. This proved to be the remedy for the block cracking that all too often in the past had been Ford's Achilles' heel in NASCAR competition.

Just how good the first of the Total Performance Fords was can be summed up in one sentence: In 1963 Ford won every single NASCAR race of 500 miles or more duration. That memorable season began on January 20th in California where Dan Gurney won the inaugural Riverside 500 with a

1963½ fastback that a member of the Holman-Moody crew described as the "best prepared car" ever to leave their shop. Then it was on to Florida for the classic Daytona 500. The first five finishers at Daytona were Fords, lead by Tiny Lund. Less than two weeks before the 500, Lund was an obscure, little known driver, but his courage, bravery and presence of mind in a moment of crisis changed that. During a sports car race on the Daytona road course, Marvin Panch's Ford 427-powered Type 151 Maserati coupe crashed and flipped onto its top. Lund saved Panch's life by pulling him out of the flaming wreck. In appreciation, Lund was given the ride in the car originally prepared for Panch.

Ford's racing success that year, which included victories in the Atlanta 500, the Charlotte World 600, and the Firecracker 400, even extended across the ocean to England. At the British Racing Driver's Club meeting at Silverstone, a 427 Galaxie driven by Jack Sears sailed forth to do battle with a gaggle of Jaguar sedans. "Saloon" racing in England had been an unchallenged domain of Jaguars, and a Jaguar had won this particular event ten time in succession. This time was different. Sears beat out Graham Hill's Jaguar for the pole position by two seconds, gained the lead on the race's first lap and went on to win with an average of 91.7 mph. In the process, he set a new "Saloon" lap record of 94.4 mph. To put this speed in the proper perspective, the record for Formula One cars at that time stood at 110.4 mph.

Ford's accomplishments during 1963 in drag racing weren't as impressive as its NASCAR record but the quality of its drag racing cars reflected the depth of Ford's committment to competition. When the 1962 drag season ended, Ford's lightweight models, weighing 3220 pounds (or some 500 less than stock), were running in the Factory Experimental Class. For 1963, a "Lightweight Body Component Kit" consisting of fiberglass front fenders, hood, deck lid and door panels plus aluminum bumpers and

Above, 1964 Ford Galaxie 500/XL

brackets was made available. This kit reduced the Galaxie's stock weight by 164 pounds. Far more impressive was the special dragstrip model Ford offered only as a two-door fastback model with a white exterior and red upholstery. Like equivalent models from GM and Chrysler this, was a "for competition only" car that its manufacturer emphasized was not suitable for operation on public roads. The lighter gauge steel frame from the Ford 300 series was used and no sound deadening material was installed. The above mentioned Lightweight Body Kit was also used. Whereas the corresponding production model weighed over 4,100 pounds, its drag racing offspring weighed approximately 3,500.

Both in 1963 and 1964 there were important distinctions between the 427 Fords intended for street use, drag racing and NASCAR competition. The volume produced engine, known officially as the "427-8V," was rated at 425 hp with an 10.7:1 compression ratio. Like all 427's, it was equipped with cross-bolted main bearing caps. The 427 intended for the drag strip was also rated at 425 hp but, thanks to a special intake manifold, cylinder heads with larger ports and a cam with slightly more overlap, it was far more powerful. Then there was the 427 NASCAR engine. With a single four-barrel Holley carburetor it was credited with 410 hp. This, of course, was ridiculous. Just a cursory look at its heads with their cavern-like ports, the wide passages of its intake manifold and a 12:1 compression ratio left little doubt about that. A conservative estimate of its true potential would be 520 horsepower. A test of a 1963 NASCAR Ford prepared by John Holman and Ralph Moody for Fred Lorenzen appeared in the February, 1964, issue of *MOTOR LIFE*. With a 3.50 rear axle the 500-plus hp, Ford moved from zero to 60 mph in 6.3 seconds. To reach 100 mph from rest took 13.2 seconds, and its top speed was 155 mph. With different gearing, these Fords were even faster. During the July 4th Firecracker 400 at Daytona both Junior Johnson and Fireball Roberts were clocked at 168.5 mph. *ROAD & TRACK* publisher John R. Bond visited Dearborn in late

November, 1963, and was extremely impressed by what he was shown. "Not even in the days of Mercer, Stutz, Duesenberg, etc.," said Bond, "have we seen such a concerted effort toward all-out racing from one manufacturer in all facets of the sport. Meanwhile, the rest of the industry sleeps on."

Mr. Bond might be forgiven for waxing so eloquently about Ford's racing prowess. After all, it wasn't everyday he saw dynamometer readings surge beyond the 500 horsepower mark. Nevertheless, Bond's remark about the tendency for others to nap while Ford raced was a bit off the mark.

The scene at the January 19, 1964, running of the Riverside 500, however, did suggest Bond was on target. Only Ford and Mercury showed up with 1964 models. Dodge and Plymouth were holding off until the Daytona 500 in February to show off their new models. As a result, the race was pretty much of a Ford romp. Fred Lorenzen broke the stock car record for the 2.7 mile sports car course with a lap of 102.5 mph and winner (for the second time) Dan Gurney was timed at 156 mph on the straight. Fords finished 1-2-4-5.

But, life wasn't so easy for Ford at Daytona. The 426 Hemi Plymouths led by Richard Petty swept the first three places. Simply put, the new Chrysler engine was at least 30 hp more powerful than the Ford 427. For a time, NASCAR had flirted with a 396.5 cid limit for Grand National cars before backing off to the old 427 upper level. For 1964, anticipating the 396.5 cubic inch regulation, Ford had been preparing a new single overhead cam racing engine whose use, in the light of the performance the Chrysler Hemi, seemed imperative, at least to Ford. NASCAR's Bill France saw things differently and prohibited its use for 1964. The sohc Ford engine was not, however, a dead duck and we will return to it shortly.

If Ford couldn't run its sohc engine, the next best thing was to jazz up the faithful 427. This was accomplished by Ford engineering which hurriedly developed the "7000 rpm kit." The use of lighter weight reciprocating parts plus an improved cam and stronger valve springs moved the 427's rev limit up from 6300 rpm to somewhere between 7000 and 7200 rpm. Since this was the area where the engine developed its peak power, the power gap between Ford and its rivals from Chrysler Corporation was narrowed. Yet, that gap still existed and during the rest of the season it was Ford's superior handling that really enabled it to stave off total defeat by the Plymouths and Dodges. For example, after winning the Atlanta 500 in April, Fred Lorenzen commented, ". . . the real secret [of winning] I guess, was the way my car handled so much better in the turns. Isaac [who finished second] could tie me on the straights, but I could run away from him anytime I wanted to in the corners."

Actually, the Ford racing record in 1964 was pretty good. After Daytona, it won every race of over one hundred miles duration until the Southern 500 at Darlington on Labor Day. There, Buck Baker's Dodge led a 1-2-3 Chrysler Corporation romp which marked the first Mopar victory in the Southern 500 since Johnny Mantz's Plymouth had won the inaugural race in 1950.

Though it wasn't apparent to race fans, the factory Fords were some 400 pounds lighter than their Chrysler competition during 1964. The use of thin sheet metal plus lightened frames reduced their race weight to just 3,450 pounds. New NASCAR rules for 1965 requiring a minimum weight of 3,990 pounds plus a wheelbase of at least 119 inches brought such dieting to an end.

The decision by NASCAR limiting use of the 426 Hemi to the Plymouth Fury model did not set well with Chrysler. Bill France reasoned that since the public could not purchase a Belvedere with the Hemi, such a combination had no business turning its wheels in NASCAR racing. Although this action coincided with the banning of Ford's new dual carburetor, high-rise intake manifold, Chrysler was

Below, 1966 Ford Galaxie 500/XL

miffed and elected to sit out the 1965 season, which became, as a result, virtually a Ford romp. In 1965 NASCAR races, Ford finished first 48 times. Between them Plymouth and Dodge managed to gain only six victories.

The street versions of Ford's NASCAR juggernaut, the Galaxie 500 XL with the 425 hp, 427 cid engine, was an extremely formidable road machine. The 427 engine was available in any Ford model except the station wagon and when the 427 was specified the almost (by this time) traditional, heavy-duty suspension, clutch and 4-speed transmission were included as required options. Other major mandatory components of the high performance package included a stronger frame, heavy-duty radiator, battery and drive train.

CAR LIFE (February, 1965) reported performance figures for a 425 hp Galaxie with 4-speed transmission and 3.50 axle that were among the best ever recorded for an American supercar:

0-40 mph: 2.3 sec.
0-60 mph: 4.8 sec.
0-100 mph: 15.8 sec.

During 1965, Ford expanded its 427 engine production capacity and for 1966 was able to manufacture about 7,500 of these engines. An interesting variation on the old 390 V-8, making its debut in 1966, was the 428 cid V-8 which might best be described as a mild mannered performance engine with a capability several notches below the 427's. By expanding the bore and stroke of the 390, Ford had no problem enlarging it to 428 cubic inches. With a single four-barrel, quiet dual exhausts, and hydraulic lifters, it produced 345 hp at 4600 rpm and a healthy 462 lbs-ft of torque at 2800 rpm.

Ford used this engine for its new "7 Litre" Galaxie which, with a C-6 version of Cruise-O-Matic, needed 8.5 seconds to run from zero to 60 mph. This wasn't quite supercar performance. Similarly, its quarter-mile time of 15.8 seconds fell short of the mark. Incidentally in 1966 Ford referred to its 427's as Cobra engines and used the

Above, 1968 Ford XL

Thunderbird label for the 352, 390 and 428 V-8's.

The running war between Bill France, Ford and Chrysler over what was and wasn't race-legal had its usual off-season skirmish prior to the start of racing in 1966.

Ford was none too happy that the Chrysler Hemi engine would be back on the tracks under new NASCAR rules. The respect that Ford had for its Mopar opponent can be measured simply by noting how strongly Ford protested the legality of running destroked 405 Hemis in 116 inch wheelbase Dodge and Plymouth models on the NASCAR supertracks. Lee Iacocca underscored Ford's position on this issue by reportedly telling France that Ford would quit racing if it had to run Galaxies against smaller Coronets and Belvederes. As we will see, much of Ford's hostility on this point related to its strong desire for NASCAR to accept its overhead cam 427 as a legal powerplant for competition.

Since this didn't happen, Ford officially sat out most of the season until it and NASCAR worked out a compromise acceptable to both sides. However, the age of the big racing Fords was over. The new NASCAR regulations made it advantageous for all competitors to race their intermediate sized cars and, thus, the Galaxie gave way to the Fairlane as Ford's standard bearer in NASCAR competition.

Just how different this era of stock car competition and high performance automobiles would have been if Ford had been allowed to use its sohc 427 makes for some interesting speculation. At the very least it is doubtful that Chrysler would have accepted this development without a struggle. In other words, an overhead cam version of the Hemi was not an impossibility and what visions of performance that thought conjures up! This didn't happen primarily because, as William Neely, author of DAYTONA USA, the official history of racing at Daytona, quotes a Chrysler official, "France looks at racing differently than we do. We want to get an extra advantage that will let us win. So does Ford. But Bill wants everything to be even . . . Essentially, we view stock car racing as a sport. He views it as entertainment."

Whether this assessment is correct or grossly out of touch with reality isn't really important. What is of interest is that Ford did develop a sohc engine that, if the history of stock car racing had followed a different path of development in the mid-sixties, might have found its way into a limited number of production line Fords. If that had happened, the

result would have been an automobile whose immense power would have made it a legend from the word go.

During the latter part of 1964, rumors were rife that Ford was planning a major counterpunch to the Chrysler Hemi. Ford eventually did respond to the speculation concerning its next move by admitting that an sohc engine did exist but that it was only "experimental." This half-hearted attempt to keep Ford's intentions known only to Ford was not taken seriously by anyone connected with the sport, particularly since internally Ford referred to this engine as its "NASCAR V-8." This was an appropriate label since the sohc 427 was an engine designed specifically as a counterweapon to the Hemi. In its earliest form, in December, 1963, the sohc existed as a 390 cubic incher, but it was soon expanded to 427 cubic inches. Many parts such as the block, crankshaft, rods, and bearings were the same as the 427 pushrod NASCAR engine, but the overhead cams, plus very large intake ports and valves, made it truly a horse of a different color. At the start of its development, the sohc 427 developed over 500 hp and, with a 12:1 compression ratio and a single four-barrel, NASCAR type carburetor, it produced 600-plus hp at 7000 rpm. There's little doubt that its potential reached very close to the 700 hp mark.

The only real problem Ford had with this engine was to convince Bill France that it was a production engine. When Ford announced that it was going to run the sohc in its 1966 race cars, NASCAR was quick to react: "No overhead cam engines permitted," its rules read, "unless approved by NASCAR." Ford didn't take kindly to this and officially sat out a good part of the 1966 NASCAR season. During 1966, Ford did offer the sohc 427 as a production option. The price was steep, $995 more than the High Performance 427 and $1963 beyond the cost of a standard 289 V-8 engined Galaxie. Prior to the running of the Peach Blossom 500 on March 13, Leo C. Beebe, Ford's racing manager, announced that the sohc engine was in production and that he would seek NASCAR's approval of it for competition. Eventually this happened. NASCAR rules for 1967 allowed

its use in cars with a 119 inch wheelbase and a minimum weight of 4,427 pounds, but this really wrote *finis* for the sohc in NASCAR competition. For one thing, the pushrod 429's were allowed to run with over 400 pounds less weight. Secondly, that 500 minimum production run requirement was just too much for Ford's limited sohc engine tooling to cope with. Also, Ford engineers weren't too thrilled with putting it in the smaller Fairlane, which, as its record shows, already was a fierce competitor with the pushrod 427 and dual four-barrel carburetors.

The role of the sohc 427 was thus limited to the dragstrip. It made its drag racing debut at the NHRA Winternationals in February, 1965, winning A/FX and B/FX classes as well as emerging as top Factory Stock eliminator. As impressive as the sohc engine's achievements in drag racing were, they really were a let down for its true domain was on the banked curves at Daytona. For this reason, it was a promise unfulfilled.

The sohc engine wasn't the only evidence offered by Ford that suggested what type of racing would have taken place if Bill France hadn't kept the lid on at NASCAR. Before both the NHRA and NASCAR announced their 427 cid limit for production cars in 1963, Ford prepared a 483 cid monster V-8 for possible use that year. It was, in design, closely related to the 406 but had a larger bore and stroke. Its block was constructed of a new type of nodular iron and its intake and exhaust ports were, respectively, 18% and 16% larger than those of the 406 engine. With dual four-barrel Holleys and 12:1 compression ratio it developed at least 500 horsepower.

In October, 1962, Fred Lorenzen, Ralph Moody and Don White drove Lorenzen's 1962 Galaxie (which had actually started life as a convertible) to 46 national and international Class B records. Their fastest lap around the ten mile circle at Bonneville was 169.4 mph. Their best two-way straight line speed was 172.26, with one run at 176.978 mph.

Above, 1970 Ford XL

15. Ford Fairlane/Torino

Nobody bothered calling it a commemorative model but it did indeed mark the 30th anniversary of Henry's fabulous flathead V-8. Furthermore, its engine displaced the same 221 cubic inches as did that earlier landmark. In this context, "it" was the 1962 Ford Fairlane and, granted that while it wasn't a bad little car, the Fairlane didn't exactly strike most people as one of the automotive greats of that year or, for that matter, of any year. Still, other legendary performance cars of the age had emerged from even humbler origins and surely a point in the Fairlane's favor was its 221 cid V-8, destined, as every enthusiast knows, for stardom. A very modest stage of tune, however, initially disguised the Fairlane V-8's robust nature. A single two-barrel carburetor, 8.5:1 compression ratio and a cam with just 0.380 inches of lift limited horsepower to a calm 143 at 4500 rpm. Quick as a whistle (well, almost anyway), Ford expanded the 221 V-8 outward to 260 cubic inches and by early 1963 the 260 had grown to 289 and its High Performance, 271 hp version was a Fairlane option. Such Fairlanes were obviously frisky Fords but they also were somewhat redundant participants in Ford's Total Performance program. To give the Fairlane a more unique place in Ford's performance sun, the decision was made late in 1963 to produce, by a NHRA deadline of December 10, 1963, a batch of fifty Fairlanes with dual four-barrel carburetor high-rise 427 V-8's for competition in Super Stock drag racing. Ford didn't spare any efforts to make the Fairlane Thunderbolt, as it was called, a competitive drag machine. A fiberglass front end, aluminum bumper, plexiglass side windows plus the removal of all sound insulation reduced its weight and special links, positioned in the rear suspension, helped traction off the line by lifting the body slightly. Other rear suspension modifications included husky traction bars and three leaf springs on the right rear side (two were installed on the left). A 150 pound diesel truck battery was mounted in the trunk as a cheap and neat better traction trick. To handle the approximately 500 hp delivered by the 427 V-8, heavy-duty Galaxie drive line components were used. Early quarter-mile tests with a 4-speed prototype were encouraging: 11.53 seconds and 132 mph. Hopes for a Ford success at the

Below, 1963 Ford Fairlane 500

10th annual Labor Day Drag Nationals at Indianapolis were quickly dashed, though. In the first round, eight Dodges and seven Plymouths ganged up on a lone Ford Thunderbolt. A Ramcharger Dodge did the dirty deed, eliminating the Ford in the first round.

During 1965, the 427 engine in street garb (410 hp or 425 hp) was a Fairlane option but the number actually constructed was low. Ford had not, as suggested by the 427's rarity, decided to deep-six the Fairlane as a performance machine. The rise to prominence of the GTO made it a virtual sure thing that Ford would counter with a mid-sized factory hot rod of its own and *presto!*, along came the Fairlane GT and its automatic transmission sidekick, the GT/A. Evidences of flattery and imitation of the GTO abounded in the new Fairlane body. This did not mean it was a bad car by any means, but it certainly invited comparison with the original Great One and, in that face-off, the Fairlane came off second best. The Fairlane's automatic transmission was manually shiftable and, along with either 3- or 4-speed all-synchromesh manual gearboxes provided a nice selection of transmissions. There weren't any grounds to fault the Fairlane's suspension, either. The GT version was about 10% stiffer than stock and a special handling package with stronger springs and shocks was also available. Although disc brakes weren't available, large, 10 inch drums were standard and wider front and rear treads also helped further the Fairlane's cause. What then was the weak link in its armor? Unfortunately for Ford, it was a big one — about 390 cubic inches to be precise. Ford rated the faithful old 390 at 335 hp, which was, (surprise!), the same as the GTO's base 389 cid V-8, but the prospective GT or GT/A street racer, unlike his GTO counterpart, didn't have the chance to select an optional, more powerful engine. Adding insult to injury, he soon discovered the Fairlane's engine became rather lethargic as the revs climbed. Yet, when set up by talent of the Holman and Moody caliber the GT/A *could* move. *CAR AND DRIVER* (March, 1966) tested just such an example and it ran the quarter-mile in 14.26 seconds and 99 mph. Although *MOTOR TREND's* test car wasn't as quick down the line, it was capable of a zero to 60 mph run in just 6.8 seconds. It was not uncommon, however, for GT/A's to be considerably slower. *CAR LIFE*

(March, 1966), found their test car unable to improve upon an 8.7 second zero to 60 mph time.

Ford was still slipping a few 427 Fairlanes with fiberglass front ends out the door but they didn't help ease the hurt felt by 390 GT and GT/A drivers as the GTO shot down their egos with disturbing monotony. This situation remained basically unchanged both in 1967 and 1968 when the Fairlane/Torino received a new and very good looking fastback body. The 390, described by *CAR LIFE* (March, 1968) as a ''neither-nor power plant'' still lacked the moxey to deliver the goods in supercar style. A far better choice for GTO baiting remained the 427 which, toned down for 1968 with hydraulic lifters, was available with 390 hp.

Ford obviously could do better and proved it early in 1968 when it rolled out the 428 Cobra Jet. Certainly its drag racing debut was classically auspicious. At the February, 1968, NHRA Winternationals, it emerged as the top Super Stock Eliminator! The foundation of the Cobra Jet engine was the not-too-exciting 428 engine best known for propelling Thunderbirds in unobtrusive fashion along the boulevards of America, which is a nice way of describing it as dreadfully dull. However, the use of 10.6:1 pistons, heavy-duty, ''big-bolt'' connecting rods, tri-metal bearings and new cylinder heads providing for 2.06 inch intake and 1.625 inch exhaust valves, plus large ports, turned a pussy cat engine into a tiger eater. It is interesting that this engine with a 735 cfm Holley four-barrel (the 390 used a 600 cfm Holley) had the same 335 hp rating as the 390. Now, however, those 335 horses moved the Torino to 60 mph in less than 6 seconds. If more verve was called for, the Ram-Air induction system, which became a factory option in 1969, was available as a 1968½ dealer installed extra.

With new looks, power and the NASCAR Manufacturer's Championship all to the Torino's credit in 1968, Ford did not tamper with its basic design the following year. The ''1969 Boss Snake,'' said Ford, ''is blood brother to the specially modified Torinos that let it all hang out on this year's NASCAR circuit.'' Ford was not content to let the Torino gain sales just on the basis of its racing successes and belated, but nonetheless very strong, supercar energy.

Plymouth's sales coup with the Road Runner called for a FoMoCo response and it came in the form of the Fairlane Cobra for 1969. All the performance pieces were standard: the 428 Cobra Jet engine, 4-speed transmission, ''competition'' suspension and F70 x 14 tires on 6 inch wheels. Whereas a Plymouth with simple and straight forward styling looked great, though, a Fairlane given a similar treatment looked dull. Apparently aware of this shortcoming, Ford gave the 1970 Torino (the Fairlane label was almost out of the picture by then) a new roofline and exterior panels. In the process of revamping the Torino's looks, its designers got a bit carried away, expanding its wheelbase another inch to 117 and adding another 4 inches to its front overhang. To propel this 4,200 pound, 206 inch long behemoth, Ford gave the 429 engine a major revamping. The base Torino Cobra engine was strong at 360 hp but a mere weak sister next to the optional-at-$229 Cobra Jet 429. Compared to its older version, the 1970 edition had larger valves, a higher 11.3:1 compression ratio, more radical cam and larger, 700 cfm carburetor. If its 370 horsepower didn't satisfy then, for another $155, the ''Drag Pack'' option undoubtedly would. Although its output was supposedly just 5 hp more, a look at its 780 cfm carburetor, mechanical lifters, forged aluminum pistons and four-bolt main bearings suggested its 375 hp rating was a little white lie.

Tucked within one of the Torino's predecessors, for example the 1966 Fairlane GT, this engine would have made performance history. That hadn't happened, however. Instead, a great engine was harnessed to an automobile with too much weight, excessive bulk and a general lack of grace. Zero to 60 mph in 6 seconds wasn't wasting time but it was also performance attainable with far less effort if Ford hadn't lost sight of the fundamental small body/big engine supercar formula. Ford certainly wasn't the only manufacturer to lose its way and sense of perspective during the late sixties, yet, just because there were other manufacturers in the same situation didn't make the last versions of the Torino Cobra more palatable.

Above, 1967 Ford Fairlane GT/A

74

16. Ford Falcon

Occasionally, during these wacky, wonderous, wild and sorely missed years, practical, let's-have-no-nonsense automobiles were touched by the fever and in quick order shed their Plain Jane look and took a turn at being a bit of a swinger. Back in 1960, it would have taken a fortune teller with a mighty accurate crystal ball to forecast that the Ford Falcon's future included such a scenario.

When the Falcon was hatched in late 1959, there were numerous reasons why many automobilists viewed it as a modern day version of Henry's 1928 Model A. It was a simple, straightforward design with an uncomplicated engine up front (where engines were supposed to be). Surely its substantial sales superiority over the Corvair, with its heretical aluminum rear engine, proved the wisdom of its ways.

It didn't take long, though, for some owners of the "New Wave" American compacts to find out what they could do on the drag strip, and within just a few months the Falcons, Corvairs and Valiants were trading insults at Daytona. The truth of the matter is that the early racing Falcons were knocked out of the ring by the hyper-active, hyper-packed Valiants. Five Falcons showed up at Daytona early in 1960 for some racing around the 3.81 mile road course. They had the drivers (Joe Weatherly, Curtis Turner and Ralph Moody, to drop a few names) but they just didn't have the right combination of power and handling to make it in the majors. Whereas the Valiants were averaging 86 mph, the best the Falcons could muster up were laps in the region of 76 mph. Even the Corvairs, with all their problems, were up around 81 mph.

Ford had, prior to the 1960 Daytona Speed Weeks, asked both Bill Stroppe's engineering firm and the Holman and Moody operation to prepare power packages for the Falcon that would be simple "bolt-on" items of an inexpensive nature. Bill Stroppe's proposal, which was far more ambitious than the H-M program, lost out because of its cost and apparently was never actually installed in a Falcon. Although they served as the nucleus of the ill-fated Falcon Florida venture, neither proposal was accepted by Ford which decided, at that point at least, that Falcon sales were doing nicely without any powerpacks. Nevertheless, these various bits and pieces would have made for a light and lively Falcon GT.

The Falcons for Weatherly and Turner were rather hastily prepared at the Charlotte, North Carolina, facility of Holman and Moody. No doubt the limited time available to get the Falcons race ready was a key reason for their dismal showing. You just can't start working on a car at 11 a.m. on a Wednesday and expect the end result to arrive at Daytona at 3 p.m. the following Friday with everything in order!

Given a more favorable set of circumstances surrounding their preparation, the Falcons would have run much stronger at Daytona. Their suspensions were beefed up with stiffer springs and heavier shocks plus a robust front stabilizer bar. Engine modifications were strictly conventional, but effective. An intake manifold sporting three dual throat Holleys was installed and the Falcon's head was milled 0.080 inches to boost compression to 9.4:1. Stronger valve springs were used, along with solid lifters and a high-lift, long duration cam. Joe Weatherly's car, fitted with a 3.89 station wagon

rear axle, would rev to 6600 rpm. Turner's car with a 3.56 axle was limited to 6300 rpm. The acceleration of the Weatherly Falcon was strong, zero to 60 mph in 10.4 seconds, and at Ford's Romeo, Michigan, track a Falcon with similar engine modifications, but with twin carburetors, reportedly reached 110 mph.

Even though the Falcon With Gusto didn't become reality it was a great idea and, instead of dying, kept bouncing back to life. Undaunted by the bad business at Daytona, Bill Stroppe jumped at the chance to build a special, one-off Falcon for Ford vice president, William Clay Ford. It was a classic engine swap, the kind every teenager without cash dreams about, and the kind that American hot rodders perfected to a fine art. The little 144 cid Falcon six was summarily removed and replaced by a 312 cid Mercury V-8, slightly overbored 0.060 inches to yield 320 cubic inches. A Holley four-barrel carburetor from a 332 cid Ford engine was used along with a 10.0:1 compression ratio and a Racer Brown street cam. Other features unique to this Falcon included a 3.10 rear axle from a 1959 Ford and a cross-flow radiator courtesy of a 1960 Ford. This car, after stirring up revived interest in the performance potential of the Falcon, faded into obscurity. Yet, it was a very important technical exercise pointing to the 1963½ Falcon Sprint.

During late 1961 and early 1962, a plan (somewhat incongruous in retrospect but viable nonetheless) evolved bringing Holman and Moody into a venture to produce a small number of ultra-quick, limited production Falcon Challengers. In terms of their mechanical form, these Falcons were to be a hodge-podge of existing components. In terms of their performance, they were to be very quick machines, worthy of being considered sports cars.

The initial Challenger I was built in ten days and was based upon a 1962 Falcon Futura body and the 221 cid V-8 Fairlane engine. At Sebring, it finished second in class behind a Chaparral. Marvin Panch and Jocko Maggiocomo shared the driving duties and had no difficulty in reaching a maximum speed of 135 mph. Challenger I later attracted considerable interest at the April, 1962, automobile show at the New York Coliseum.

Later that summer, Holman and Moody showed off their Challenger II which they planned to market until Ford decided to go with the Sprint program. Its engine was the Fairlane V-8, now with 260 cubic inches and fitted with the solid lifters and four-barrel carburetor used in the early Shelby Cobras. A cam with greater lift than the normal 260's was also installed. With a Borg-Warner 4-speed transmission the Challenger had good (0-60 mph in 9.3 seconds) but certainly not outstanding acceleration. Its quarter-mile marks of 11.6 seconds and 83 mph were of a similar caliber.

Aside from its mechanical features, the most interesting aspect of the Challenger II was its appearance. By cutting 3 inches from its body just below the lower window line, Holman and Moody gave the Challenger II a taut, no-nonsense appearance.

An even more extreme Falcon modification, the Challenger III not only had a 3 inch section removed from its body, but had the same amount cut from its top, which

was also reshaped into a fastback form. Holman and Moody gave serious thought to building one hundred of these cars in order to compete in the F.I.A.'s Grand Touring Class. In order to do so, their engines were sleeved down to reduce displacement to 243.968 cubic inches, just under the 4-liter sports car limit. A Holman-Moody cam was installed that was slightly milder than those used in the 1962 Ford stock cars they prepared. Intake and exhausts, virtually identical to those used in 1957 by Ford, were utilized along with a four-barrel carburetor from the 406 cid Ford V-8. With an appropriate compression ratio of 10.5:1, the Challenger III engine delivered somewhat more than 230 hp to the 4-speed transmission used in the 406 Ford.

As noted earlier, Ford's decision to market its own, sportified version of the Falcon wrote a quick end to the Challenger saga but the experimental work performed by Holman and Moody was an important basis on which the Falcon Sprint was developed. As a result of the Challenger program, it became evident for example, that the Falcon rear axle couldn't handle the power of the 260 V-8, that its brakes were totally inadequate and that more front end chassis strength was needed. As a result, the Falcon Sprint used many Fairlane components, including brakes, rear axle and torque box.

Early in January, 1963, the Sprint, along with other 1963½ Ford offerings, was introduced by Benson Ford at Monte Carlo. Mr. Ford's speech on behalf of his company's products and the rationale behind their form was an interesting discourse on Ford's attitude towards performance and competition. Stressing the view that the Americans and Europeans were drawing closer together via trade, he maintained that the gap between U.S. and European cars was lessening. Thus, since the Ford Motor Company was an international corporation, Mr. Ford added, "Now we draw upon a new source of strength that is essentially European . . . the characteristics that in Ford products we call lively — high performance with economy of weight and power, good driving and handling characteristics, all of the things that add pleasure and zest and safety to driving . . . The Ford products that are being displayed for the first time at this conference," Ford continued, "were influenced by this product philosophy. They wed the sports car and the typical family vehicle to create what we believe is important product innovation."

Benson Ford went on to depict racing as "stimulating interest, concern, even passion for automobiles with the general public." Fords were already familiar sights in drag racing and NASCAR competition. Now, with Benson Ford adding rallies to the list of events that, he claimed, improved engines, drive trains and suspensions, it really came as no surprise when the Falcon Sprints entered the 1963 Monte Carlo rally. They made an extremely impressive debut. A win wasn't theirs, that honor went to Paddy Hopkirk's Cooper S, but the Falcon did finish second, overall, and captured first and third in the over 2500 cc class. Bo Ljungfelt's Sprint set the fastest time in all the special tests (sharing one with Hopkirk's Cooper). This marked the first time in Monte Carlo history that one car had dominated that portion of the rally so convincingly.

As would be expected, the Rally-Sprints were far different than the stock versions. Much of their bodywork was constructed of fiberglass and there were many chassis and mechanical modifications. The Monte Carlo Sprints were powered by 260 hp, 260 cid Cobra engines capable of 7000 rpm. A 4-speed transmission and a 4.51:1 Galaxie, limited-slip rear axle were also used. Although the Sprint's top speed was only 118 mph, its zero to 60 mph time was a quick 7.5 seconds.

To cope with the expected and realized rigors of the Monte, Ford outfitted its Rally Sprints with a very tough suspension. Koni adjustable shocks, set on their firmest ratings, were used and, in order to prevent rear axle windup, extra leaf springs were installed at the rear.

After their Monte Carlo debut, the Sprints went on to score overall victories in the Tulip, Geneva and Mexican rallies. They came away from the Alpine Rally with a class win and finished 2-3-4 in the Trans-Canada Rally, a performance earning them both the Team and Manufacturer's awards.

In comparison to their competition versions, the production Sprints were pretty tame, but zero to 60 mph in just 11 seconds was pretty snappy for a car with a relatively small 260 cid, 164 hp V-8. The Sprint could have developed along lines similar to that of the Chevy II but that wasn't in Ford's crystal ball. The arrival of the Mustang in 1964 really gave the Sprint the *coup de grace,* although the Sprints continued to fare well in rally competition that year.

By 1966, the Falcon was using the Fairlane/Comet body and was headed for oblivion. Replaced by the Maverick in 1970, it was a victim both of corporate fratricide and the phenomenal success of the Mustang.

Above, 1964 Ford Falcon Sprint

17. Ford Mustang

Nothing succeeds like success and of all the supercars the Mustang was the greatest success of them all. It was a super seller of the sixties, an automobile whose personality kept pace with the times and, if less than perfect in some ways, did evolve into an extremely strong performer.

Successes, both past and present, weighed heavily upon the early development of the Mustang. The success of the original two-seater Thunderbird was still a very pleasant memory at Ford. The success of the Falcon, after the Edsel debacle, had vindicated the work of the market researchers and the signals that an affluent youth market was out there, up for grabs, were too strong to be passed by. The success of Chevrolet's Corvair Monza couldn't be ignored. Finally, there were the Ford executives, probably best exemplfied by Lee Iacocca, who were, to say the least, highly success-motivated.

Amidst the characteristics given the Mustang during its development were several that were crucial to its performance character. Certainly the most dominant was an inherent quality of sportiness. An automobile with trim proportions, bucket seats, floor shifter and a name that connoted good times, was bound for the big time.

The initial hoopla surrounding the Mustang's April, 1964, introduction (it wasn't every week that Lee Iacocca showed up on the covers of both *TIME* and *NEWSWEEK* and a somewhat critical attitude on the part of some journalists towards the Mustang, tended, temporarily at least, to put its performance character in the background. In August, 1964, Mustang was the third best selling car in the U.S., headed only by the Chevrolet Impala and Ford Galaxic 500. For the bulk of the year, it outsold every Chrysler and AMC car on the market and very nearly outsold the Chevelle, with sales of 240,373 to the Chevelle's 256,750. With sales like that, who cared if *CAR AND DRIVER* postulated, "Nobody will ever say its a great car," or that in reference to the early rear-engined Mustang I, *MOTOR TREND* lamented, "It's rather a shame that the Mustang name had to be diluted this way."

But, the Mustang, by virtue of future features, was destined for greatness and "diluted" would soon cease to be applicable to any Mustang save for the basic six- and eight-cylinder models. Ranging from the six's 101 hp to the 164 hp, 260 cid and 210 hp, 289 cid V-8's, these engines were strong enough to keep most Mustang owners happy, but not until mid-summer did the Mustang's first, serious high performance engine come on line. This was the 271 hp, 289 cid V-8 that had sparked the AC Cobra to sensational performance times. With a 10.5:1 compression ratio, solid lifters, high rise manifold and a single Holley four-barrel, this engine was expensive ($435.80), but, in terms of the product it delivered, most enthusiasts found it was worth every penny.

When the Mustang II, the production model's kissing cousin, was trolled before the sports car crowd at Watkins Glen in the fall of 1963, it was powered by this engine. Lee Iacocca, making the most of the teaser appeal of the Mustang II, wryly commented, "271 horsepower in a car weighing about 2,500 pounds could offer interesting and sporty transportation combined with the ability to idle along in traffic whenever necessary." Just how "interesting and

sporty" the production Mustang with 271 hp could be was a point of pride for virtually everyone connected with its development. A Ford test driver, for example, told *HOT ROD* magazine that a 271 hp Mustang with the special handling pack could "more than hold its own with a Sting Ray Corvette on a tight-handling course." This was no mere idle boast for a 271 hp Mustang with the special handling suspension lapped the 1.5 mile Waterford Hills, Michigan, sports car track just 0.6 seconds under the lap record then held by a Cobra. A heavy-duty chassis was a required option with the 271 engine. The special handling feature included even higher rate springs, shocks, quicker steering, 15 inch wheels and high speed tires. No small wonder that Ford competition manager, Frank Zimmerman predicted that in SCCA racing the Mustang would "come in second to Cobras and ahead of Sting Rays."

In light of the great success the Shelby-ized Mustang achieved in sports car competition, it's interesting to consider how the early Mustang first fared at the hands of the sports car press. Initially *ROAD & TRACK* was quite enamoured with it. The Mustang was, they said, "definitely a sports car, on a par in most respects with such undisputed types as the MG-B, Triumph TR-4, or Sunbeam Alpine." Once *ROAD & TRACK* had the opportunity to test a production Mustang, its ardor cooled considerably. "The Mustang we tested," concluded its driver, "if given the blindfold test, would be indistinguishable from any of a half a dozen other Detroit compacts. There's just nothing different about it in this respect." These less than laudatory comments were followed by other lukewarm judgements. "As for the street version, "*ROAD & TRACK* continued, "there seems little excuse for such frankly sloppy suspension on any car with the sporting characteristics which have been claimed for the Mustang." From *ROAD & TRACK's* perspective Ford had missed a golden opportunity to build a quality road car. "Instead, they simply built all the familiar characteristics, for which the typical American sedan had been cursed so long, into a sporty looking package."

In this respect, the Mustang was suffering the same type of unbounded criticism that had earlier afflicted the Thunderbird. The times had changed, however, and in the early sixties Ford's avid interest in competition virtually assured frequent racing appearances by Mustang and, as a production model, it steadily improved as a performance machine. Starting in September, 1964, Kelsey-Hayes disc brakes became available for the front wheels and if the Mustang in convertible form (which served as the pace car for the 1964 Indianapolis 500) wasn't sporty enough, then the 2+2 Fastback, debuting as a 1965 model in September, had to satisfy even those hard to please customers. The looks were there, the handling (via options) was there and, thanks to the 271 horsepower engine, performance of zero to 60 mph in 7.5 seconds was also on tap.

A month before the 2+2 Fastbacks went on sale, two hardtop Mustangs took part in the 3,500 mile Spa-Sofia-Liege Rally. Both the Mustangs and their drivers (Bo Ljungfeldt/Fergus Sager and Peter Harper/Peter Procter) had their work cut out for them. In 1963, only 20 cars of 129 starters finished. The 1964 rally was considerably tougher but this didn't deter Leo C. Beebe, Ford Division special

vehicle manager, who said, "We found out last year that this rally lived up to its reputation and decided to enter again this year to see just how rugged this new car of ours really is."

Equally impressive was the stirring performance of the Mustangs of Messrs. Peter Procter and Peter Harper in the 1964 Tour de France. Their cars won 13 of 17 speed tests and finished first and second in class. At the opposite end of the performance spectrum—drag racing—a Class A, Factory Experimental Mustang was outfitted by Ford Engineering with a 600 hp sohc 427 V-8. Equipped with a 5.14 rear axle and close ratio 4-speed transmission it leapt from zero to 60 mph in 3.7 seconds and then continued on to complete the quarter-mile in 11.7 seconds at a speed of 128.6 mph.

Good timing, and lots of it, seemed to be something the Mustang had in abundance during the early years of its existence. It first appeared when the nation's population distribution couldn't have been more favorable, and the opportunity to use the New York World's Fair as the location for the Mustang's debut was a true, once-in-a-lifetime dream come true for Ford.

Similarly, what better racing medium was there for the Mustang to strut its stuff than the SCCA's Trans-American Sedan Championship? Its first race took place on March 25, 1966, at Sebring the day before the 12-hour endurance run. It wasn't exactly an auspicious Trans-Am opener for Mustang. The winner was an Alfa Romeo GTA. Second, and winner of the over-two-liter class, was Bob Tullius' Dodge Dart followed by two Plymouth Barracudas. The Mustang of A.J. Foyt was strong early in the race but bit the dust after 32 laps. Things improved rather quickly, however, for the second TransAm held at Wentzville, Missouri, on June 12th was won by a Mustang. This victory was followed by three others and, just like that, Mustang won the manufacturer's title for Ford.

The 1967 Mustangs, with new sheet metal below the beltline plus a new roofline for the 2+2 fastback, were longer and wider than before but still instantly identifiable as America's first ponycar. The task of updating the Mustang's appearance without losing the significant form that had helped sell considerably more than one million cars

in less than two years, was not an easy one but it was effectively accomplished.

All the anguish the Ford stylists and executives experienced during the Mustang's first major facelift notwithstanding, a far more fateful move was the decision to offer Ford's 335 hp, 390 cid V-8 as a $158.08 Mustang option. To this point, the Mustang's performance image was based upon trim size, relatively lightweight and a small, high revving engine. To continue along these lines, however, was to ignore the large and growing market for big engined street machines. Furthermore, the danger existed that if Mustangs weren't to be had with big engines, even those faithful to its 289 V-8 might be lured away by the siren song of a 389 Pontiac V-8 installed in a GTO.

In effect, then, Ford really had no choice but to go full bore with development of a big engined Mustang, yet, the use of a 390 cid V-8 in a Mustang brought its own set of problems. The most serious was that bugaboo of all automotive designers, and the special bane of chassis engineers, weight. The 390 engine increased the Mustang's weight by 500 pounds beyond that of a six-cylinder model and added to the burden on the front wheels by 379 pounds, up 79 from that imposed by a 289 V-8. To cope with those extra pounds, the 390 Mustang was equipped with stronger, 260 lbs-in front springs. 245 lbs-in and 220 lbs-in springs were used in Mustangs with 289 V-8 and six-cylinder engines, respectively. A larger, 0.72 inch instead of the usual 0.69 inch diameter front stabilizer bar, was also included in the 390 suspension group. If these handling helpers weren't enough, then another handling option with even stiffer front springs was available. The result was an automobile with sporty proportions, quick acceleration (zero to 60 mph in 7.1 seconds with select-shift Cruise-O-Matic that also offered manual shift control) and handling that belied the 390 Mustang's road weight of 3,897 pounds.

If there were any doubts about Ford's intent and ability to keep the Mustang in the midst of the most sustained power struggle in automotive history, they were blown away in 1968. Although it was not available with a manual trans-

Above, 1965 Ford Mustang 2+2

mission, a 390 hp, 427 V-8 with lightweight pistons and connecting rods kept the Mustangs moving along very briskly. Until mid-model time, this engine was the Mustang's top power option. Then came the 428 Cobra-Jet, a product of Ford's Special Vehicles Department. Its credentials were impressive: 10.6:1 compression ratio, a Holley 735 CFM four-barrel carburetor, and enlarged intake and exhaust ports. The 427 high performance V-8 contributed its cylinder heads, valve springs and dampers. A 290° duration cam plus "header-type" exhaust manifolds were also included. *HOT ROD* magazine's reaction to the 428 Cobra-Jet Mustang was to declare it "the fastest-running Pure Stock in the history of man." It was possible, *HOT ROD* discovered, if all accessory belts were removed, to run the Mustang Cobra-Jet throught the quarter-mile in a thundering 13.5 seconds, which corresponded to 106.44 mph. This "Dearborn rocket sled" also ran from zero to 60 mph in 5.9 seconds. If more and less was your game, *more* go was possible, thanks to a special order option that allowed for *less* weight by the removal of virtually all sound-deadening material. *HOT ROD* described riding in such a vehicle as "motoring about the countryside in a 50-gallon steel echo chamber." The Cobra-Jet engine, which was available with either a 3-speed automatic or 4-speed manual, was ticketed at $420.96 beyond the cost of a 289 V-8 equipped Mustang.

The first engine that made the Mustang a great per-former, the 271 hp, 289 V-8, was not available in 1968. Taking its place in a roundabout sort of way was a new 302 cid tunnel-port V-8. As the powerplant for the Trans-Am Mustangs, it was treated rather rudely by "Mr. Nice Guy," Mark Donohue, and his Penske-prepared Camaro. Mustang had won the Trans-Am title in 1967 but this time around it managed only 3 victories, far behind the Camaro's 10 wins.

Obviously, the 302 engine, as hundreds of thousands of Trans-Am race watchers were to discover, was destined to enjoy a happier future. Yet, during 1968, the tunnel port engine did pretty well for itself out on the streets. A mild version with hydraulic valves, dual four-barrel carburetion and flat-top, 10.5:1 compression ratio pistons was offered with a conservative 240 hp rating. Far more stimulating to the performance enthusiast's soul was the 302 tunnel-port available in very limited numbers as a dealer installed option. Compared to the older 289 V-8, the 302 had a longer, 3.00 inch stroke plus considerably larger valves. Its intakes measured 2.12 inches in diameter, compared to the 289's 1.773 inch units. Respective exhaust valve sizes were 1.54 inches and 1.44 inches. This engine with very light, domed pistons, 12.5:1 compression ratio, solid lifters, a forged crankshaft and twin Holley 540 cfm four-barrel carburetors was virtually identical to the 1968 Trans-Am engine. No power rating was released but, judging from its performance, it was near the 400 hp mark — sufficient to provide a zero to 60 mph time of 5.4 seconds. From zero to 100 mph the tunnel-port 302 with 3.91 axle and 4-speed manual transmission needed just 12.5 seconds. Quarter-

Below, 1967 Ford Mustang 2+2

mile speeds above 106 mph were possible.

The Mustang received its third major styling change in 1969. As before, the basic appeal of the first model was retained but there now was a stronger, more assertive look particularly in the Sports Roof version that was a very worthy successor, in terms of appearance, to the earlier fastback Mustangs. In its "let it all hang out" performance version, the Sports Roof Mustang (which was 0.9 inches lower than the hardtop model) was known as the Mach I. Earlier, in 1966, the first Mach I, a two-seater showcar, had appeared but, if anything, the production car was better looking. Thanks to the Cobra Jet in Ram Air form with a 735 cfm Holley four-barrel (which carried the same 335 hp rating as the normal 428) the Mach I also took the Mustang up to a new point in the performance stratosphere. The Mach I was available only as a fastback and was delivered with a galaxy of nice goodies that underscored the fact that this was no ordinary, six-cylinder Mustang that some cute secretary was committed to for 36 payments. Among the more notable, and noticeable, of these goodies were a hoodscoop, rising from a matte-black hood, NASCAR hold-down pins, scoops for the rear brakes mounted high upon the rear fenders, body color coordinated streamlined mirrors, side stripes plus high back bucket seats. Also available were Goodyear Polyglas tires that were a big help in the handling department. The Mach I, powered by the Cobra Jet Ram-Air 428, made a very favorable impression upon *CAR LIFE* which declared it both the "Best Mustang Yet and Quickest Ever" and "the Best Ponycar of 1969." The Cobra Jet Mach I had lots of straightline get up and go; there was no doubt about that. With Cruise-O-Matic, the *CAR LIFE* test car achieved a quarter-mile time and speed of 13.90 seconds and 103.32 mph. The only car tested by *CAR LIFE* to do better was a 427 cid Sting Ray. Although *CAR LIFE* had high praise for the Mach I's cornering power, *CAR AND DRIVER* viewed it as the car's greatest shortcoming. "The beak-heavy machine," reported *CAR AND DRIVER*, "just won't corner with any dignity at all." Even with its standard equipment, higher rate front and rear springs, stiff anti-roll bar, high control shock absorbers (staggered at the rear), bias belted tires and six inch rims, the Mach I's underpinning had its work cut out for it. Of the

Mach I's 3,607 pounds, some 2,140 or 59.3%, rested on the front wheels.

It's entirely possible that if Ford had not been coming under strong external pressures to do otherwise, the Mach I Cobra Jet might have gone down in history as the point of apogee for the Mustang's performance career. Fortunately, it didn't work out that way at all. The success of Chevrolet's Z/28, of which some 7,000 were sold in 1968, did not sit well with anyone at Ford, especially its President, Semon Knudsen. Since the early sixties, Ford had more or less seized the initiative away from Chevrolet in developing new marketing concepts and this Chevrolet thrust had to be countered quickly.

Ford also had some housekeeping to tend to in the NASCAR frontlines. There, its "Blue Crescent 429" in order to be eligible for competition needed to be sold to the public in a minimum amount of 500 vehicles. Chosen for this task was the Mustang. Thus, at 1969½ model time another set of vigorous Mustangs were released from the corral, the Boss 302 and Boss 429.

The specification sheet of the Boss 429 reads like a super dream machine come true. Aluminum heads, ultra large ports and valves (2.3 inch intake and 1.9 inch exhaust), a 285° duration cam, 735 cfm Holley four-barrel and, of course, a quasi-hemi head were indeed the parts from whence performance dreams come. Ford rated this engine at 375 hp at 5200 rpm but at that engine speed it probably was producing at least 400 hp. The Mach I heavy-duty suspension system was the starting point for the Boss 429's. At the front, the suspension was moved outward approximately one inch to provide room for the very hefty 429. To handle its torque, the strongest rear axle and limited-slip differential in the Ford inventory were used. The only transmission offered was a close-ratio 4-speed. *CAR LIFE* magazine's Boss 429 test car quarter-mile performance of 14.09 seconds and 102.85 mph didn't quite match the Mach I Cobra Jet's, but the fact remained that the NASCAR 429's were capable of 570 hp and thus while the Cobra Jet was near its peak the Boss 429 had a *long way* to go in this regard. This situation plus very strong brakes and certainly

Above, 1969 Ford Mustang Grande

passable handling made *CAR LIFE's* assessment of the Boss 429 as "the best enthusiast car Ford has ever produced" valid until the opportunity to wind out a Boss 302 arrived. To *CAR AND DRIVER* (June, 1969) the Boss 302 was "easily the best Mustang yet and that includes all the Shelbys and Mach I's." Not everyone would agree with this judgement, particularly those who liked to play with big engines. Yet, there can be little resistance to declaring the Boss 302 as the best Ford-produced (to distinguish it from the Shelby versions) example of just how good the original Mustang design philosophy was. Unlike the Mach I, it didn't suffer from excessive nose heaviness. Like the Mach I, its appearance, with a matte black hood, front spoiler, clean side flanks sans scoops plus an optional rear "venetian blind," was seductively sensational. It was also easy to rave about its suspension, which followed along earlier Mustang heavy-duty lines, plus new front spindles to move the wheels a bit further apart. Goodyear F60-15 polyglas tires mounted on 7 inch wheels necessitated wider wheel openings that certainly didn't detract from the Boss' appearance.

The 302 engine didn't have tunnel ports but it did have big, canted valves, that were capable of breathing very deeply. Its intakes were of 2.23 inch diameter, just 0.02 inches smaller than the Hemi 426's. Exhaust valves measured 1.71 inches in diameter. A Holley 780 cfm four-barrel carburetor, high-rise manifold and solid lifter were

Below, 1970 Ford Mustang Boss 302

also used. Ford credited the street version of the Boss 302 with 290 hp at 5800 rpm and 290 lbs-ft of torque at 4300 rpms. Its zero to 60 mph time of 6.0 seconds plus consistent runs through the quarter-mile of 14.5 seconds and 98 mph suggest otherwise. More likely, its maximum horsepower approached 400.

For Trans-Am racing, the Boss 302 was naturally considerably more potent with a runner-type intake manifold, two four-barrel 1100 cfm Holley carburetors and numerous beefed up internals. Alas, these features plus drivers Peter Revson, Dan Gurney, Parnelli Jones and George Follmer couldn't prevent the Donohue-Penske gang from winning the Trans-Am title for Camaro. The following year though things improved and the Mustang came to the finish line the winner.

The 1970 Mustangs, aside from detail changes, were performance carbon copies of the year earlier models. The next year things started to come unglued. The new Mustang was larger, and heavier. Although the 429 was still available in Cobra Jet, Ram Air and Super Cobra Jet form, there was no 428 and the 302 was phased out. Its replacement, the 351 HO Cleveland engine, rated at 330 hp, was no slouch however, and the Boss 351 with this powerplant and its strong suspension was by no means a paper tiger. Nor were the 429s, rated at 370 hp with or without Ram Air and 375 in Super Cobra Jet Form, but they were the last performance Mustangs. No 429 engines were to be had in 1972, leaving the limited availability 351 in 275 (net) hp HO form to close the door on Mustang's golden years.

18. Ford Thunderbird

The Ford Thunderbird's career as a high performance automobile was short and bittersweet. It had its moments of glory intermingled with ridicule, most of it misdirected and based upon prejudice, and before it really had a chance to evolve into a sports car different from the Corvette, but a sports car nonetheless, its entire personality was irrevocably altered.

The Thunderbird originated in the same type of environment that encouraged Chevrolet to create the Corvette. Early fifties America was conducive to the growth in popularity of two-seater sports cars. Since most of the British manufacturers utilized components from low priced sedans as the basis for their sports cars, it seemed logical that their American counterparts would do likewise, if and when they decided to challenge the imports.

The most adamant critics of the Thunderbird seemed determined never to regard it as a sports car. Yet, on every reasonable criteria, it could pass for, at the very least, a close facsimile. *MOTOR LIFE* (January, 1955) concluded, "The Thunderbird, not advertised as a sports car by its creators, is very close to being one." In similar fashion, *ROAD & TRACK* (May, 1955) favorably passed judgment on the Thunderbird, observing "The Ford Motor Co. refrains from calling this car a sports car, but we think this policy is being overly cautious . . . The Thunderbird is a touring sports car, designed to give sports car qualities up to a point."

Actually, in the early stages of the Thunderbird's promotion Ford referred to it as "a completely new kind of sports car." Tom McCahill, who seldom got hung up on the business of splitting hairs over the issue of what car was or wasn't a sports car, was in basic agreement with Ford's description. In spite of the T-bird not being a car with inherent competition potential, it was, in his view, "a full-blown sports car."

In retrospect, the debate over the T-bird's virtues or lack of them as a sports car was a silly one. Perhaps it didn't match the ideals established by the most exotic Europeans but it was reasonably priced at $2,695 and few two-seaters at that price could match its performance, reliability and overall versatility.

In its original form, the T-bird was powered by Ford's 292 cid V-8 with 193 hp when hitched to either a 3-speed manual or overdrive transmission. Fordomatic Thunderbirds with 198 hp were capable of zero to 60 mph runs under ten seconds when in a good state of tune. Stick-shift models did slightly better. Lots of discussion took place about the Thunderbird's top speed. *ROAD & TRACK* reported questioning five Ford dealerships about the top speed of the Thunderbird and receiving answers ranging from 125 to 150 mph. In its own test of a 198 hp Fordomatic Thunderbird, tuned by the Clay Smith shop, *ROAD & TRACK* achieved a top speed of 112 mph and a zero to 60 mph time of 9.5 seconds. Veteran sports car driver Jack McAfee did most of the performance testing for *ROAD & TRACK* and reported "the car felt very safe and stable during the timed speed runs."

Tom McCahill, who put his money where his mouth was, purchased a new Thunderbird and pegged its top speed with overdrive at 130 mph. He was not the least bit uncomfor-

table describing the Thunderbird as "the finest production American sports car ever built, bar none." At Daytona, the Thunderbird's success made, wrote McCahill *(MECHANIX ILLUSTRATED,* May, 1955) "some early automotive critics of this car appear for the rest of the year as if they'd been stuffed with red neon tubes." For the record, the T-bird won the under $4,000 sports car class at 121.992 mph, the American Sports Car Class at 124.633 mph and finished third in the acceleration runs behind two Ferraris with a speed of 84.66 mph. In this event, the best a Jaguar XK 120M could do was 79.542 mph and none of the production Jaguars were faster than the Thunderbird in the high speed events.

If the performance of a Thunderbird either in its stock form or as the specially prepared, but easily duplicated, Daytona Champion wasn't enough, McCulloch offered a supercharger that boosted the T-bird up to 260 hp. This enabled the twin-seat Ford to out-accelerate virtually every stock, production car in the world. Zero to 60 mph took only six seconds of your time and the zero to 100 mph time was a phenomenal 16 seconds. Top speed was a true 131 mph. Such a Thunderbird was not a stock model, of course, but the possession of such potential obviously spoke well of the basic quality of the Thunderbird.

After being quite pleased with the virtues of the first Thunderbird, *ROAD & TRACK* (August, 1956) came away from the firsthand acquaintance with the 1956 version with considerably less enthusiasm. "Personal car is the right terminology," concluded *ROAD & TRACK,* "for the T-bird has flown in competition as if its wings were clipped — this is no sports car by any stretch of the imagination, and Ford never claimed otherwise." *ROAD & TRACK* was not only wrong on the last count but in its overall assessment. It's true the Thunderbird didn't do well in sports car racing but Ford, unlike Chevrolet, had chosen not to provide the means, in the form of racing options, to make its two-seater a competitive machine. As events proved in 1957, the potential was there, however. Furthermore, at the 1956 Daytona Speed Weeks the performance of the T-bird required no apologies or excuses. The 292 cid V-8 was still available, now rated at 202 hp, but only in conjunction with the manual 3-speed transmission. For the Overdrive and Fordomatic T-Birds, the "Thunderbird Special V-8" with 312 cubic inches was used. The automatic transmission still received the more powerful, 225 hp engine, whereas the O/D equipped Thunderbird carried a 215 hp rating. The only difference between the two engines was their compression ratios, 9.0:1 and 8.4:1 respectively.

Although the T-bird's ride was softer for 1956, due primarily to rear springs with four instead of five leaves that were longer, (50 inches to 48 inches), there was no significant change in its road manners. *SPORTS CARS ILLUSTRATED* (June, 1956) reported "the T-bird corners remarkably good" and at Ford's Kingsman track in Arizona a stock 1956 model had no difficulty lapping at 119 mph. Even though it was no longer calling the Thunderbird a sports car, *ROAD & TRACK* could not fault its performance. Its 225 hp Fordomatic test car turned zero to 60 mph in 9. seconds and reached a maximum speed of nearly 114 mph.

In time for participation in the Daytona Speed Week

competition for 1956, Ford offered, on a limited basis, a super performance version of the 312 V-8 with dual four-barrel Holley carburetors and 10.0:1 compression ratio heads. In essence, this 260 hp engine was Ford's stock car racing unit with larger intake and exhaust ports, a limited advance ignition, high lift cam and tubular pushrods among its high output features.

At Daytona, Chuck Daigh's 260 hp Bird left no doubt about its viability as a performance machine. At the drag-strip with a 4.56 rear axle, it turned the quarter-mile at just over 100 mph. During the Speed Week standing start mile acceleration runs, it had no difficulty in exceeding 130 mph. Daigh had drawn first blood in the Chevrolet-Ford feud on February, 22nd, when he had gotten the best of Zora Arkus-Duntov's Corvette in the acceleration runs, 92.14 mph to 89.75 mph. Neither car, however, stood up to post run scrutinizing and were eventually assigned to the modified sports car class. Nonetheless, another ''stock'' Thunderbird won the production sports car class at 88.78 mph. In the flying mile competition, John Fitch's Corvette was the easy winner at 145.54 mph but the Thunderbird's best speed of 134.40 mph was certainly respectable. For the record, it's worth noting that the T-Bird was slightly faster than the highly respected Jaguar XK140MC, the fastest example of which peaked at 134.08 mph.

If this wasn't enough, Bill Frick (the creator of earlier era Fordillacs and Studillacs) offered, for $5,750, a Thunder-bird with a McCulloch supercharged Cadillac V-8 that broke the 6 second mark from zero to 60 mph.

All the self-serving nonsense about the T-bird's status as a sports car was shot to pieces after the 1957 Daytona Speed Week. The Thunderbird's achievements in Florida have always been overshadowed by the aura of the 283 hp, fuel injected Corvette, but they were very substantial and need no excuses or rationalization. Ford was up to its corporate armpits in racing at this point and while the AMA anti-racing decree of June, 1957, did a number on the T-Bird's future as a performance automobile, it was more than good while it lasted. It was spectacular.

Ford was after Chevrolet's hide at Daytona in 1957. Peter De Paolo was harboring a stable of fearsome Fords in whose ranks were two very special modified Thunderbirds built by Frank Coons and Jimmy Travers. These were out-and-out competition sports cars, perhaps a notch or two below the SS Corvette, but very close to the European concept of a racing sports car. Their bodies had been completely gutted of extraneous (for competition) items. Their production dashboards had been replaced by a simple panel of in-struments, and an aluminum cowl covered the passenger seat. To reduce overall weight, *SPORTS CARS ILLUS-TRATED* (July, 1957) reported, ''all body, hood, decklid and cowl stiffeners are moth-eaten with super-size lightening holes.'' When the T-Birds were sent out for high speed runs, a full length belly pan was installed. There were many other mechanical changes from stock made in these cars including Lincoln and Mercury front suspension com-ponents, semi-elliptic rear springs with height-adjustable rear shackles and a Halibrand rear end. Drum brakes with 2½ inch wide linings were used front and rear. Ford's experiences with the Lincolns in the Mexican Road Race surfaced in the form of heater blower fans fitted to direct cool air to the T-Bird's rear brakes.

A harbinger of things yet to come manifested itself on February 9th when one of the racing Birds appeared with a 430 cubic inch, supercharged Lincoln engine. Unfortu-nately, it never really had a chance to strut its stuff in the Flying Mile runs for experimental cars since it quickly embarrassed everyone at Ford by blowing its engine. Its compatriot, propelled by a 312 cid V-8 fitted with a McCulloch supercharger, didn't come away a winner but managed a one-way run at 153.125 mph. Several days later the Lincoln-Bird redeemed itself with a victorious 96.065 mph run in the standing one-mile acceleration runs. The blown, 312 Thunderbird driven by Chuck Daigh finished third at 93.312 mph. In the stock sports car competition, a Thunderbird won top honors with a 130.725 two-way speed run. The Lincoln-engined T-Bird also claimed the high speed championship in its class with a strong 160.356 mph two-way average.

In 1957, for the first time, sports car races were held at New Smyrna Beach in conjunction with the Daytona Speed Week. While the 312 cid engined Thunderbird, running without the supercharger, didn't win, its second place finish behind Carroll Shelby's 4.9 Ferrari was hardly a dishonor. Certainly it was an impressive achievement for an auto-mobile so often disparaged for not fitting into the purist's definition of a sports car.

In its strictly-stock forms the basic engine for the 1957 Thunderbird was the veteran 292 V-8 with a 9.1:1 com-pression ratio, single two-barrel carburetor and 212 hp. A step up to 245 hp was achieved by equipping the 312 cid ''Thunderbird Special V-8'' with 9.7:1 compression ratio heads and a four-barrel carburetor. The same engine in ''super'' form was available with either Fordomatic, over-drive or conventional 3-speed transmission. Output was a healthy 270 hp with an ''extra-high-performance'' version with a high lift cam pumping out 285 hp. The king of the '57 T-Birds, however, was the F7-engined model of which just 211 were built. This version, equipped with a McCulloch variable-ratio supercharger, single four-barrel carburetor and the high-lift cam of the 285 hp engine, was given a 300 hp rating which was probably on the low side.

Initially, the first four-passenger Thunderbird of 1958 was not eligible for NASCAR stock car competition since Bill France's organization considered it a sports car. (Later NASCAR accepted the T-Bird for racing; Ford reciprocated by offering a 430 cid, 350 hp engine and heavy-duty 3-speed transmission for racing.) This really didn't matter, for the high performance segment of the Thunderbird's career, for all practical purposes, was over. There were, however, some interesting variations on that theme that make for highly desirable collector's items today. In 1960, a 350 hp, 430 cid engine was offered as an alternative to the stock 300 hp engine and, for the 1963 model run, a 400 hp, 3-carb version of the standard 390 cid Thunderbird V-8 made a short but glorious appearance. Ford played around during 1968 with a 429 cid Thunderbird with a hotter-cam and modified ignition that could run the quarter-mile in the low 14's, but by that point in time the Thunderbird's personality was actually in opposition to an infusion of speed tonic. However, this takes nothing away from the Thunderbird's very credible high performance heritage. It was far more of a sports car in its early days that its critics ever gave it credit for, as the record clearly shows.

Rules the road
and America knows it!

Standard trim and other
specifications and accessories
are subject to change without notice.

HUDSON HORNET

sets new sales records every month with this fabulous line-up—

MIRACLE H-POWER — So eager to go! That's the thrilling new, high-compression H-145 engine! And it's engineered to give you long years of power-packed driving pleasure! Built to outlast any other engine on the market.

HYDRA-MATIC DRIVE* — Miracle H-Power makes Hydra-Matic Drive a brand-new thrill! Completely automatic four-speed transmission with the sensational new H-145 engine frees you from driving drudgery and gives you effortless mastery of the road!

*Hydra-Matic Drive optional at extra cost

"STEP-DOWN" DESIGN — Different and better way to build cars is a big factor in Hudson Hornet's popularity! Exclusive recessed floor provides sleek, low beauty—most room in any car—and America's lowest center of gravity for the steadiest, safest ride ever known!

HUDSON HORNET WINS! — Flashing first across the finish line in a grueling test of power, stamina and safety, the fabulous Hudson Hornet outruns a field of 71 entries of almost every make to win the 160-mile National Championship Stock Car Race at Daytona Beach!

Hudson . . . most **DURABLE** car your money can buy!

Four rugged custom series— lower-priced Pacemaker — renowned Super-Six luxurious Commodore and fabulous Hudson Hornet

1951

84

19. Hudson

Hudson's role in American performance history was, in many ways, a unique one. Firstly, it has to be recognized as far and away the only independent to play a really significant role in that area. American Motors did, of course, earn a couple of Trans-Am titles, but that achievement really pales in contrast to Hudson's outstanding participation in NASCAR racing over a span of time lasting four racing seasons.

Scarcely less impressive than the magnitude of this achievement is the way in which it was attained. Hudson always prided itself on the quality of its six-cylinder engines and it was upon a supposedly obsolete flat-head six that Hudson built its reputation. Then, too, there was the issue of image. In spite of the quality of their handling and performance, the Hudsons of the 1948-54 era were anything but flamboyant machines. Unlike Pontiac, which used success on the tracks and hot acceleration as springboards for change, Hudson, except for a really excellent facelift in 1954, remained unmoved. The people who purchased Hudsons were, by and large, solid citizen conservative types who usually purchased Hudsons for other reasons besides their racing success. Their size, styling and overall, old-fashioned image virtually made it a sure thing that Hudson was not to be a young person's car in spite of its long string of NASCAR successes. Yet, Hudsons were super road cars, incredibly tough, well built and designed — a classic example if there ever was one, of an automobile that proved beauty really is only skin-deep.

Hudson's propensity for racing and record setting ran deeply through its history. Its 76 hp Super Six of 1916, touted as the "first high speed engine," had the stamina to average nearly 76 mph for 24 hours to set a mark that took a 491 cubic inch Marmon V-16 to break in 1931. In the early 1930's, both Hudson and Terraplane set hundreds of speed records and, when Reid Railton, the man who designed John Cobb's land speed record car, was looking for components to assemble his own car, he chose Hudson. The result was an automobile with a 110 mph top speed and a zero to 60 mph time of 9 seconds. No wonder the AUTO-CAR described it as "10 years ahead of its time."

With the war shutting down automobile production in Europe, Hudson sent its restyled 1940 model with a 255 cid, 120 hp eight to Bonneville where it set new mile and 12-hour records for Class C sedans.

Hudson's initial post war offerings were its 1940 models very slightly warmed over. At that, the Hudson Eight with 128 net hp was hardly a performance has-been.

However, the excitement of getting production of its new models going in late 1947 and the eagerness of Americans to purchase any new automobile made any move by Hudson to wave the performance flag both impractical and unnecessary. Judging from the remarks of its president, A. E. Barit, however, Hudson hadn't turned its back totally on its tradition. Prior to its introduction, Barit promised the new Hudson would have the lowest center of gravity of any American car and that its engine would "produce more horsepower than any other 'six' on the market."

When they did appear, the new Hudsons were certainly decent performers for their time. THE AUTOCAR reported the 128 hp Commodore Eight as capable of a 91 mph top

speed. Zero to 60 mph was a respectable 18.4 seconds. THE MOTOR praised its handling, finding there was "practically no roll at any time and the car takes 60 mph corners in its stride."

The Super Eight was still Hudson's most powerful engine, but lurking just behind it was a new 270 cid, 121 hp six that in 1951, with a larger 3 13/16 inch x 4 1/2 inch bore and stroke, powered the Hudson Hornet. With 145 hp and 257 lbs-ft of torque, it effectively eclipsed the old eight in power. It was destined also to shade the eight as Hudson's greatest performer. Although no one knew it then, it was also destined to be Hudson's last.

The Hornet was not cheap — a Hydra-Matic equipped four-door sedan sold for over $3,000 — but it gave its owner the distinction, among many others, of driving one of America's fastest cars. MOTOR TREND magazine's test of an H-M Hornet netted a top speed of 97.51 mph. The Hornet's ability to move from zero to 60 mph in less than 15 seconds was only slightly less impressive.

At this point in Hudson's history, its path crossed that of Marshall Teague whose name would become forever linked with the "Fabulous Hudson Hornet." Teague was a seasoned competitor in stock car racing and his garage in Daytona Beach was a first class operation with the talent and technical skill to turn out first class racing machines. It may be apocryphal but one likes to believe that, as HOP UP reported in November, 1953, when Teague first drove a Hornet in 1951 he was so impressed he bought the car on the spot. Before long, Teague and the Hudson Company were in cozy collusion, the former asking for and suggesting options to enhance Hudson's racing prowess and the latter seeing that he got them.

For Hudson, Teague and NASCAR, nothing would ever be quite the same after February 11, 1951. That was the date of NASCAR's Grand National race at Daytona Beach. During its 26th lap, when Tim Flock pitted for fuel, Marshall Teague's Hudson moved into the lead and went on to score his first victory with the Hornet. Teague's qualifying speed of 96.83 mph was impressive but not overpowering. Flock's 1950 Lincoln had been the fastest qualifier at 102.20 mph and the 1950 Oldsmobile of brother Fonty Flock had also out distanced Teague's Hudson with a fast 99.31 mph mark. Over 160 miles of racing, though, the Hudson's 82.39 mph average had been more than either the Lincoln and Oldsmobile could match.

Teague's Hudson could not be considered as anything but a dark horse for this race since just a few days before the race neither his nor anyone else's Hudson had been even listed among the entrants. Even after the fact, the Hudson triumph was not taken seriously, with many drivers considering its success at Daytona as a lucky shot. There were even several days of suspense before NASCAR officially awarded the Grand National victory to Teague. At race end, Hudson had not officially delivered the Hornet's specifications to NASCAR and not until they were received and checked against those of Teague's car did his victory become official.

During the next several weeks, Teague added two more victories to his record and moved into the lead on the Grand National Circuit. After his victory in a 150-miler at

Phoenix, Arizona, Teague had kind words for his car that were sweet music to Hudson. "Proof of the durability of the Hornet is provided by the fact that this car has gone through four hard races," Teague said. "Based on the amount of measurable mechanical wear, I feel that each race is the equal of 50,000 miles of hard highway driving." Continuing to wax rather eloquently about Hornet's virtues, Teague explained, "A good deal of my success is due to the reduction of pit stops because tire wear with the Hudson Hornet is held to a minimum because of the lower center of gravity and the resulting magnificent balance of the automobile."

It wasn't long before other NASCAR drivers followed Teague's lead and started campaigning Hudsons. One of the best of this group of early NASCAR chargers was Herb Thomas, who drove one of Teague's Hudsons, often referred to as Teaguemobiles, to the 1951 NASCAR Championship. During a four week span during the summer, Thomas scored four consecutive victories, the most impressive being his triumph in the Darlington 500. From the start of qualifying to the final wave of the checkered flag, Darlington was one of Hudson's finest racing hours. Teague led all 81 qualifiers with an 86.21 mph average for 10 miles, which was also a new track record. When Teague's Hudson was forced to retire as an aftermath of a collision, Thomas' car took over the lead and went on to pace the Hudsons to a 1-2 finish. The third place car, incidentally, was six laps behind Thomas' at race's end. It was quite a day for the Hornets. They led the field for 356 of the 400 laps, were the fastest qualifiers and, of the 47 cars finishing the race, five were Hudsons. No wonder Hudson could rightfully boast, "Here again is proof that the *stamina, durability,* and *power* of Hudson cars are far ahead of any other American-made automobile. Here again is proof that the Hudson Hornet 'takes over where the others leave off.'"

Darlington was by no means the last victory for Hudson in 1951. It was, however, with the exception of Teague's win at Daytona, the most significant one since it was the first time Hudson tested its Twin-H Power option. There was nothing particularly fancy about Hudson's dual carburetors and revamped manifold. Teague once said that the basic components had been kicking around at Hudson since

1944, but it did symbolize, in no uncertain terms, that Hudson was willing to provide Teague and other race drivers with the wherewithal to continue to win races.

Marshall Teague didn't come back a winner from the 1951 Mexican Road Race, but a sixth place finish in that torture test, with what Troy Ruttman called the only stock car in the race, was more than credible. The only major deviations from pure stock to be found in Teague's 1951 Hornet Club Coupe were its dual exhaust system and relieved block. Teague pegged its horsepower at 170 and rated the Hudson as a 125 mph automobile. The only cars exceeding Teague's 85.2 mph average were two Ferraris, a super-hot Chrysler, Ruttman's highly modified 1948 Mercury and a wildly worked-over Packard.

Hudson's 1952 models were little changed from the previous year's offering but this hardly restrained respected testers such as Tom McCahill from writing, "They are America's finest cars from the very important standpoint of roadability, cornering and steering." From the first Grand National Race of the 1952 NASCAR season, it was also apparent that Hudson was also America's finest stock car. At West Palm Beach, Florida, on January 20th, Tim Flock's Hudson was both the winner and the fastest qualifier. This event was overshadowed by the drama, romance and sheer class that the Daytona Beach Grand National had going for it. Included in the 62 car field were 160 hp Oldsmobiles, 180 hp Chryslers and 190 hp Cadillacs. The Hudsons with their 155 hp Twin-H flatheads appeared to have their work cut out for them. Hudsons weren't even close to the top in the two-way measured mile runs on the beach for American stock cars but, on the fourth lap, Teague's car, which had started in 13th position, took the lead and never gave it up. Averaging 84.65 mph, Teague lead Herb Thomas to a 1-2 victory for Hudson. As usual, the race's tempo took its toll as only 37 of the 62 car starting field made it to the end, and, as usual, the Hudsons hung tough with six of the finishers Hudsons.

By April, 1952, Hudson had swept the first five Grand National events. On the first day of that month Hudson began equipping Hornets with option E, or Twin-H Power at the factory. Within a few weeks, over 50% of all Hornets

Above, 1950 Hudson Commodore

being delivered were Twin-H powered and well over 10,000 were produced during the model year.

Hudson had, during the 1951 season, offered a Heavy Duty Suspension kit consisting of export springs and shocks plus heavy-duty wheels and hubs. To handle the rigors of racing Hudson also made available shot-peened spindles and steering arms.

The 1952 season was, if anything, even more incredible for Hudson. Its competition simply seemed unable to mount a serious challenge to the Hornets as they swept the first five NASCAR Grand Nationals. Out of the first 15, Hudson won 13, with Oldsmobile and Chrysler each managing just a single victory. In May, Marshall Teague with an eye toward expanding his racing career, switched from NASCAR to AAA competition where he won seven victories and accumulated 1,980 points, more than any other AAA stock car champion in history. Tim Flock gave Hudson another NASCAR Grand Championship and when Herb Thomas won a NASCAR Grand National at North Wilkesboro, North Carolina, in late October, it was Hudson's 44th stock car victory of the season! Both Tim Flock and Marshall Teague were recognized by *SPEED AGE*, respectively, as NASCAR and AAA Stock Car Driver of the Year.

During the 1952 season, Hudson made certain its Severe Usage kit, which was very similar to the earlier mentioned Heavy Duty Suspension Kit, was available to whoever wanted it. Also offered as a $50.00 dealer installed option, was a Twin Exhaust Manifold and Pipe Kit.

Hudson officials held firm to the belief that racing was of great value to the company. Parts merchandising manager, H. L. Temphin, for example, was convinced observing, "The publicity covering Hudson's many 'wins' has been of untold benefit to us." If Hudson was pleased with its racing success, its competitors weren't. As a result, various alibis were created to explain away Hudson's long string of wins. Pat Kirkwood, a Chrysler driver, maintained, "the Hudson wins because of Marshall Teague and the Hudson factory." That really didn't enlighten anybody. More objective was Wilbur Shaw's remark in *POPULAR SCIENCE* that, "The real secret of Hudson's track performance is its cornering qualities plus acceleration." Concurring with this opinion were *ROAD & TRACK* (July, 1952), "It does handle better than other American cars of the same size and weight," and *MOTOR TREND* (August, 1952), "This is one of the best cars for all-around handling qualities that *MOTOR TREND* has tested." One thing was certain, however, after every one of Teague's wins on the AAA circuit, his car was checked over by race officials and declared absolutely stock.

Teague again demonstrated the toughness of a stock Hudson in the 1952 Mexican Road Race. This time around he competed with his 1951 Twin-H powered four-door Hornet that usually served as the tow vehicle for his race cars. Like all of his Teaguemobiles, this Hornet was a carefully built and meticulously prepared machine whose top speed was 115 mph. During the race he was consistently in the top ten leaders of the stock class and finished seventh behind 4 Lincolns and 2 Chryslers. After the race he noted, "The superior roadability of the Hudson and the outstanding traction of the new Pure Oil Company tires enabled me to get through the mountainous curves even better than the much talked about European cars [Porsche, Lancia and Jaguar] with a total weight of 4,900 pounds ready to race."

Hudson had uncovered a virtually free performance bonanza with the discovery that when cylinder heads from the Pacemakers and Wasp models were installed backwards on Hornet engines a very substantial boost in compression ratio from 7.7:1 to approximately 9.2:1 was attained. However, for the 1953 season, something slightly more dramatic was needed to keep the Hornets out front. The competition, particularly Oldsmobile, were determined to take the sting out of the Hornets on the stock car track and Hudson had to be on its toes if it wasn't going to become a has-been.

Early in January, 1953, Hudson took a strong step in the right direction by offering a "Skeleton Engine Assembly" plus a higher lift cam as dealer installed options. Later, in August, Hudson dropped this nondescript title and labeled this option the "High-Performance 7X Skeleton Engine Assembly." At $385.00, the 7X was not cheap but, said Hudson, "For those who want extra high performance, the new Hudson 7X Engine completely fills the need. Initially engineered for police cars and high altitude work, the 7X Engine is becoming increasingly popular with drivers who desire even greater acceleration and higher top speed."

The 7X engine wasn't a dashing step forward designwise for Hudson, but it provided enough extra power for the Hornet to again win the NASCAR and AAA stock car titles. The primary differences between the 7X and a standard engine were the 7X's knurlized pistons, cam, larger valves, and combustion chamber shape. Also important was the use on the 7X of an iron cylinder head that, said Hudson, "creates considerably higher compression, as compared to the Standard Hornet." Horsepower figures for the 7X weren't released but when Hudson made it the standard Hornet engine in 1954 the 7X was rated at 170 hp. With 2 inch intake valves, hot cam and large ports the 7X, without question, was capable of developing 200 hp when set up for racing.

It certainly needed that much to keep ahead of its competitors in 1953. Both Dodge and Oldsmobile defeated the Hornet in the first two Grand Nationals of 1953. At Daytona, the Hudsons could only manage a fourth place finish behind two Oldsmobiles and a Lincoln. Writing in *SPEED AGE* (June, 1953), Roger Huntington concluded, "it looks like the Hornet may be in for some rough going, what with Olds and Lincolns coming to life. If so, Hudson may find they have a lion by the tail." Despite this and other forecasts of doom, the Hornet was by no means washed up. Unfortunately, Hudson nearly was. The company lost some ten million dollars in 1953 and, with survival at stake, there wasn't much left over to maintain the Hornet's supremacy in the face of a determined V-8 spearheaded assault by the opposition.

The Hornet still was the car to be reckoned with in racing, however, and in 1953 and 1954 it was both the NASCAR and AAA stock car champion. On the road, the last of the true Hudsons was no sluggard. Zero to 60 mph in 12.2 seconds, a quarter-mile time of 18.5 seconds and a top speed of over 106 mph were performance figures very similar to what a stock 162 hp Chevrolet V-8 could achieve in 1955.

All things, be they good or bad, run their course and fade away. For the Hornet, the end of its racing career came on February 6, 1955, at West Palm Beach, Florida Speedway. Against a field that included several 1955 Oldsmobiles and Chryslers, Herb Thomas led Hudson to a 1-2 finish. That was the end. The future belonged to the Chrysler 300, not to a car powered by a flat-head six. Hudson did get a V-8 engine for 1955, but it also became a kissing cousin to the Nash and, thus, whereas it once had been fabulous, the Hornet became, in 1955, just another car.

20. Lincoln

Lincoln's high performance game plan trailed both Cadillac's and Chrysler's but did not follow the same pattern of development. Cadillac, carefully nurturing its hard won and well earned prestige status, did not directly engage itself in performance activities. Chrysler, on the other hand, did consort with Briggs Cunningham's racing efforts in the early fifties, but, by and large, didn't get intimately involved in competitive affairs until the halycon days of the C-300.

Lincoln tuned in on a different wavelength and the age was better for it. Acting for all the world to see like an Americanized and upsized Mercedes-Benz, the Lincolns of the 1952-54 era won three consecutive victories in what was widely regarded as one of the roughest, no-quarter-given-so-don't-even-ask road races ever conceived by man, the Carrera Panamericana.

They weren't called the Road Racing Lincolns when they debuted on February 6, 1952, but there was no denying the new Lincoln's attractive styling and impressive engineering. The appearance of the first new postwar Lincolns (of 1949-51) still generates lively debate between their admirers and detractors but few voices of criticism can be heard about the looks of the 1952 Lincolns. It's an overworked term, yet ''purposeful'' best describes their overall appearance. Mounted on a 123 inch wheelbase (down 2 inches from 1951) and with nearly 11 inches less overall length, the new models obviously rejected the notion that bigger was better. Equally important, in terms of what the future held, was the reduction of the Lincoln's road weight by nearly 500 pounds.

If Ford had chosen to restrict Lincoln's changes to these for 1952, the end result would have been regarded as a step in the right direction. After all, a smaller, lighter luxury car with, for the age, clean and simple styling had to be highly regarded, but Lincoln went much further than this and produced a car that would have made Henry Leland (the marque's founder) proud. A new ball-joint front suspension with widely angled upper and lower A-arms provided not only easier servicing and greater durability but also a wholly new driving experience for American luxury car owners. If there was a car that successfully refuted the old adage that American sedans wallowed instead of cornered, it was the new Lincoln. *MOTOR TREND* (June, 1952) gave credit where it was due, noting that ''without a doubt, the most outstanding characteristic of the Lincoln is its handling ability.''

In contrast to handling that made life in the turns invigorating, the Lincoln's new V-8 seemed just a tad weak in the power department, at least to those whose experiences included time behind the wheel of an Olds 88. Tom McCahill, obviously rooting for Lincoln but still calling the shots as he saw them, reported in *MECHANIX ILLUS-TRATED* (February, 1952): ''The Lincoln with overdrive is a real 100 miles per hour car. But it falls short of being a performance leader in its class, especially in the low pick-up ranges . . . I hope to be able to report in the round-up in the December issue that the new job, slightly changed, finally put itself up in front with Chrysler and Caddie in the performance department. In style, comfort and luxury, it is a magnificent automobile right now.''

Lincoln obviously had goofed by introducing its new 317 cid V-8 with only 160 horsepower. It was all too easy to compare this rating with Cadillac's 190 and Chrysler's 180. Lincoln's excellent MacPherson strut ball joint front suspension just didn't carry the same public image clout as a healthy horsepower rating. The next year, however, Lincoln had it all: looks, handling and horsepower in abundance. With 205 horsepower, Lincoln became, said *THE AUTO-CAR* (December 26, 1952), ''the first manufacturer in the world to offer more than 200 hp in a standard quality-production saloon.''

To achieve this output, Lincoln engineers found a displacement increase unnecessary. Instead, they pursued the path of refinement with a good deal of finesse and with outstanding results. Included among the 1953 engine's new features were a four-barrel carburetor (optional), a higher 8.0:1 compression ratio (up from the previous year's 7.5:1), a low pressure dual exhaust system, an larger intake manifold, a higher lift cam and larger (1.98 inches to 1.74 inches) diameter intake valves.

Lincoln for 1953 was very much a car worthy of Ford's Golden Anniversary, and what better way was there to celebrate the occasion than by going road racing? In effect, that was the question put to Benson Ford by Bill Stroppe whose partner, Clay Smith, and Troy Ruttman had finished fourth in the 1951 race behind two Ferraris and a Chrysler. After some hesitation, Ford gave Stoppe the green light and work soon began in the Long Beach speed shop of Smith and Stroppe on a team of three ''Road Racing'' Lincolns. Chuck Stevens, who was to drive his Lincoln to victory in the 1952 Mexican Road Race, reported that when Smith and Clay had completed their work the Lincoln's V-8's output was ''a lot higher than the 205 horsepower punch it rated in showroom condition.'' Although a solid lifter cam from the Ford F-8 truck engine was used, Stropope directed most of his attention to the small details that, from his years of experience, he knew meant the difference between victory and defeat. Thus, care was taken, for example, to match the Lincoln's ports and manifold. Although Lincoln offered a dual exhaust system option just prior to the Mexican Road Race, the Lincolns entered used a single exhaust system without mufflers. Stroppe preferred this arrangement over the duals since he felt the proximity of the left exhaust pipe to the fuel pump might cause vapor lock. He also preferred to run the team cars with overdrive transmissions but this was not possible since Lincoln offered only Hydramatic in 1953. They were, however, carefully tuned and adjusted to shift from third to fourth gear under maximum throttle at 84 mph.

It came as a surprise to some that the Mexican Road Race Lincoln was not a strong zero to 60 mph performer. After all, a time of 15.4 seconds really wasn't very impressive, particularly since the factory claimed a stock model's zero to 60 mph time was approximately 12 seconds. The racing Lincolns were, however, racing cars not drag racers and their engines, with the highest torque peaking speeds of any American car, were tuned to deliver power hour after hour across 1,900-plus miles of Mexican roads.

Prior to their introduction on November 25, 1952, Lincoln had tested its 1953 engines in 1952 chassis at

Bonneville. One car, driven by Bill Stroppe, reached a speed of just over 117 mph. The typical 1953 production model wasn't quite as fast but at 110 mph it was, as *ROAD & TRACK* (March, 1953) noted, "unquestionably . . . the fastest stock car in America." When *ROAD & TRACK* tested one of the Mexican Race veterans it reached a maximum speed of 116.9 mph. However, on this point let Bill Stroppe have the last word. Writing in *HOP UP* (March 1953) he reported, "We found that the Lincoln would run about 120 to 125 mph depending on the smoothness of the road, wind and how level the road was." John Bond of *ROAD & TRACK* reported that the MRR Lincoln "rolled very little in a turn. It rode like a truck." Obviously, the

latter liability was the price paid to create a car that could average 90.9 mph in the 1952 race.

There wasn't anything particularly startling about the racing Lincoln's suspension. At the front were dual Houdaille shocks with a second set at the rear. Export, heavy-duty springs were fitted front and rear with airlifts installed inside the front shocks.

Firestone 6-ply (8.00 x 15) racing tires were used. One hundred were taken to Mexico for use by the Lincolns and were changed nightly. To keep the Cop-Sil-Loy treated rear

Above, 1952 Lincoln Capri
Below, 1953 Lincoln Capri

brake linings cool, twin heater fans were mounted in the trunk and constantly blew air on the rear brakes.

After whipping all comers in Mexico, the Lincolns ran into a hornet's nest at the 1953 Daytona Speed Week. In the flying start measured mile runs, the Lincoln's best speed of 107.88 mph was bettered both by Oldsmobile (113.38 mph) and Cadillac (110.85 mph). Similarly, the Lincoln didn't win any laurels in the acceleration trials across the measured mile from a standing start. Its speed of 69.61 mph was again easily exceeded by Oldsmobile (75.41 mph) and Cadillac (73.21 mph). Even a 1953 Packard was quicker at 71.12 mph, but instead of casting the Lincoln's performance into the shade these figures place it in a better perspective. Simply put, the Lincoln possessed a knock-out punch not unlike that of a heavyweight boxing champion. There were faster and quicker cars, but like a great pugilist the Lincoln, long after its challengers had shot their wads, was still in one piece and ready for more when the checkered flag was in sight.

Thus, the Lincolns swept the first four places in the 1952 Mexican Road Race with second place finisher Johnny Mantz setting a new record for stock cars of 115.40 mph on the last leg. The previous record of 113.35 was held by Tony Bettenhausen's 1951 Chrysler. Chuck Stevenson's winning average of 90.96 mph compared well with Karl Kling's 300 SL's (winner of the sports car class) speed of 102 mph.

With the Carrera Panamericana (then part of the F.I.A. sanctioned the world's championship for sports cars) in 1953 came a revision in its regulations. The Lincoln "racing kits" of 1952 were disallowed and modifications to cars running in the stock cars were limited to suspension, brakes and tires. In addition, all cars were required to arrive in a secured impound area within three hours after each day's racing. As a result, the Lincolns ran without the Ford truck cams and solid lifters, but it seemed to hardly matter. Although Bill Vukovich's Lincoln dropped out on the first leg with transmission failure, other Lincolns finished in the top four places, led by Chuck Stevenson and Clay Smith in the same car that had been victorious a year earlier.

The 1954 Lincoln's power rating remained unchanged at 205 hp. There were, however, a number of worthwhile changes and modifications. A new four-barrel carburetor, which Lincoln shared with the 1954 Mercurys, was used as were larger, by one inch, diameter brakes that significantly improved the Lincoln's stopping ability.

The Lincolns in the 1954 Mexican Road Race didn't have things as easy as they had in previous years but they still finished 1-2. Clay Smith's untimely death in August deprived the team of one of its greatest assets and, although 14 of the 29 entries in the large stock car class were Lincolns, four factory cars failed to complete the first leg. In spite of this debacle, a Lincoln driven by Ray Crawford was the class leader. Crawford had driven in all the Mexican races but had never finished higher than eighth. The 1954 race changed all that. In spite of a strong challenge from Keith Andrew's Cadillac, Crawford's car (a private entry receiving factory assistance) and Walt Faulkner's Lincoln were the first two stock cars across the finish line.

The decision of the Mexican government to end the Panamericana classic brought the Lincoln's road racing career to an end. This decision left Lincoln the undefeated winner and still champion of American stock cars. As far as Lincoln's role in high performance history is concerned, this development couldn't have come at a better time. Lincoln advocates have to shutter when they contemplate the fate of their cars if they had been forced to square off against the Chrysler C-300 in a 1955 Mexican Road Race. The 1955 Lincoln with a larger (341 cid) and more powerful (225 hp) engine was a fine car, but it was hardly the C-300's equal. This judgement hardly brings dishonor to the Road Racing Lincoln. At a time when too many Americans regarded performance as meaning only quick acceleration, they offered much more. Cars of great versatility, strength, stamina and speed, they pointed ahead to the best years of the age when the American supercar reached the zenith of its development.

Above, 1955 Lincoln Capri

MERCURY announces its newest sizzler, the...

Marauder

Even the styling says "go." Note that racy new hardtop roof. It's not only beautiful, its aerodynamic styling cuts air resistance. Choose from two models: the Marauder with a big 390 V-8 standard engine . . . or the Marauder S-55, with console-mounted transmission selector, bucket seats, and 4-barrel Super Marauder 390 V-8 standard engine. Talk about hot! Talk to your Mercury dealer.

 MERCURY
MONTEREY·MONTEREY CUSTOM
MARAUDER and S-55

COMET · METEOR · MERCURY: PRODUCTS OF MOTOR COMPANY · LINCOLN-MERCURY DIVISION

21. Mercury

It's no secret that Ford had problems with its medium-priced offerings during the fifties and early sixties. Its unhappy experience, for example, with the Edsel contained enough disasters of assorted dimensions to spawn several full length books. Less dramatic, but still promoting insomnia as a corporate malaise at Ford, were the difficulties Mercury faced in successfully competing with General Motors' horde of mid-range automobiles. Eventually Ford struck reasonably profitable pay dirt by recreating the Lincoln-Mercury division and portraying the Mercury as a car cast in the Lincoln Continental tradition. This move, beginningin the mid-sixties, also made it unnecessary for Mercury to pursue an active role in performance activities. Thus, several years before the Brave New World of the seventies succeeded the Rapid Transit Transportation of the sixties, Mercury had left the task of maintaining a strong performance image to the smaller Cougar and Cyclone models.

Even when its competition and performance program was in full swing, Mercury had to play second fiddle to Ford's effort which received the lion's share of the company's racing budget. Perhaps the greatest irony of Mercury's on again, off again, "what am I doing out here on a dragstrip anyway?" split-performance personality was the contrast it made with earlier Mercury history. Back in the pre-1948 days, Mercury enjoyed a slight, yet discernable performance advantage over Ford. True, it was more expensive but it was also just a tad quicker. Even the heavier, 1949-53 models, particularly those of 1949-51 whose smooth lines just invited the customizers to come out and try their hand, gave Mercury an image edge over Ford.

Image can hold up only so long, however, when you square off against an opponent whose products aren't also powered like yours, which is to say with an engine dating back in origin to the early Depression days. Mercury learned that lesson the hard way. Early fifties Mercs with dual pipes sounded mellow but they were no match for the Rocket-engined Oldsmobiles.

Ford engineers weren't standing still and, in 1948, in the midst of Henry Ford II's massive corporate rebuilding program, a project to bring Ford's engines out of the dark ages was begun. The eventual result was a new family of modern, overhead valve V-8 and 6-cylinder engines for every Ford product. Mercury's new V-8 arrived in 1954. There wasn't anything terribly exotic about its design but with 256 cubic inches, thanks to a bore and stroke of 3⅝ inches and 3 1/10 inches respectively, and 161 hp at 4400 rpm, the new ohv V-8 gave Mercury a long overdue performance advance. All Mercurys had a 7.5:1 compression ratio, four-barrel carburetor and mechanical lifters that Ford guaranteed would not float below 5500 rpm. With Merc-O-Matic and 3.54 axle, the Mercury's zero to 60 mph was an acceptable 14.9 seconds.

Thanks to engines with 292 cubic inches, the 1955 Mercurys with new bodies and a top rating of 198 hp lowered their zero to 60 mph time into the 12 second zone, still not quick enough to remove all the tarnish from their performance image. The situation was far from hopeless,

however. Bill Stroppe, one of the guiding geniuses of the Lincoln's road racing days, fielded a team of Mercury stock cars during the 1955 season that scored several major West Coast victories.

Touted as "The Big M," Mercury became a separate Ford Motor Company Division in 1956. This helped Mercury's position both in the marketplace and its effort to create a new look for itself. Back in 1954, Mercury had first used a new ball-joint front suspension and now, after two years of subtle refinement, handling emerged as one of its strongest points. Most knowledgeable drivers came away after a stint behind the wheel of a '56 Mercury raving about its stability in the turns, its resistance to roll and its excellent steering. The greatest compliment came from those with firsthand experience with the road racing Lincolns who generally regarded the 1956 Mercury as a worthy successor to that outstanding automobile in the cornering department. "If you could drive this car blindfolded," promised *MOTOR TREND* (March, 1956), "you'd swear it was a pre-1956 Lincoln — it feels just the same."

Not all of Mercury's efforts for 1956 had been directed toward improving its handling. Early in the season, the top Mercury engine was a 3.86 inch bore, 3.44 inch stroke engine with 312 cubic inches, top rated at 225 hp with a four-barrel carburetor and dual exhausts. A short time later, this engine was augmented by a 312 V-8 with dual four-barrels, a high-lift cam and 9.75:1 compression ratio. These 260 hp units were scarce but some were provided Bill Stroppe for both USAC and NASCAR competition. The Stroppe Mercurys were at their best on twisting road courses as demonstrated by their victories at Elkhart Lake and the Paramount Ranch circuit.

Stroppe also built a Mercury nicknamed "The Thumper" that the official Mercury racing team entered in the 1956 Daytona Speed Week. Externally, the only tip-off that this wasn't your usual Mercury Custom two-door hardtop was its Halibrand magnesium wheels. The real reason it was put into the Prototype Class was found under the hood: a 1956 Lincoln engine with its bore upped by 1/8 inches to yield 391 cubic inches. Forge True Pistons, a Herbert roller tappet cam, special, large valves plus ported stock heads had been installed by Stroppe. No horsepower estimates were made by Stroppe who preferred to let "Thumper" speak for itself. Its best two-way average through the flying mile, running a 3.31 axle, was 147.269 mph. Its best one way run, 152.931 mph was exceeded by a post Speedweek mark of 153.649 mph. The Stroppe-Mercurys scored several racing victories in 1957 but ran into bad luck at Daytona where, after a victory in the NASCAR convertible race, 3 of 4 Mercurys entered in the Grand National suffered pushrod problems that rendered them noncompetitive.

Any 1957 Mercury was available with the Turnpike Cruiser engine, a 368 cid V-8 top rated at 335 hp. By using this engine, which was, in effect, the 1956 Lincoln engine, Mercury was beginning the practice of turning to its higher-priced sibling for its high performance powerplants. This policy reached its zenith the following year when the first "Marauder" engine became a Mercury option. There were actually two Marauder versions. The first, with 383 cubic inches, was the fourth largest in the industry. The second

Left, 1963 Mercury Marauder

with the same 4.3 inch bore but a longer stroke was, at 430 cid, the largest U.S. built automobile engine. This monster, weighing in at nearly 750 pounds was, with a single, four-barrel carburetor and 10.5:1 compression ratio, rated at 360 hp. Some analysts considered this a bit optimistic but it did push the bulky Mercury from zero to 60 mph in 9.5 seconds. Some of the credit for this capability had to be given to the new, dual-range Multi-Matic Merc-O-Matic transmission. Although it was linked to a miserable push-button setup it was, said *MOTOR TREND,* "without a doubt, the best automatic transmission that has ever been available in any car." When the "High Performance Range" button was pushed the transmission started in first gear and, under full throttle, would shift from second to high at about 75·mph. Thus, even with the standard 2.91 axle, the Mercury could run from zero to 60 mph in less than 10 seconds. The most imposing "Big M's" for 1958 were those with the Super Marauder engine. This 400 hp V-8 required a beefed up Multi-Matic to handle its extra power, which came from triple, two-barrel Holley carbs. These carburetors and their

Above, 1962 Mercury S-55

94

special intake manifold were also marketed as dealer options but the stronger transmission plus fancy, chrome plated rocker arm covers were only available on factory built Super Marauders. The abandoning of a plan to use hotter cams in these brutes was hardly mourned since the 400 hp Mercurys were zero to 60 mph in under 8 second machines even with a mild cam.

The overdone and exaggerated styling Mercurys were afflicted with in 1958 was inconsistent with their road manners. Alongside a sleek Plymouth the Mercury looked like the box the Mopar had been shipped in. Yet that big, square hulk could handle surprisingly well. *MOTOR TREND* alluded to this attribute, by remarking, "a big engine in a light chassis has always been the ideal of hot rodders, and these Mercs are the closest thing to this ideal that Detroit has ever produced." More to the point was the decision of the California Highway Patrol to purchase 325 Mercurys for patrol use. "Any resemblance," said *HOT ROD*, "between the new Highway Patrol Mercury Police Special and Mexican Road Race Lincolns is strictly emphatic." In appearance, the CHIP's Mercury was a Monterey two-door sedan, but underneath this mild mannered demeanor were the elements of a formidable road machine. At the front, larger Park Lane model front suspension components including spindles, hubs, brake drums, bearings and steering idler arm were used along with "export" coil springs. The standard four leaf rear springs were replaced by seven leaf station wagon "export" springs. Mercury's large 11 inch x 3 inch front drum brakes were left unchanged but the stock, 11 inch x 2½ inch rear brakes were replaced by larger 3 inch diameter versions. With a 360 hp, 430 cubic inch engine and 2.91 axle plus Multi-Matic, the heavy police cars finished the quarter-mile at 82.50 mph.

Mercurys built from 1959 through 1961 held little appeal for performance enthusiasts. The 1959 versions were huge beyond logic. The least expensive Monterey had a 126 inch wheelbase and that of the Parklane stretched out to 128 inches. The 430 cid V-8 was carried over but the Super-Marauder version was no longer offered. A lower, 10:1 compression ratio contributed to a down rating of the 430 engine's power to 345 at 4400 rpm.

Mercifully, the Mercury was downsized for 1960 with a 120 inch wheelbase. Historically, the 1960 Mercurys were of interest as the first models of the marque to be available with six-cylinder engines. This was also the last year for Mercurys with the 430 V-8, which was further down rated to 310 hp for 1960. The following year its use was restricted to Lincolns and Ford trucks. Mercury used Ford V-8s with displacements of 292, 352 and 390 cubic inches. The most powerful Mercury used the 390 V-8, developing a not too exciting 300 hp.

Mercury's 1962 power lineup was virtually unchanged but late in the year, in very limited numbers, Mercurys became available with the Ford 406 cid engine either with 385 hp (one four-barrel holley) or 405 hp (triple two-barrel Holleys).

To celebrate its return to high performance respectability, Mercury introduced its S-55 two-door hardtop and convertible models. Although part of the S-55 package's $379.90 cost went for fancy front seats and an all vinyl interior, the bulk went for its 406 engine, 4-speed transmission, heavy-duty clutch, driveshaft, radiator and suspension. The S-55 was also delivered with 15 inch wheels fitted with nylon tires and quicker, 22:1 instead of 30:1, non-power steering.

In evaluating the new Mercury, *HOT ROD* (November, 1962) observed, "Mercury is deadly serious about regaining the performance image it used to enjoy." By the fall of 1962, when the 1963 models were starting to roll off the line, intentions were turning into actions. Fran Hernnandez, a veteran of the early Southern California Timing Association days and a former Autolite performance manager, became Mercury's product performance and evaluation manager. Associated with this development was an announcement from Bill Stroppe that he would be returning to both USAC and NASCAR racing with a team of Mercurys.

There were bigger engines waiting out in the wings but Mercury's most powerful engines for 1963 were initially the twin 406 V-8s. On special order was a 330 hp version of the 390 engine fitted with mechanical lifters and a long duration cam.

As its part of the Ford Total Performance program Mercury introduced its fastback Marauder S-55 as a 1963½ model. Bill Stroppe estimated that its new, smoother roofline added 4.5 mph to the Mercury's top speed. To give Stroppe the needed power for racing, Mercury also offered a 427 V-8 with either a single four-barrel and 410 hp or two four-barrels and 425 hp. The only difference between these engines and their Ford counterparts were the names on the rocker arm covers. Mercurys 427's were uncommon automobiles. In its July, 1964, issue, *CAR LIFE* reported that only 57 had been so equipped.

Stroppe's racing successes with the 1963 Mercury didn't equal Ford's but Darel Dieringer did win the last major race of the season, The Golden State 400, on the 2.7 mile Riverside Raceway Course. Earlier, Parnelli Jones set a new stock car record at Pikes Peak with a Stroppe-prepared Mercury. A total of·11 racing successes in 1963 and early 1964 enabled Ford to tout the 1964 mercury as the "Proved Performance Champion of the Medium-Price Field."

Mercury's highwater performance had already been reached at that time, though there were no engine changes for 1965 but the Mercury's wheelbase and overall length grew by 4 inches and 8.4 inches, respectively, as they became more little Lincolns than fancy Fords.

The 427 racing V-8 wasn't available in 1966. The 428 cid, 345 engine used by the Thunderbird became the top Mercury powerplant. Although, a for-police-use-only 392 hp version was also offered.

Suggestive of earlier high performance Mercurys was the Marauder X-100 introduced in 1969. Its 429 cid, 360 hp gave it a strong zero to 60 mph time of 7.5 seconds but its awkward size, rather distasteful styling and poor cornering were negative attributes hard to ignore.

An image of luxury, size and prestige just below the Lincoln's was Mercury's as the sixties ended. It had never been totally at ease with the high performance crowd, which in turn was often a bit unsure about the intentions of the "Big M."

ALL NEW! COMET CYCLONE . . . WITH A HERITAGE 100,000 MILES LONG!

CAPTURES THE SPIRIT OF DAYTONA. Racy, sporty, elegant. That's Cyclone, a just-out model inspired by Comet's incredible Durability Run at Daytona, where 4 specially equipped Comets each clocked 100,000 miles averaging over 105 mph! In every Cyclone: new Super 289 cu. in. V-8, tach, bucket seats, chrome engine fittings, competition-type wheel covers. (The vinyl covered roof is optional.)

COMET A MERCURY PRODUCT
WORLD'S 100,000-MILE DURABILITY CHAMPION

Ride the
Magic
Skyway

FORD MOTOR COMPANY EXHIBIT
NEW YORK WORLD'S FAIR 1964-1965

LINCOLN-MERCURY DIVISION (Ford) MOTOR COMPANY

22. Mercury Comet/Montego

Like the first Falcon from which it was derived, the 1960 Mercury Comet was totally devoid of any performance attributes. An American car with a 90 hp engine that needed almost 24 seconds to accelerate from zero to 60 mph not only was a super *slow* car but also one with performance that was almost hazardous to the occupants' health and safety. There also wasn't much to be said in favor of the Comet's styling. It had a longer wheelbase and overall length than the Falcon, but whereas the Ford's lines were trim and well proportioned, the Comet appeared ungainly and awkward. Of course, with the nation going compact car crazy, the Comet's sales blasted off in spectacular fashion. nearly 200,000 were sold in 1960, even though they weren't available until the spring of that year.

Good sales aside, Mercury was well aware of the Comet's performance deficiency and took a step in the right direction by offering the 1961 version with a 170 cid six developing 101 hp. The Comet still was far from living up to its name in acceleration, but zero to 60 mph in just over 15 seconds helped Comet drivers breathe a lot easier as they merged into fast moving interstate traffic from entry ramps.

The Comet didn't get into the compact car racing scene as did the Falcon. Perhaps Mercury felt such behavior was unbecoming for a "senior compact," but the enthusiasm, and thus sales potential, represented by the public's interest in Chevrolet's dolled-up Corvair Monza persuaded Mercury to loosen the Comet's corset a bit. The result, first shown at the 1961 New York Automobile Show, was the Comet S-22. Neither its engine nor its running gear differed from other Comets, but semi-bucket front seats plus a dividing console gave it just a little more spice. A steering wheel fitted with vinyl handgrips and slightly upmarket carpeting and upholstery were also part of the S-22 package. Externally, S-22 insignias were apparent and standard equipment on all S-22's included whitewall tires, and chrome wheelcovers.

The movement away from basic transportation represented by the S-22 continued, but at a slow pace. Late in 1962, Mercury announced a 4-speed manual transmission (adapted from the English Ford Zephyr) for the Comet and, for 1963, a convertible model of the S-22 was offered. What the S-22 really needed to make it more competitive in the sporty-car market was improved styling and more power. Both of these needs were met by the 1963½ S-22 fastback powered by Ford's 260 cid, 164 hp V-8. Obviously, this Comet was a close kin to the Falcon Sprint but, successfully upgraded by Mercury, the S-22 was clearly a spring board for future Comet performance enterprises. To handle the additional 65 hp and 200 pounds of the 260 V-8, Mercury strengthened the Comet's integral body/chassis in 14 areas. Torque boxes from the Meteor were also installed. The V-8 powered S-22's used 5-bolt wheels, 7.00 x 13 tires plus larger wheel bearings, tie-rod ends and drag links. Front spindles from the Meteor were also used as were rear axle shafts from the Ford Econoline trucks. These changes, plus the usual stiffer springs and shocks, contributed significantly to the Comet's surprisingly good handling. "Our S-22," reported *MOTOR TREND* (August, 1963), "could

be pushed through turns at a very rapid rate in perfect safety. There's very little body lean . . . When it comes to handling, few other Detroit sedans can match it."

The 164 hp 260 V-8, which was available in every Comet model, was not by any stretch of the imagination in a high output form. Its compression ratio was a mild 8.7:1, and a small two-barrel carburetor was used along with a single exhaust system. Yet, with a 4-speed manual, the S-22 could accelerate from zero to 60 mph in 11.5 seconds.

The S-22's fastback roofline was a styling step in the right direction but, to *CAR LIFE*, the S-22 was still somewhat of an ugly duckling. "It has always seemed," said *CAR LIFE* (July, 1963), "that Mercury stylists must have labored long to come out with such a homely car." Well, you can't win them all.

This criticism notwithstanding, the evolution of the Comet into a performance automobile was preceding quite well. The S-22 Sportster put a lot of distance between itself and the early 90 hp weaklings of 1960.

Distance was something the Comet proved very good at covering in giant strides from September 21 to October 30, 1963, at the Daytona Speedway. Beginning at 8:30 on the 21st, a team of five 1964 Comet Calientes began a run that eventually would be the wherewithal for an advertising program proclaiming Comet as the car that covered "A hundred thousand miles at a hundred miles per hour on the track of the Mighty Big D."

It's hard to imagine a more sensational demonstration of the Comet's coming of age than this epic run. To put the Comet's achievement into some perspective, consider just one item. In 1952, a Jaguar XK-120 coupe had made motoring history by averaging 100.65 mph for 10,000 miles. Among the 100 plus records broken by the Comet was the World and American mark in the unlimited class for *50,000* miles. The Comet covered this distance, five times greater than the Jaguar's, at 108.828 mph.

The five Daytona Comets were all equipped with 289 cid, 271 hp V-8's built by Ford's Cleveland Engine Plant at Brookpark, Ohio. This solid lifter engine, which was available in 1964 Comets, was fitted with such factory options as a high performance cam, heavy-duty alternator and a larger oil pan. With a 3-speed manual transmission and a 2.70:1 rear axle, they were capable of a 112 mph speed at 3600 rpm, which was just 200 rpm above the maximum, 312 lbs-ft torque output. Running at this speed the Comets still delivered close to 12 mpg!

With the exception of a few spills on the banked curves (during the run a major hurricane passed through Daytona), the Comets ran like the proverbial clocks, stopping only every two hours for fuel, tire checks and driver switches. At 76,446.6 miles one of the Comets suffered a broken valve spring. The car was quickly repaired and completed 100,000 miles. F.I.A. regulations prevented it from taking part in the official record breaking however. A second Comet earlier lost its ignition system and returned to the track on October 8 with a retuned engine and a 3.25:1 axle. Since it was out of the 100,000 mile run it set out to grab some high speed records. It easily broke records for 500 and 1,000 miles held by Bugatti since 1936 with respective speeds of 131.697 mph and 129.847 mph. The Comet

Left, 1964 Mercury Comet Cyclone

engine blew at 2,000 miles but with a second engine it went on to break another dozen or so records, including 10,000 miles at 124.421.

Prior to the 100,000 miles at Daytona, the 289 engine had successfully completed a 15,000 mile "feasibility test" conducted by Ford Engineering. After 100,000 miles, the Comet engines were disassembled and found in surprisingly good shape. The greatest wear was evident in their piston pins, and timing gears. The valve springs had lost some of their strength but wear in the bores, rings, bearings and crank journals were judged to be well within "recommended limits for service use."

The Daytona run was obviously a very effective marketing tool that helped sell Comets but even without the favorable publicity of Daytona the 1964 Comets would have done well in the market. The 1964 models were given their first major restyling and the result was generally favorable. Underneath, a wider rear tread plus wider rear springs helped make the Caliente, Comet's new upmarket model, "a car with excellent handling characteristics, ranking closely behind the Dodge Dart in this respect," according to CAR LIFE (January, 1964).

At mid-season model time, the Cyclone model, visually a Caliente devoid of much of its basically superflous side trim, and mechanically a fairly strong performer, appeared. The very potent, but also very rare, 271 hp version of the 289 was available but the standard engine for the Cyclone was the 289 with a four-barrel carburetor, hydraulic lifters and 9.0:1 compression ratio. Early 4-speed Cyclones were delivered with a Warner-Gear gearbox. This transmission detracted from the car's performance because of the wide gap in ratios between third and fourth gear. The change over to a Ford-built 4-speed, whose ratios were far more compatible to the 289's power and torque curves, was a positive performance step since it reduced the Cyclone's zero to 60 mph time by nearly one second, to 9.7. Mercury's excellent Multi-Drive, 3-speed, Merc-O-Matic was offered as a $189.60 option for the Cyclone. Closely related to the Fairlane Thunderbolt were a small number of special Comets built and campaigned during the 1964 drag racing season. All were assembled by Ford Engineering and such drag masters as Don Nicholson, former Chevrolet driver Tom Sturm and Jack Chrisman were early recipients of these Comets which were placed in the A/FX or factory experiment class by the NHRA. The Comet's 427, twin four-barrel engine developed in excess of 480 hp and one A/FX

Comet held both the class elapsed time — 11.02 seconds — and quarter-mile speed — 128.04 mph — records in 1964. The extensive use of fiberglass body panels plus plexiglass side windows lowered the Comet's race weight to 3,085 pounds. CAR LIFE (September, 1964) tested a A/FX Comet with a 4.57:1 axle and recorded the following acceleration times: 0-60 mph, 4.2 seconds; 0-100 mph, 9.4 seconds; standing start quarter-mile, 12.0 seconds, 121 mph.

"Comets for 1965 — the durability Champions." That's how early 1965 Comet ads were headlined and, this time at least, it wasn't just an idle boast.

During 1964, a team of six Comets took part in the 3,100 mile East African Safari. While they didn't win, two of the Comets finished, one in 18th position. For the record, only 21 of the 100 starters also finished. These Safari Comets were jointly prepared by Bill Stroppe and Ford of England's competition department. All had the 271 hp engine, 4.57:1 axle, Ford's new close-ratio, 4-speed gearbox, heavy-duty suspension and drum brakes with metallic linings.

To kick off publicity for the 1965 models, a set of "strictly stock" Comets left Ushuala, Argentina, on September 12, 1964, destined for Fairbanks, Alaska. Forty days and 16,247 miles later they arrived at their destination, ending what was another legitimate performance durability test.

Lincoln-Mercury division continued its policy of touting the Caliente as the luxury version of the Comet and portrayed the Cyclone as its performance leader. The Caliente was available as a four-door sedan, two-door hardtop or two-door convertible. The Cyclone, on the other hand, was offered only as a two-door hardtop with front bucket seats. The only engine offered in the Cyclone was the familiar 289 cid V-8 with a four-barrel carburetor and a rating of 225 hp. In its Comet guise, it was identified as the "Comet Cyclone Super 289 V-8" and was available as a Caliente option. In a demonstration of pure nonsense, L-M labeled the Caliente's 200 hp V-8 (it was also available with a 120 hp six) the "Comet Cyclone 289 V-8," yet did not offer it as a Cyclone option! The 271 hp, 289 V-8 was no longer available, although on a very limited basis a fiberglass hood derived from the A/FX Comet but with non-functional scoops was a Cyclone option. With this hood and its own distinctive grille, the Cyclone conveyed an impression of fleetness

Above, 1963 Mercury Comet S-22

and, with a 4-speed manual transmission and 3.00:1 axle, it delivered quite nicely on this promise. Zero to 60 mph in 8.8 seconds was respectable for a small engined automobile. Comets had a good reputation for stability and the Cyclone scored high in this area. Axle hop was a problem under full throttle acceleration, but the optional "performance handling kit" for the Cyclone held it to a tight line in the turns.

It was almost inevitable during the mid-sixties that both full-sized cars and compacts grew on an almost annual basis. From its inception, the Comet had been a product of this type of automotive evolution and its 1966 version, based upon the Fairlane body shell, was a prime example of its operation. A wheelbase of 116 inches and an overall length of 203 inches gave the Comet dimensions that would have made it a full-sized car in years gone by, but in 1966 placed it in the intermediate-size category. The earlier demise of the Mercury Meteor made the Comet's increased size a good marketing move. For performance fans, it also marked another step up for the Comet for it now had the wherewithal to effectively take advantage, along Pontiac GTO lines, of the classic small car, big engine combination. Thus, for 1966, appeared the Cyclone GT. Its engine? The ubiquitous Ford 390. On paper, the new Comet seemed to have everything the ideal supercar needed: a big engine with 335 hp, an optional handling kit, front disc brakes and either a 4-speed manual or an automatic transmission ("Sport Shift") that allowed the driver to control its operation. Thanks to its new chassis, the Comet's rear tread was increased by 2 inches, thus holding out the promise of improved roadability. To its credit, a Sport Shift Cyclone turned in a strong zero to 60 mph, 6.6 second time. The 390 V-8, however, tended to weaken at the top end as its hydraulic lifters started to pump up near the 5000 rpm mark. Another liability of the 390 engine as a Comet engine was its weight, some 433 pounds more than the 120 hp six. *CAR LIFE* (April, 1966), was less than enthralled with the result, observing that although the Comet behaved itself in a straight line, "less-than-straight roads are less pleasing and here the overbalance of weight makes for a nervous driver. Overall handling is not, then, a highpoint with the Cyclone GT."

A year later it was turnabout time for the Comet. For one thing, the Comet name was on the way to oblivion. By 1969, it would be nowhere to be found. Of greater interest was *DRAG RACING* magazine's naming of the Mercury

Below, 1968 Mercury Cyclone GT

Cyclone as its "Performance Car of the Year." In drag racing, Don Nicholson's 135 victories deserve a good deal of the credit for this award, but primary credit had to go to that workhorse of Ford's Total Performance program, its great 427 engine. With this engine, either with 410 or 425 underrated horsepower, the Cyclone came of age as a performance automobile.

After another redesign, the 1968 Comets, just 16 inches shorter than their full-sized sibling Mercurys, had abandoned all vestiges of their humbler days. Even the Comet name was found on just one model with the rest of the line being identified either as Mercury Montego or Mercury Cyclone models. With victories in both the Daytona and Atlanta 500 races, the Cyclone had matured into a formidable Super Track car. In its 428 Cyclone form it also had taken the final step to street performance greatness. The Cyclone's Cobra Jet 428 used the best from Ford's 427 and 428 engines to serve up 335 very healthy horsepower at 5600 rpm. With Ford's heavy-duty, 3-speed automatic, 3.91:1 axle and Goodyear Polyglass tires, the Cyclone could flirt with the 6 second time from zero to 60 mph. Furthermore, it also possessed a first class set of brakes whose performance *CAR LIFE* characterized as "nothing short of phenomenal in a car weighing 4,000 lbs." In a similar vein, the Cyclone's handling also drew rave reviews. In sum total, it was a near perfect supercar: a tough car in competition, quick on the street, sure footed in the turns and able to stop in a straight line from high speeds without losing its composure.

The Cyclone GT remained a great performer for 1970. A standard 429 cid, 370 hp Cobra Jet engine saw to that. Its styling was surprisingly understated (with the exception of its "bulls-eye" grille). The Cyclone's designers abandoned the fastback profile of the earlier 1968-69 models in favor of a long hood, short rear deck appearance that gave the 1970 version a no-nonsense-all-business type of personality. It's tempting to dismiss the high performance Spoiler model as merely a Cyclone gussied up to take advantage of what was then a common styling cliche, but a car whose standard equipment included, in addition to front and rear spoilers, a ram air intake, Hurst shifter and a new cross-flow radiator that made a two-inch lower hood possible was a lot more than just a decal special.

The 1970 Cyclone's increased size made it less than the perfect supercar. Yet, in the total perspective of Comet/Cyclone performance cars, this wasn't a major spot upon their record. Few cars of the age matured into greatness with the style and form of the Comet. It started slow but ended up very, very fast.

23. Mercury Cougar

The way a lot of people saw it, the Cougar should never have gotten involved in high performance fun and games at all. It was, argued these naysayers, "a Mustang with class," a car "for the man on his way to a Thunderbird." Thus, they said, a spruced up, stretched out, semi-luxury car had no need to nuture a rough and ready high performance image. Its prospective customers were older and more affluent than the supercar crowd and a car with good looks and typical big V-8 power would suit them just fine.

This wasn't exactly the perspective Lincoln-Mercury had of the Cougar's public image. It's true the Cougar was intended to curry favor among customers accustomed to paying more for their cars than were typical Mustang owners. Along those lines, the Cougar's three inch longer (111 inch) wheelbase and stretched overall length of 190.3 inches were intended to put some visual distance between it and the Mustang. In addition, more sound-deadening material plus the use of voided rubber bushings in the Cougar's rear suspension gave it a ride far quieter than a comparable Mustang. Also, not to be ignored, was the exclusively V-8 engine line-up for the Cougar. This assured that if they weren't the first away from the stop light, at least no Cougar would be last, either.

There was another element of the Cougar personality needing to be reckoned with and that was its strong European Grand Touring flavor. The SR-7 Cougar's array of instruments and gauges set in a walnut dash, plus its leather upholstery, were clear indicators that Lincoln-Mercury welcomed a little "Old World Tradition" inside the Cougar. On this point, Lincoln-Mercury aroused the ire of Jaguar which complained that the initial Cougar emblem with its lithe "big cat" silhouette too closely resembled Jaguar's feline symbol. Anglo-American friendship was preserved by the positioning, in large letters, of C-O-U-G-A-R just below the Cougar's cougar.

Even the selection of this name reflected a mentality prone to sport. Lincoln-Mercury could have chosen a far more stately label but, instead, it followed the dictates of a marketing survey reporting the public's association of Cougar with swiftness, silence and a lithe manner.

Within the Lincoln-Mercury hierarchy, key men who were strongly pro-racing and pro-performance were in positions to influence the Cougar's performance potential. Not the least were Fran Hernandez, L-M performance specialist, and Frank E. Zimmerman, Jr., the former special vehicles manager for Ford during its Le Mans and Indianapolis programs. Zimmerman left his position as general marketing manager at Lincoln-Mercury to become its general sales manager, but this switch brought more strength to Lincoln-Mercury as his old job was filled by Leo Beebe, Ford's former performance head.

If Trans-Am race fans knew where to look during the 1966 season, they would have discovered yet another tipoff to the Cougar's future: at every Trans-Am race, representatives of Lincoln-Mercury were in attendance.

A review of the Cougar's engine offerings didn't provide any earth-moving revelations. Its two 289 cid V-8's with 200 hp and 225 hp ratings were familiar workday engines and the optional 320 hp, 390 V-8 with a fairly mild cam and hydraulic valve lifters was also a well-known and un-exciting entity.

But a closer look often reveals what was missed in the first once-over. Along with the 390 engine, plus, of course, the payment of $323, came the GT Performance Group. This included a low-restriction exhaust system, power front disc brakes (11.38 inch Kelsey-Hayes), and Firestone Wide-Oval tires on 6 inch wide rims. For another $31, there were more goodies available for the Cougar as the "Performance Handling Package" including a suspension with solid rubber bushings, stiffer front and rear springs, and larger Gabriel heavy-duty shocks.

The possibility that the Cougar would be a Trans-Am participant in 1967 was enhanced by Lincoln-Mercury's application to the F.I.A. for certification of the Cougar along with the Comet 202 as Group Two Touring cars. It became a sure thing when L-M published a four page brochure detailing a long list of dealer installed features which made for some pretty interesting reading. Included were aluminum pistons, high-lift cam and a choice of manifolds allowing either dual four-barrel Holleys or four two-barrel Webers to be used. At one time, Ford had offered the latter carburetors for the Mustang and claimed a 306 hp rating for 289 engines so equipped. Various horsepower claims were made for the Trans-Am Cougar engines. *CAR AND DRIVER* (July, 1967) quoted output as 361 hp. An early 1967 Autolite ad referred to the dual four-barrel carburetor Cougar "Group 2" engine as producing 341 horsepower.

Frank Zimmerman told *SPORTS CAR GRAPHIC* (November, 1966) that, "we share the conviction of Ford Motor Company that racing improves the breed, that things learned on the race track enable us to build better and safer cars. And, sedan racing seems to us to be one of the most useful opportunities presented by automobile racing to 'improve the breed,' because the rules specify that the cars must be production with minor modifications."

The talent gathered together to improve the genetic composition of the Cougar was substantial. Bud Moore was responsible for the preparation of the Team Cougar cars, with Dan Gurney and Parnelli Jones put on the payroll to handle the driving choices. Gurney's All American Racers Company was eager to play a role somewhat analogous to Carroll Shelby's relationship to the Mustang. Specifically, Gurney wanted the chance to develop and sell special Cougar high-performance accessories for the 289 V-8. Working with Harry Weslake, A.A.R. produced cylinder heads for both the 289 cid and the 302 cid V-8's, which became the base Cougar engine in 1968. A Cougar with these Gurney-Weslake heads plus an intake manifold for a single four-barrel was capable of 14.2 second quarter-miles. Unfortunately, this rose never got beyond the bud stage. Gurney wanted to develop, produce and sell the Cougar speed parts to Lincoln-Mercury. The company didn't think much about that idea since they wanted direct control of their manufacture. Predictably, the result benefited no one. All American Racers missed an opportunity to diversify, Lincoln-Mercury lost a chance to gain access to very specialized racing technology and, of course, the possibility of the Cougar becoming the top cat of the small-engined pony cars fell apart.

The unhappy scenario did not, fortunately, detract from the Cougar's showing in the 1967 Trans-Am racing circus. At the season's opener, The Daytona Trans-Am, Team Cougar was very competitive. Both Jones and Gurney qualified on the first row. Jones' car was the fastest in practice, turning a lap of 105.02 mph. On the straights, the Cougars came close to speeds of 175 mph. Although Jones led for the first 24 laps, a broken rocker arm hobbled his effort which eventually ended with a third place finish.

This mechanical failure was not to be a common Cougar malady, but in the first few races it was apparent the Cougar's handling was not up to a race winning level. After the Green Valley, Texas Trans-Am, however, where Gurney and Jones finished 1-2, the Cougars were very competitive. Helped by Peter Revson's victory at Lime Rock in his first race with a Cougar, they became very tough and finished the season a strong second to the Mustang. This interdivisional competition, which at times bordered on fratricide, wasn't smiled upon by corporate leadership which decreed there would be no such behavior in 1968. Thus, there was no Team Cougar for the 1968 Trans-Am. This did not, fortunately, spell a complete end to the Cougar's competition career. NASCAR, eager to grab a piece of the pony car action, created its GT racing class that year and it proved to be the domain of the 1968 Cougars. The Bud Moore Cougars won 10 of 19 races and team driver Tiny Lund won 9 of them.

The availability of the 390 hp, 427 cid V-8 (with hydraulic lifters) for the 1968 Cougar was a less than happy development for those who preferred a well mannered road car. The 427 Cougar GT-E with the XR-7 suspension wallowed in the turns and possessed a degree of understeer

Above, 1967 Mercury Cougar

that represented a heavy price to pay for a zero to 60 mph in 7 seconds performance.

The Cougar was obviously unable to resist the trend toward big and heavy engines that eventually led to the demise of the pony cars. In 1969, for example, the Cougar with new styling was available powered by the CJ 428 V-8 with or without Ram Air, but far better balanced machines that more accurately portrayed the Cougar's quasi-European character were those with 351 cid, four-barrel V-8s. With a healthy 290 hp output, they came close to 428 performance without a serious handling handicap.

SPORTS CAR GRAPHIC (October, 1968) was apparently quite pleased with the 1969 Cougar, noting it, ''appears to be the most improved of all the Pony Cars.'' On a limited basis, special Dan Gurney Cougar models with the 351 cid high performance engine and a special handling package were available.

Cougars' top 1970 performance model, the Eliminator, was regarded by some industry watchers as representing an effort to regain its former, Trans-Am/NASCAR performance image. The potential of the Eliminator with the aerodynamic spoilers and high-output 302, 351, 428 and 429 cid V-8's was undeniable. The Boss 302 was a 290 hp pavement stomper, the 351 with its canted valves delivered an untempermental 280 hp, the Cobra-Jet 428's were strong 335 hp engines and the 429 ''NASCAR'' V-8 was an awesome supplier of 375 hp. Obviously, Cougars weren't anemic in this aspect of performance, but they had lost much of the individuality that had earlier distinguished them from their contemporaries.

The following year the Cougar was restyled but, unfortunately, the key changes were more length and more width. The Cougar, like the other pony cars, had lost much of its original attractiveness by succumbing to the bigger must be better philosophy.

sedate it ain't

400 CID V-8. Full 115-inch wheelbase. Heavy-duty springs, shock absorbers, shaft. Sway bars, front *and rear*. High-performance axle. Dual exhausts. Beefed-up wheels. White-Line or wide-oval Red-Line tires. Bucket seats. Louvered hood. Higher oil pressure. They're all standard goodies at one modest price. Available also, if you wish—Rocket Rally Pac, UHV ignition, superstock wheels, front disc brakes and the like. Put one into action and you'll agree: 1967 Olds 4-4-2 is the sweetest, neatest, completest anti-boredom bundle on rubber!

OLDS 442 **GM**

ENGINEERED FOR EXCITEMENT...TORONADO-STYLE!

OBEY LAWS DRIVE SAFELY | Olds thinks of your safety, too, with GM-developed energy-absorbing steering column that can compress on severe impact up to 8¼ inches; with four-way hazard warning flasher; outside rearview mirror; dual master cylinder brake system, plus many other safety features—all standard!

MOTOR TREND / DECEMBER 1966

24. Oldsmobile

Oldsmobile, like most of the other automotive superstars of the Golden Age of high performance, did not enter that era with particularly impressive credentials. Oldsmobile's image was essentially that of a motorcar more often than not owned by a individual of solid but not unlimited financial status who perhaps had risen from the blue collar ranks to become a manager, or, perhaps, a plant superintendent. Such folks were not especially concerned about performance, that kind of goings on was for the younger set, most certainly not for the owners of Oldsmobiles.

A lot changed in the early fifties, and the car that set the pace and established the big engine, light body pattern that typified the American supercar in its definitive form was Oldsmobile.

The development of the ohv Olds V-8 that powered the Olds 88 (which used the same basic body as Chevrolet) into the record books had its origins in the mid-thirties. As early as 1936, Cadillac engineers had been working on a ohv, high compression V-8 and, while the 1949 Oldsmobile and Cadillac V-8 engines were the product of separate projects, they reflected a common design heritage.

In June, 1947, Charles Kettering, GM's engineering wizard, gave the S.A.E. a peek at what was in store when he presented a paper dealing with the potency of an overhead valve, high compression engine. Experiments with a 181 cid, ohv six-cylinder engine developing 95 hp and with a 12.5:1 compression ratio had left no doubt among Oldsmobile engineers that the L-head straight eight properly belonged to the past. By October, 1947, a 287 cid, ohv V-8 was definitely in Oldsmobile's future and, just over a year later, on November 3, 1948, production began of this engine, expanded to 303.7 cubic inches. After that moment, it seemed almost as if God himself had a liking for fast cars. Events that exemplified the new found performance prowess of the Olds 88 happened so fast and blended into each other so perfectly that it's hard to believe they weren't the product of divine intervention. At Indianapolis, in May, 1949, the pace car was an Olds 88 convertible and, when NASCAR both literally and figuratively got rolling that summer, the car that won most of the races (six of nine) was, you guessed it, Oldsmobile. The following year, Oldsmobile not only captured ten victories but emerged the winner of the first Carrera Panamerican race in Mexico.

Obviously, the new Oldsmobile V-8 was an engineering milestone. At 668 pounds it wasn't exactly a lightweight, though it weighed a good deal less than the L-head, 257 cubic inch eight it replaced. It was, however, as tough as nails, could absorb all kinds of abuse once some teething problems (easily burnt valves to cite one example) were solved and, most importantly, its 135 hp propelled the relatively light Olds 88 in a most impressive fashion. When Tom McCahill tested one *(MECHANIX ILLUSTRATED,* July, 1950), he found it the "best all-around highway performing stock car made in America today." With Hydra-Matic, the 88 needed 13.4 seconds for the zero to 60 mph run, but a stick-shift Olds dropped this down to only 12 seconds. Uncle Tom coaxed his test car up to a top speed of 96.9 mph, faster than the 92.11 mph *MOTOR TREND*

managed, but *MOTOR TREND* could still report the Olds 88 was the first car it had tested capable of a 90 mph top speed. The Oldsmobile's performance was clearly a performance benchmark for postwar American cars.

If there were any diehards who refused to believe the Olds 88 was as good as its proponents said, their ranks were thinned out after the 1950 Daytona Speed Week. Joe Littlejohn coaxed a stick-shift Oldsmobile up and down the beach for a 100.28 mph average. Pretty heady goings on for nineteen fifty, and for a time Oldsmobile got quite caught up in racing. During the 1951 racing season it won nearly 50% (twenty of forty one) of the NASCAR Grand Nationals. The following year, the Hudson Hornet proved to have more gumption than the 88 but Oldsmobile came back strong in 1953. A half-dozen, specially prepared Oldsmobiles showed up for the annual NASCAR beach party early in 1953. No official horsepower figures were ever released for these cars but they utterly and completely dominated the flying mile competition. Bob Pronger broke Littlejohn's old record with a two-way average of 113.38 mph, and, in the acceleration runs, Pronger won again at 74.41 mph. Finally, in the Grand National race, the 1-2 Oldsmobile triumph left no doubt the 88 was a powerhouse. Among the heavy-duty parts fitted to the engines of these super-hot 88-s were 8.5:1 compression ratio heads, high-lift cams, solid lifters and blocked manifold heat risers.

While Hudson bent over backwards to help keep its cars competitive in racing, Oldsmobile tended to back off from serious involvement in competition after the 1953 Daytona Speed Week. Oldsmobile took a long hard look at the benefits it would gain from racing and decided, since its cars were priced beyond the means of most racing fans, that the direct impact of winning races upon sales would be minimal. Oldsmobile was turning away almost completely from enhancing a reputation that was literally international since for three years in succession (1950-52) it had won the Francorchamps Stock Car Race in Belgium.

As a pioneer of the age of high performance, Oldsmobile had been a trail blazer but, in the mid-fifties, it was definitely taking a backseat to Hudson in NASCAR competition. Irregardless of this power shift, the 1953 Super 88 was still one of the top performing American sedans. Its engine, now with a 8.0:1 compression ratio and the Rochester Quadra-Jet four-barrel carburetor, developed 165 horsepower, sufficient when linked to the new Dual-Range Hydra-Matic to achieve a zero to sixty mph time of 12.3 seconds and a 110 mph top speed. Such movability from a 4,000 pound automobile with an automatic transmission was hardly lethargic.

"The Olds that Couldn't Wait" described the 1954 Oldsmobile, which supposedly had been originally planned for the following year. Actually, "the family hot rod" was a better description of the new Oldsmobile. A new body just over sixty inches high plus GM's panoramic wraparound, but-watch-your-kneecaps windshield were the big news that year. Performance was as good as ever thanks to a boost in engine displacement to 324.3 cubic inches, and a higher, 8.5:1 compression ratio. Horsepower jumped up 20 to 185 and maximum torque stood at a healthy 300 lbs-ft. at 2000 rpm.

Left, 1967 Oldsmobile 4-4-2

The introduction of Chevrolet's new V-8 in 1955, plus the arrival of the Chrysler C-300, put Oldsmobile in a performance bind. The fact of the matter was, of course, that it really didn't matter as far as Oldsmobile sales were concerned. In 1954, well over 400,000 were sold and a calendar year output of 433,810 represented Oldsmobile's best production performance of its history. Yet, at the same time, it just didn't seem right for Oldsmobile to allow the 88 to become an over-the-hill road runner. Like it or not though, that's basically what the 88 was in 1955 and 1956. Its advocates liked to describe its performance as mature but that was nothing less than calling it stodgy. An enterprising Oldsmobile enthusiast could break the 10 second mark from zero to sixty and exceed 113 mph, but such combinations were rare.

The 1957 models initially offered nothing that even vaguely suggested a change in Oldsmobile's performance status might be imminent. The Super 88, like all the Oldsmobiles, had all new styling but it was at best uninspired, at the worst dated and, at the least, dull. By jumping the Rocket V-8's bore and stroke 1/8 inch and 1/4 inch, respectively, Oldsmobile engineers increased its displacement to 371 cubic inches, which boosted advertised horsepower to 277 at 4400 rpm. The result was, as expected, good, but certainly not thrilling, zero to sixty mph runs hovering around the 10 second mark. It seemed just about everybody was producing a quicker accelerating car than Oldsmobile, but, at this low ebb, the old performance spirit that had once made the 88 the car to be reckoned with at the red light or drag strip was resuscitated via a triple carburetor/manifold option known as J-2. Oldsmobile had used the appellation to identify the various performance kits it had offered in the early fifties. Now, it meant 300 hp at 4000 rpm, thanks not only to the triple carbs but also to a 10.0:1 compression ratio achieved by use of a thinner head gasket. At $83, the cost of those extra horses wasn't exactly a bargain, but if cost was no object, or if the ultimate Oldsmobile performance experience was desired, an over-the-counter dealer option consisting of an Iskenderian E-2 cam and solid lifters was a must. The J-2 engine with these

items developed 312 hp. A 300 hp J-2 Olds Super 88 could flirt with the 9 second mark for the zero to 60 mph run and, with 312 hp, come in well under it. A 312 hp Oldsmobile 98, which weighed over 420 pounds more than the Super 88, checked in with an 8.6 second run in a *MOTOR TREND* (March, 1958) test. *MOTOR TREND* concluded that "a J-2 in a Super 88 will be a thing to deal with on the strip." *HOT ROD* (July, 1958) added, "A stiff set of shocks and most of the so-called foreign sports cars will never know which way they went." Neither of these remarks were just empty statements, judging by Lee Petty's winning the NASCAR Grand National Point Championship with his Oldsmobile.

Despite the obvious transformation the J-2 made in Oldsmobile's performance, it was dropped by Oldsmobile at the end of the 1958 run. Triple carburetors were great only if they got plenty of exercise but disuse brought gum and sticky deposits which in turn led to unhappy owners of Oldsmobiles.

There was actually little performance degradation due to the J-2's demise thanks to the 394 cubic inch version of Oldsmobile's V-8 that, along with the older 371 cid model, was offered in 1959. With larger intake valves, a four-barrel Rochester carburetor, and a new four-port exhaust manifold, the 394 developed 315 horsepower at 4600 rpm. Not every automotive journal was pleased with the considerable bulk of the '59 Oldsmobile, but *HOT ROD* (June, 1959) did report that its 315 hp Super 88 test car attained a favorable zero to sixty mph time of 8.4 seconds.

Lee Petty's victory with a 1959 Oldsmobile in the inaugural Daytona 500 notwithstanding, Oldsmobile passed into the decade of the sixties with virtually no performance image at all. Its annual production level tended to stagnate around the 340,000 mark, far below the 485,000 total for 1956 and even under its 1950 output of 408,000 automobiles.

Oldsmobile's sales slip was traceable to many factors: The nibbling away at the auto market by domestic compacts and foreign imports and the corresponding decline of the

Below, 1952 Oldsmobile Deluxe 88

full sized car as a social status were certainly two causes. In contrast to the emergence of the youth market for automobiles, however, these were less important to Oldsmobile. What was needed for an Oldsmobile renaissance was a Youngmobile and, towards that end, several key developments came to fruitation in the early sixties. The first had its genesis in the go ahead given by GM to Pontiac, Oldsmobile and Buick to develop so-called "Senior Compacts" based roughly on the body components of the Corvair. The resulting Oldsmobile F-85, in its initial form, was a nice car but of very limited appeal to performance enthusiasts. This sentiment was given a major push toward the positive by Oldsmobile's announcement late in the summer of 1961 of a turbo-charged F-85. This project originated in October, 1959, and, before the introduction of the F-85 in 1961, a prototype had already been tested on the road. Both technical problems and parts delays postponed the Turbo-Olds' introduction until the spring of 1962, by which time interest in small, high performance cars was clearly on the rise. The 215 hp Jetfire Sports Coupe was certainly quick enough. With Hydra-Matic, its zero to 60 mph time was 8.5 seconds, but it suffered from two inherent shortcomings. The first, a lack of a manual transmission, was corrected in 1963 when the Warner T-10 4-speed gearbox was offered. The Jetfire's second liability, the inability of a small displacement engine, even with a turbocharge, to compete on even terms with the big bore V-8's, was not so easily overcome. Like its Chevrolet counterpart, the Corvair Monza Spyder, the Jetfire was too European in its performance philosophy and, thus, was alien to the American hot rodders from which much of the Yourth Market had inherited its automobile preferences.

On the surface, the Oldsmobile Starfire, which had been first introduced in 1962 and given a facelift for 1963 that tidied up its exterior, seemed a more likely candidate for Oldsmobile to place its high performance mantle on, but in spite of a 345 hp, 394 cid engine, the Starfire (which weighed over 4,500 pounds) could do no better in acceleration than the Jetfire and was priced at a then hefty

Above, 1955 Oldsmobile Super 88

$4,129.

Obviously, Oldsmobile had a handle on what would make for an attractive performance car: namely, good looks, a potent engine and chassis/suspension components that made for decent handling, but they were scattered helter-skelter amidst the Oldsmobile lineup, thus diluting their overall impact.

Whether by accident or design, the introduction of a new V-8, the first since the Rocket V-8 of 1949, and a new, larger body for the F-85 represented Oldsmobile's best chance of getting out of the performance doldrums. The new engine was substantially smaller and lighter than the 394 V-8 but proved to be relatively inexpensive to develop since it utilized much of the tooling from the older model. Initially appearing with a displacement of 330 cubic inches, this V-8 was optional on the 1964 F-85. It was also the standard powerplant for the new Jetstar 88, a lightweight version of the larger 88 series. With 290 hp, the new Olds engine had a respectable output per cubic inch ratio, a reasonable weight (at 560 pounds it weighed approximately 100 pounds less than the 394 V-8) and the potential for future power and displacement boosts.

Thus, when the F-85, along with the Buick Skylark and Pontiac Tempest, grew out of their Corvair-sized format and became true mid-sized automobiles in 1964, the stage was set for what could be regarded as the reincarnation of the Olds 88 of 1949. Officially, it was Option Number B-09 Police Apprehender Pursuit, but, on the boulevard and dragstrips and for evermore, it was the 4-4-2, a 1964¾ offering that evolved into the finest performance Oldsmobile of them all. The 4-4-2 handle first symbolized a car with four on the floor, four-barrel carburetor and dual exhausts. This obviously implied performance, but it also suggested the 4-4-2 was an automobile with lots of go-power but short on cornering power. Such misshapen machines did mar the best years of America's high performance age, but none of them ever bore the 4-4-2 label. Oldsmobile's chief engineer, John Beltz, once remarked that from the outset of the 4-4-2's development, "We wanted to come as close as we could to a true sports car, but in a package that would give practical street

transportation for 4-5 passengers in everyday driving. We decided right off that we weren't just going to stick a big engine in a little car for maximum 0-60 acceleration. We have spent as much effort on improving the handling and stability of this car as the acceleration.''

As a result, the 4-4-2 package, which retailed for $285.14, included heavy-duty front and rear springs and shocks, the usual large front anti-roll bar *plus* one at the rear. With 7.70 x 14 red line tires (Royal XP-800 Tiger Paws), the 4-4-2 had far less body lean and understeer than the normal F-85 Cutlass and deservedly received high grades for handling from the critics. *CAR LIFE* (August, 1964) noted, ''So set up, our Cutlass was the best handling of any GM car we've been exposed to (except for the Sting Ray) and far superior to its identical cousins from the other divisions. There is, in our judgment, hardly a better handling passenger sedan produced in this country.''

The 4-4-2's high standard of handling was matched by a first class engine. A wilder cam, stronger valves, and extra-quality precision main bearings and rods set the 4-4-2 engine apart from lesser things. Undoubtedly, its 310 hp rating, up just 20 from the most powerful Cutlass V-8, was a conservative one. With its standard 3.23:1 axle and 4-speed transmission, the 4-4-2 accelerated from zero to 60 mph in 7.4 seconds and to 100 mph from rest in just 20.7 seconds. If there was a weak spot in the 4-4-2 performance profile, that short-coming was found in its stock brakes. Even with cooling flanges on their drums, they couldn't even approach the levels of competence attained by the 4-4-2's handling and acceleration. GM's famous metallic linings were available as part of a heavy-duty brake package but they should have been part of the standard 4-4-2 design.

For its full-sized, 1965 models, Oldsmobile opened up the basic 330 cid engine of 1964 to 425 cubic inches. In the Jetstar I and Starfire models, a top rating of 370 hp was available, making these cars fairly rapid conveyances. They were still inferior in the performance department to the 4-4-2, which for 1965 was an automobile with a 400 cubic inch displacement engine, four-barrel carburetor and dual exhausts. The 4-4-2 engine differed in its basics from the 425 V-8 only by its smaller (by 0.125 inch) bore. Olds pegged this engine, with the same 10.25:1 compression ratio as 1964, at 345 hp and 440 lbs-ft of torque. The 4-4-2 package, in addition to the handling modifications of the earlier version, included stronger wheels, rear axle, drive-shaft, suspension arms and bushings, engine mounts, a 70 amp battery and an 11 inch clutch. Standard transmission for the 4-4-2 was a new all-synchro 3-speed gearbox for which a floor shifter was available for $43.04. The 4-speed, close-ratio unit, unchanged from 1964, was priced at $188.30, and a Special Duty Jetaway 2-speed automatic transmission was ticketed at $209.82. These prices made the $156.02 price of the 4-4-2 package appear to be even more of a bargain.

Like the earlier versions, the 1965 4-4-2 received lots of high grades for its handling. Roger Huntington, in *MOTOR TREND* (May, 1965), described it as ''certainly one of the top-handling American passenger cars available today and certainly the best of the General Motors'.'' Tom McCahill *MECHANIX ILLUSTRATED*, (March, 1965) depicted the 4-4-2 both as ''a high performance car at a comparatively low price that will beat the brains out of almost anything on the road when the traffic light turns green,'' and as a car whose ''suspension, for an American sedan, is close to being magnificent.''

Although it was offered only in 1966, the availability of a three-carburetor/manifold option midway through the model year represented a significant step in the 4-4-2's evolution, as did the W-30 cold air package. The 4-4-2 had tended to lag behind its GTO brethren-adversary in straight-line acceleration. Now, with 360 hp at 5000 rpm, this disparity virtually disappeared. When the GM high priests went on one of their periodic anti-performance exorcising tirades, the 3-carb setup was given the old heave-ho treatment, but the voodoo doctors at Oldsmobile weren't so easily dissuaded. The 1967 edition of the 4-4-2 had to breathe through a four-barrel carburetor, but the use of a Toronado cam and a higher compression ratio held the 4-4-2's power loss to just 10 horsepower. A strong plus for the 4-4-2 in 1967 was its new Jetaway 3-speed automatic transmission (actually Turbo Hydra-Matic in disguise with a higher rpm shifting valve body and a revamped convertor for greater initial torque) with manual control over first and second gears. Olds engineers claimed that a Jetaway equipped 4-4-2 and one with a manual 4-speed would end a quarter-mile drag race in a dead heat. As had been typical of

Above, 1964 Oldsmobile Starfire

earlier 4-4-2's, the 1967 received accolades for the overall excellence of its road manners. *HOT ROD* (October, 1966) called it ''a sophisticated engineering package, not just a straight-liner.''

The 400 cubic inch engine of the 1968 4-4-2 carried the same 350 hp rating as in 1967, but it was now wrapped up in a very sensual and extremely good looking body that had the added bonus of being slightly shorter than before. The trend towards lower priced, smaller engined supercars encouraged Oldsmobile to offer its Cutlass model W-31 form for approximately $300 less than a comparable 4-4-2 model. The forced air induction system of the W-31 Cutlass S, operating through twin oval scoops on the front grille's under panel that fed into tubes attached to the carburetor air cleaner, boosted its 350 cid engine's horsepower from 295 to 310. But as *CAR LIFE* (April, 1968) noted, ''This has to be the strongest additional 15 hp to come from Detroit in recent years.'' At its press introduction, a Cutlass S with open exhaust headers and a 4.66:1 rear axle turned a quarter-mile in 13.65 seconds and 106.64 mph.

Since the W-31 cold air kit included the 4-4-2 suspension, it kept faith with the Oldsmobile philosophy that its supercars were to handle in the turns as well as they went on the straights. From this strong position, the W-31 went on to greater strength the following year. By virtue of new cylinder heads, larger valves, a wilder cam and smoother flow exhaust manifolds, the W-31 engine was worthy of a rating of 325 hp at 5400 rpm for 1969. With the model 300 Turbo Hydra-Matic, the W-31 needed only 6.6 seconds to travel from zero to 60 mph.

With GM forbidding its divisions to produce A-body cars with engines larger than 400 cubic inches, it was inevitable that someone outside the corporation would drop one of GM's super-size V-8's into the waiting engine bin of a 4-4-2. That someone turned out to be George Hurst. In 1966, Hurst had fabricated two special Oldsmobile ex-

hibition cars that probably reaped him (and Oldsmobile) ten times their cost in free and highly favorable publicity. One of the Hurst Olds was a 4-4-2 with twin 432 cid V-8 (425's with slight over bores) equipped with fuel injection and superchargers. The second creation was only slightly less outrageous: a 1966 Olds Cutlass with four wheel drive and two 425 cid Toronado engines.

The first Hurst effort in 1968 at marketing a limited production Hurst-Olds was, by contrast, a very modest venture, being in essence little more than a stock 4-4-2 with some minor detailing. The next year, however, it was quite a different story. A ''see me a mile away'' color scheme of gold on white, plus a big fiberglass hood scoop and a rear deck spoiler, made the Hurst-Olds 4-4-2 something far removed from a shrinking violet type of automobile. With its standard 400 cid V-8, the 4-4-2 was a performance heavyweight but the men from Hurst wanted even more. Out went the 400 V-8 and in came the 455 in Police Pursuit form with special cylinder heads, stronger valve springs and a wilder cam. Other changes included a recalibrated ignition, a better breathing intake manifold and new exhaust headers. All this coughed out 380 hp at 5000 rpm, good enough for zero to 60 mph times of 6.2 seconds and a 132 mph top speed.

Bad times were just around the bend but Oldsmobile ended the decade of glory with style. The W-31 continued with its 325 horsepower, ''select fit'' components, 308° duration high-lift cam and hydraulic lifters that could withstand 7000 rpm before floating. Both the W-31 and 4-4-2 (which received the 455 engine in 1970) could be equipped with the W-25 twin hood scoop/ram air option.

With few exceptions the high performance Oldsmobiles of the 1950-1970 time span were best remembered for their balance, good looks and for the good times they gave their owners and fans. Like the first Rocket 88 the 4-4-2 moved with class. Certainly not as blatant as some of its competitors it nevertheless was a superb supercar with class.

Below, 1970 Oldsmobile 4-4-2

Plymouth has been pulling some fast ones.

Or more accurately, specially equipped Plymouths, and some pretty good drivers have been really romping the last 12 months.

Plymouth, USAC Champ

Norm Nelson's and Paul Goldsmith's Hemi-Powered Belvederes wrapped up both 1st and 2nd place in the '65 USAC Stock Car Championship. (Jim Hurtubise's Plymouth was in 4th place, point standing.)

NASCAR: 13 starts—6 records

And Richard Petty. Although the Hemi-Powered Belvedere didn't run until July (then only on short tracks), Petty still racked up some fine finishes. Out of 13 starts, he took four 1sts, four 2nds and two 3rds. And qualified on the pole seven times . . . six of them with a new qualifying lap record. With this warmup, and NASCAR '66 rules allowing Hemi-Powered Plymouth Belvederes on the big tracks, watch out for Plymouth at Daytona.

NHRA's 11 Top Stockers

At the NHRA Winternationals the only cars to qualify for Top Stock Eliminator were 11 Plymouths! And Plymouth took nine class wins as well.

SCCA: 2 championships!

In the sports car world, Scott Harvey's Plymouth Barracuda carried him to his second consecutive Sedan-Class National Championship in SCCA road racing. While Dennis and Sally Koelmel drove their Plymouth Barracuda to the

SCCA National Rally Championship.

USAC-FIA world's record

And, in case you're interested in '66, there's the Bonneville record run made by a '66 Plymouth Belvedere. The Hemi-Powered Belvedere, completely showroom stock except for tires and pipes (and a healthy roll cage), made a USAC-FIA timed and sanctioned two-way flying mile run to average 156.35 mph for a new record in Class B, American closed stock cars.

Which about sums up Plymouth's winning ways to date. Oh yes, in

addition to our hot performers we do make a variety of economy and luxury cars in all lines—like VIP, Fury, Belvedere, Valiant and Barracuda.

So go to your Plymouth Dealer's and ask him to show you the '66s. It's worth the trip.

25. Plymouth

It was Labor Day, 1950. What had been, just months earlier, a cotton field outside of Darlington, South Carolina, had been transformed into a mile-and-a-quarter track for stock car racing, and the first Southern 500 was going full blast. Well, that might be somewhat of an exaggeration, but the Olds 88's, Fords and Cadillacs were mixing it up pretty good. Who won that race that really got NASCAR rolling? It was Johnny Mantz driving a 1950 Plymouth! That's right, a $1,700 Plymouth sedan with a 97 hp flathead six beneath its black hood.

A close look at the how and why of this Plymouth triumph reveals that Mantz won by using common sense rather than brute power. Yet, in those early NASCAR days Plymouths proved to be pretty rugged spear carriers. As far as any sort of real performance, Plymouth was the wheeled equivalent of the Invisible Man, though. Furthermore, Plymouth was having no trouble gaining a reputation as one of America's true blah cars. A conservative styling policy brought the Chrysler Corporation to the brink of disaster in 1954, but the following year it was turnabout time as the cars with "The Forward Look" made their debut.

In comparison with the roly-poly 1954 models, the new Plymouths, displaying the strong, undisguised influences of jet aircraft and sports cars, were a pleasure to look over. For those who were faithful to the venerable L-head six, it was still available with 117 hp for 1955, but, like Chevrolet, the big news from Plymouth engine-wise was its new V-8. Some 1954 Dodge truck owners had actually previewed Plymouth's Hy-Fire V-8 since it had been used in some late 1954 models with a rating of 145 hp and a displacement of 241 cid.

With over 65% of all 1955 Plymouths equipped with V-8's, its acceptance certainly exceeded the expectations of its designers but, not surprisingly, Chrysler still followed a conservative line in explaining the rationale behind the Plymouth V-8. For example, J. C. Zeder, director of engineering and research for Chrysler Corporation, commented early in the model year, "We are not seeking to develop higher speed and greater power than anyone else. The increased horsepower and torque in the 1955 Plymouth, when combined with the PowerFlite transmission, results in improved performance in low and middle ranges plus greater economy."

Yet, Plymouth, like just about every other manufacturer, wasn't immune to the influence of the horsepower race's stepped up tempo. And, although it was the last of the low priced three to do so, Plymouth was soon offering a power pack consisting of a four-barrel carburetor, special intake manifold and dual exhausts. This engine, rated 177 hp at 4400 rpm, had the same 260 cid as the 167 hp Super Hy-Fire V-8. The least powerful V-8, the Hy-Fire, displaced 241 cubic inches and developed 157 hp.

The Plymouth V-8's were not the performance equals of their Chevrolet adversaries but were roughly on a par with the Ford V-8's in acceleration. The typical 167 hp Plymouth with the 2-speed PowerFlite transmission ran from zero to 60 mph in approximately 14 seconds. The powerpack dropped this by a second or so, certainly not enough to worry any pilots of 180 hp Chevys.

Plymouth described its 1956 styling as having a "delta shape" which was, in retrospect, paving the way for the revolutionary look of the 1957 models. As far as its development into a performance car was concerned, a more important move was Plymouth's operation of a new "Qualimatic" engine plant turning out a virtually all-new 277 cubic inch V-8. Its ancestry obviously included the 260 V-8 of 1955, but with larger valves, better breathing ports and a more efficient combustion chamber (still called "polyspherical" by Plymouth) and mechanical lifters, it possessed far more potential. The zero to 60 mph time of 9.9 seconds still didn't make the 1956 Plymouth with its most powerful 200 hp engine the "Hot One" but it was getting warmer.

Plymouth's big breakthrough from its old, staid lifestyle came in January, 1956, at Daytona Beach. What better place was there in the U.S., with the possible exception of Bonneville, for Plymouth to turn loose its razzle-dazzle Fury model? Plymouth would have loved to have had the Fury compete in the February Speed Weeks but NASCAR required that any model with a new, larger displacement engine be available for a minimum of ninety days before it could be accepted for competition.

This technicality didn't prevent Plymouth from turning Phil Walters, of Cunningham racing fame, loose on the beach in a 3-speed Fury with a 3.54 axle. The results were impressive. The Fury broke the old record (80.428 mph, held by Cadillac) for the standing-start one mile with a speed of 82.54 mph. Through the flying mile, Walters' best run was 126.611 mph, with a two-way average of 123.440 mph. This easily shattered the year-old 112.295 mph mark set by a 1955 DeSoto. The Fury was Plymouth's strongest foray yet into the high performance zone and it wanted the whole world to know what it was all about. Thus, the deluxe Belvedere two-door hardtop which served as the Fury body was spruced up with gold-colored, anodized aluminum side trim and grille plus special wheel discs and Fury nameplates. Plymouth's interior designers came up with a gold and black interior motif for the Fury's seats and door panels which blended together quite well.

By boring and stroking its 277 cid V-8 to 303 cubic inches (using a single four-barrel carburetor with large jets and throats than that of the 200 hp V-8), a less restrictive exhaust system plus stronger valve springs and a 9.25:1 compression ratio, Plymouth was able to claim 240 hp at 4800 rpm and 310 lbs-ft of torque at 2800 rpm.

The first Fury, thanks to dearched rear leaf springs and shorter front coil springs, had both a lower center of gravity and a one inch lower height than other Plymouths. On the road, these changes, along with Oriflow shocks normally used on Chryslers, translated into a stiffer ride and the Fury's ability to take turns considerably faster than a normal Plymouth. *SPORTS CAR ILLUSTRATED* (May, 1956) observed, "The ride handed out by the Fury is totally different from that of any other Plymouth past or present. It is not stiff but neither is it soft or mushy. Firm would probably be the best description." Since the Fury's springs were about 45% stiffer than stock, "firm" was certainly an accurate description. The Fury's front drum brakes were of 11.5 inch by 2 inch dimensions. At the rear were 10 inch by 2 inch units borrowed from the 1956 Dodge. Total brake area was 173.5 square inches. With an F.O.B., Detroit, price of $2,832, the Fury was a good performance bargain. Most road tests of stick-shift Furys reported zero to 60 mph times of around 9 seconds and top speeds of 115.5 mph.

The sum total of the Fury's attributes was quite acceptable to *ROAD & TRACK,* which concluded after its road test, ''The Fury is a car which should not be dismissed lightly even by the sports car set. It does in fact have many sports car-like attributes over and above the performance which is truly 'furious' if not actually sensational.'' Sometimes *ROAD & TRACK's* reserve was just a little too much. After all, during the February Speed Weeks at Daytona, the same Fury that had mixed up the sand in January returned for an encore performance. During the interim it had spent some time in Detroit having its engine motivated to produce a few more horsepower. Once again, Phil Walters did the driving, and he did it well. Running in the experimental class, the Fury made a best one-way run of 143 mph and recorded a two-way average of 136.41 mph.

''Three years ahead . . . the only car that dares to break the time barrier!'' Thus proclaimed early ads for the 1957 Plymouth. Just exactly who was going to be eating Plymouth dust wasn't spelled out, but by implication, Plymouth obviously hoped it would be Brands ''C'' and ''F.'' Time and the rust worms haven't been kind to the 1957 Plymouths, but in their day they represented as radical a change as any postwar car has ever made. In their standard form, the new Plymouths were outstanding both in regard to their looks and cornering power. Cadillac may have been first, in '48, with fins, but the '57 Plymouth and its immediate antecedents took them about as far as they could go. As a result they became a passe styling theme very quickly, but it's important to realize that rear fender fins were a world-wide phenomenon, appearing on automobiles as diverse as Mercedes-Benz and Ferrari. Matched against the efforts of many imitators, the Plymouth appearance ranked with the best.

The icing on the cake was, of course, that outstanding torsion-bar suspension nestled beneath that provocative Virgil Exner-styled body. If such a thing as a postwar landmark in handling existed for American sedans, it was the 1957 Plymouth.

The high marks earned by the ''normal'' Plymouth were, however, totally eclipsed by the capabilities of the 1957 Fury. If it was true that you were three full years ahead when you drove a Plymouth, then you were three light years ahead when you drove a Plymouth Fury. This statement might be dismissed as mere hyperbole, but *MOTOR LIFE* (April, 1957) had no qualms declaring, ''This new Fury qualifies as a really outstanding road car . . . It stuck to the road so well that winding, curvy roads and mountainous stretches didn't slow it up.'' Racer Brown, of the *HOT ROD* editorial staff, came away from testing a Fury with equally impressed senses. At the conclusion of his runs, he wrote, ''I was ready to take on all comers to prove the Plymouth was the most roadable passenger car ever built in this country . . . After driving the Fury for over 1,500 miles, I'll say that there isn't a more roadable car that can be purchased in 'over-the-counter' form available in this country at any price.''

The basic essence of the Fury's potency was a careful refinement of a first class engineering job into an excellent performance machine. The Fury engine, for example, used the same 1.84 inch intake and 1.56 inch exhaust valves installed on all Plymouth V-8s but had a longer, 3.31 inch stroke that resulted in a 318 cubic inch displacement. From this point on, things became much more interesting. Dual four-barrel Carter carburetors were used along with a fairly radical cam and special, 9.25:1 compression ratio domed pistons. The result was 290 hp at 5400 rpm and 325 lbs-ft. of torque at 4000 rpm. The relatively high rev point where the Fury V-800 engine reached its peak torque output was its only serious shortcoming as a performance engine. A drag race between a Fury and a conventional Plymouth with a 235 hp, 301 cid V-8 saw the Fury trailing its subordinate for the first 100 feet. after that, the fury picked up steam, winning handily with a 16.30 second, 83.87 mph finish. Obviously, the Fury wasn't the quickest super stock, but with a 3-speed manual transmission and 3.54:1 axle it was a zero to 60 mph in 8.5 seconds automobile.

Although the total Fury package retailed for approximately $700 more than a comparable hardtop model, its performance components could be ordered for any Plymouth model for $290. Besides the 290 hp engine, the package included a heavy-duty frame, larger (1.09 inch instead of 1.04 inch) diameter front torsion bars and six, rather than five leaf rear springs.

The details of the Fury's brakes were less impressive. They were the same 11 inch by 2 inch units used by all Plymouths and the Fury needed better brakes. Fortunately, Plymouth did offer larger, 12 inch by 2½ inch ones as optional equipment.

By virtue of an all new body, not to mention the excellent TorqueFlite transmission, Plymouth made an extremely strong showing in 1957. Its sales success the following year was far less impressive; the down turn of the economy plus a backlash against the below par construction competence too common to Chrysler Corporation products took their toll upon Plymouth's 1958 sales.

Plymouth had the company of virtually all the Chrysler car line-up in watching its fortunes tumble during 1958, but in the performance category Plymouth was stronger than ever, thanks primarily to the brand new Golden commando engine. This V-8 with bore and stroke of 4 1/10 inches and 3⅜ inches yielding 350 cubic inches, was a derivative of what Chrysler called its ''B'' engine and was destined for a long and fruitful performance life. With a larger bore, similar versions were used in 1958 DeSoto and senior Dodge models which obviously helped Chrysler keep production costs low. Actually, economics was a major factor in the development of this engine. Many critics weren't terribly happy to see the Hemi V-8 bite the dust and be replaced by an engine with wedge-shaped combustion chambers, but with 1.95 inch intake and 1.60 inch exhaust valves, plus a healthy cam with lift of 0.390 inches, the Golden Commando had plenty of muscle, along with a weight of 630 pounds, some 120 less than the 331 Hemi's.

The standard engine for the '58 Fury was the ''Dual Fury V-800'' which, except for the new model Carter carburetors, was little changed from the 290 hp engine of a year earlier. The Golden Commando engine, also with two four-barrel Carter carbs and 10.0:1 compression ratio, was rated at 305 hp at 5000 rpm. In practice, valve float started near the 5000 rpm mark, but, on the other hand, peak torque of 370 lbs-ft was achieved at 3600 rpm, some 400 revs less than that of the Dual Fury V-800 engine. This feature wasn't an insignificant one. For example, *ROAD & TRACK* (March, 1958), which headlined its Fury road test with the admonition ''Sports cars, watch out'' noted, ''. . . the forte of this engine is its tremendous low speed flexibility and torque.'' *ROAD & TRACK* also praised the Golden Commando engine as ''Mechanically . . . an outstanding

piece of engineering.'' Either with 3-speed manual or TorqueFlite transmission, the 305 hp Fury consistently flirted with the 8 second mark in zero to 60 mph runs. This lusty acceleration was accompanied by the excellent road performance for which Plymouth had very quickly gained a reputation. Typical of assessments of the Plymouth's handling was this comment made by *MOTOR LIFE* (January, 1958): ''. . . the vehicle's greatest claim to fame is the positively magnificent roadability it offers. Indeed, the Plymouth is the best-handling sedan on the road today. It even surpasses many sports cars in this category.''

A will o'-the-wisp option for the '58 Fury was Bendix ''Electrojector fuel injection.'' When the 1958 Plymouths were first shown in the fall of '57, the Bendix system was touted as raising the Golden Commando's horsepower to 315. However, *HOT ROD* (January, 1958) reported, ''at this writing, the availability of these units is uncertain, and the price will probably stop most buyers from considering one.''

Hurting Plymouth sales once again was the low level of its workmanship. Misaligned moldings and loose bits and pieces of interior trim were even more glaring examples of incompetence when they showed up on a luxury prestige car such as the Fury.

''America's greatest sports-luxury car has now become a complete line at new low prices!'' Thus spoke Plymouth as it attempted to exploit, and thus inevitably dilute, the Fury image. Now Furys were four-door hardtops and sedans and somehow that didn't quite square with the original Fury formula. All was not lost, however, for at the top of the Fury lineup were a two-door hardtop and convertible identified as Sport Furys. Plymouth was in the last phase of its three year style cycle and, hoping to keep its appearance from being too old hat-ish, its stylists gave it a pretty thorough face lift. Like the earlier '57 and '58 models, the new Plymouth's weakest point was a rather undistinguished front end. It always seemed strange that Chrysler's designers could create such fluid and dynamic profiles and rear decks but fail so miserably when it came to front grillework.

Above, 1958 Plymouth Fury

A quick look under the Sport Fury hood suggested retrogression was taking place in performance. Its base engine was a 260 hp, 318 cid V-8 based on the old 1955 polyspherical model. The optional Golden Commando, bored out an additional 0.060 inches to 4.12 inches and with the same 3.38 inch stroke, now had a 361 cubic inch displacement. However, no matter how hard anyone looked they would find only one four-barrel carburetor attached to the Golden Commando engine. The dropping of the dual-carb option wasn't as bad as it appeared since both the '58 and '59 engines were rated at 305 hp and the newer version produced more torque (395 to 375 lbs-ft) at a lower (3000 to 3600) rpm mark. Similarly, the 1959 Golden commando reached its maximum horsepower at 4600 rpm whereas the older engine peaked at 5000 rpm.

Plymouth reduced the length of the front torsion bars on its 1959 models by 2 inches and added a front stabilizer bar. These two changes left its handling virtually unchanged. For the Fury the factory ''Firm-Ride'' option consisting of heavier front torsion bars, stronger rear springs and heavy-duty shocks was well worth the investment.

Automotive history has tended to banish the 1960 Plymouths into the dark realms of outer space, dismissing their ultra-fins as nothing less than a bad expression of a dated styling cliche. Since Chrysler Corporation was then sinking into one of its all-too-frequent, self-imposed depressions, they certainly don't stand out as super sales phenomenons.

Yet there was more—much more—to the high performance Plymouths of 1960. Chrysler, by making an abrupt change of pace the next year, didn't make it easy to defend the fins of '60 but, even so, there were worse looking cars on the road than the '60 Plymouth.

In the matter of workmanship, the new Plymouths exhibited substantial improvement over earlier models. The sloppy, almost haphazard assembly so common on '57 and later Plymouths was a very serious impediment to Plymouth's attempt to expand sales in the '60's. ''Ever since the '1960' models of 1957,'' wrote *MOTOR LIFE* (December, 1959), ''Plymouth has been plagued by assembly faults. Sheet metal did not fit properly, accessories failed to work and minor trim attachments would even fall

off. This has been the most serious problem on what, otherwise, was one of the best engineered cars in America.''

The '60 models weren't perfect, but there was lots of evidence that Chrysler was trying to build them better. The best part of the Plymouth story for 1960 was that Plymouth was building them *a lot* hotter. For 1960, there were five very strong engines to choose from: two based on the 361 cid engine and a trio of 383's. Lowest engine on the performance pole was the 361 cid Golden Commando V-8 with one four-barrel, 10.0:1 compression ratio and 305 hp. Then came, said Plymouth, ''America's first production ram induction engine, the 361 cid SonoRamic Commando V-8.'' Since the principles of ram-induction were reviewed in regard to the Chrysler 300, there's no need to retrace them here. Instead, let's just look at the SonoRamic's specifications. With two four-barrels sitting out in left and right field on top of those long intake tubes, and 10.1 compression ratio, it developed only 5 more horsepower at 4800 rpm than the base Golden Commando V-8, but this was deceptive since the ram engine pumped out 435 lbs-ft of torque at just 2800 rpm, considerably more than the Golden Commando's 395 at 3000 rpm. The result was a very quick Plymouth. With TorqueFlite and 3.31:1 rear axle, its zero to 60 mph time was 7.5 seconds. The quarter-mile statistics were 15.6 seconds and 90 mph.

If this wasn't enough, then all you had to do was to step up to your Plymouth dealer and request a special order of 383 muscle tonic power in any one of three stages of potency. The SonoRamic 383 with twin four-barrels pounded out 325 hp at 4600 rpm. Interestingly, its torque rating was identical to the 361 ram V-8.

At the NHRA National Drag Championships held in Detroit on Labor Day, 1960, a 330 hp Fury with TorqueFlite and a 4.10 axle won the Super Stock Automatic Class with a best run of 15.34 seconds/98.25 mph.

Two 383 cid Golden Commando V-8's rounded out the tribe of potent Plymouth engines. The first, with a single four-barrel carried 325 hp and 435 lbs-ft credits. Finally, a 383 fitted with a runner-type manifold and dual four-barrel carburetors checked in with 330 hp at 5200 rpm and 425 lbs-ft of torque at 3600 rpm. This engine was the best Plymouth mustered up for high rpm competition. Whereas the 383 Sonoramic's power started to drop off above 4800 rpm, this engine continued flexing its biceps.

Although Plymouth had access to Chrysler's new 3-speed manual transmission, only the single carburetor Golden Commando was available with stick shift. All the other big engines were linked to a beefed-up TorqueFlite with increased oil pressure to assure rapid shifts under full throttle.

For under $30, the big 12 inch diameter brakes used on the Chrysler 300 were available on any of the 1960 Plymouths. Chrysler had softened the Plymouth's suspension for 1960, but for under $10 the good old days of outstanding Plymouth roadability could be back for an instant replay. The heroes, available on special order, included heavy-duty shocks, torsion bars and springs identical to those used on Plymouth police cars.

An interesting version of the ram-tuned 383 that almost, but didn't, make it into production used the solid lifter cam of the 400 hp, 413 cid Chrysler 300-F engine. Unfortunately, shortly after the February, 1960, Daytona Speed Weeks, Plymouth decided not to offer such an engine. It did, However, make some runs at Daytona driven by Paul O'Shea. With a 2.93 axle, it was clocked at over 147 mph. Later, a 3.31 axle was installed (Plymouth offered eight different rear axles ranging from 2.93 to 4.89). On the dragstrip, its best effort was 15.0 seconds/95.64 mph.

Plymouth abandoned fins with a vengence in 1962, turning instead to the experimental XNR roadster for its styling inspiration. The result wasn't all that pleasing and probably the best to be said about the look of the '61 Plymouth was that it was original. (so were the looks of the

Above, 1962 Plymouth Sport Fury

Cyclops that gave Odysseus and his buddies such a hard time!)

Only very minor adjustments were made in the power department for 1961. The 383 Golden Commando with dual carburetors, for example, was slightly boosted in power to 340 hp. Late in the year, a few Plymouths were shipped out with Chrysler 413 engines rated at either 350 or 375 hp.

Strange things happened to Plymouth in 1962. Nowhere to be found were 413 V-8's or even 383's, much less ram-induction manifolds. Along with improved looks, the new Plymouth was considerably smaller than the 1961 version. Wheelbase was cut two inches to 116 and overall length dropped to 202 inches from 209.5 inches. None of these changes were, in themselves, detrimental to Plymouth, indeed, most were positive steps, but they seemed to augur decline for Plymouth's position among the supercars. There was a bit of the old thunder lacking, no doubt about that. However, a Sport Fury with the top engine available (a 305 hp, 315 cid V-8 and a new redesigned TorqueFlite transmission) was no slouch; zero to 60 mph in 7.7 seconds was still rapid transit. In the turns, thanks to smaller (by one inch) torsion bars, there was more lean, but the Sport Fury was still an excellent road car. "Up in the mountains," claimed *MOTOR TREND* (April, 1962), "it will take an awfully good driver in an awfully good import to pass an equally good driver in the Sports Fury."

Plymouth soon realized that the decision to go with a 350 cid engine in the midst of a very rough and tough power struggle was akin to the old "are you going to send the kid up in a crate like that?" act and brought back the 330 hp, 383 cid engine option for 1963. This was welcome news but it only took a quick run down some twisty pavement to discover that changes for 1963 included more than new

Below, 1963 Plymouth Belvedere

sheet metal and a resurrected 383. In their desire for Plymouth to compete more effectively with Chevrolet, Chrysler management had latched onto the soft ride of the GM products as a key sales advantage. All that was needed to give Plymouth a similar attribute was to throw away a front suspension bar, and soften up the shocks. The result? A bouncy ride, sloppy handling and an abandonment of a great heritage. "Although the car goes down the road like a shot with its tremendous in-and-out of traffic acceleration," remarked *CAR LIFE* (February, 1963), "it lacks the fineness of handling so necessary to maintain safety at speed . . . Plymouth, heretofore, has been rated as one of the best handling domestic vehicles. The '63 doesn't seem to continue the tradition, unfortunately."

This type of follow-the-leader-even-if-what-he's-doing-is-dumb was doubly unfortunate because in other areas Plymouth was honing its performance capabilities to a fine edge. The outstanding Warner T-10 4-speed transmission was now available and, with Plymouth sharing the Super Sport 426 engine with Dodge, its competitiveness in drag racing took a quantum jump forward. Early in 1963, Plymouth (along with Dodge) made a lightweight drag-package available. Consisting of an aluminum hood, front fenders, stone shields and front bumpers, it reduced ready to race weight to just over 3,200 pounds. At the 1963 NHRA National Championships, the muscular Mopars with these body components and the 426 S/S engines were the dominant contenders in super stock competition. A TorqueFlite Plymouth had the low stock elapsed time, 11.95 seconds, of the meet and another Plymouth with 3-speed manual transmission had the top trap speed of all the super stocks: 119.1 mph.

It was also a year of triumph for Plymouth in stock car competition. USAC awarded its Manufacturers trophy to Plymouth for winning more USAC-sanctioned, late-model

races during 1963 than any other make. Of 16 races, Plymouth won 6, and finished second 7 times. Added to these achievements was a record of setting the fastest qualifying times in 6 different races. NASCAR's championship was won by Joe Weatherly with a Pontiac but Plymouth's Richard Petty had scored more firsts than any other driver.

In the history of high performance American cars, there were many, perhaps innumerable, moments of glory and greatness, but future researchers will be hard pressed to find a twelve-month time span that matched 1964 for sheer sensationalism. It was the year of the first Mustang and the year of the first Pontiac GTO, but if brute horsepower was the prime mover of the age then the event that counted for the most was Daytona, 1964. Brock Yates called it "one of the most stunning automotive debuts in recent racing history" and there was only one engine that Yates could be talking about, the Hemi 426.

Ford came to Daytona riding the crest of its Total Performance campaign. At the conclusion of racing on that dark (for Ford) February 23, an awful lot of buttons (compliments of Plymouth) reading "Total What?" were being displayed in the pits.

On the eve of the race, reports were rife about Plymouth and Dodge cars that had lapped the Goodyear five mile track at San Angelo, Texas, in excess of 180 mph. One of the key men in the Chrysler venture at Daytona was Ray Nichels, the highly regarded racing mechanic from Highland, Indiana. In October, he had been introduced to the Hemi in high style at San Angelo by Paul Goldsmith who gave him a 185 mph ride around the course. After the Daytona 500, Nichels recalled, "It was a tough secret to keep. We knew we had something that should go better than anything that had ever run at Daytona many weeks before the race, but . . . few of us realized just how strong it would really prove to be on the race track."

Ford put up a strong front of optimism but this mood turned very gloomy once the Plymouths of Richard Petty and Paul Goldsmith started lapping unofficaly at 175 mph. Gloom turned to foreboding, to a sense of impending rout once the qualification runs were completed. The first *five* qualifiers, led by Goldsmith's Plymouth at 174.91 mph, were either Dodges or Plymouths and the fastest Ford (Marvin Panch, at 167.068 mph) was qualifier number 8. Fred Lorenzen tried to sound positive prior to the race's start, remarking, "We've proved our endurance, and that's a new engine they've got. It doesn't count unless you make 500 miles." Up to the 1964 Daytona 500, Ford had won 10 straight 500-or-more-miles stock car races. Thus, Lorenzen did have a point . . . but not that day. A. J. Foyt's Ford proved the only Dearborn product capable of running with the Hemi and he went out ignominiously on lap 129 when his engine blew up. Plymouth went on to sweep the first three places.

New model introductions tend to be more pomp than substance but it wasn't that way when Paul C. Ackerman, Chrysler's engineering vice-president, did the honors for the Hemi . . . "The new Chrysler 400-plus horsepower engines," he explained, "have a number of outstanding design features which result in greatly improved performance potential especially for sanctioned competitive racing events . . . our engineers," continued Ackerman, "have been able to combine effectively the best features of all our past, present and even experimental designs into this engine and have obtained outstanding results." Indeed, the new Chrysler engine was so outstanding that Ackerman

reported, "existing dynamometer and equipment just didn't have enough capacity for the new engines. . . Included in the new testing equipment are engine dynamometers which can absorb 600 horsepower at 10,000 rpm."

Plymouth labeled the Hemi the Super-Commando and then released output information that was ludicrously conservative. Drag racing Super-Commandos were available with either 11.0 or 12.5:1 compression ratios. The former had a rating of 415 hp at 6000 rpm and 470 lbs-ft torque at 4600 rpm. The 12.5:1 engine's respective outputs were 425 hp and 480 lbs-ft. All drag racing Hemis carried dual four-barrel carburetors with ram-tuned manifolds and were available with either TorqueFlite or manual 4-speed transmissions. The track version, having to comply of course to NASCAR regulations, was delivered with a single four-barrel mounted on a dual-level intake manifold. Its ratings with 12.5:1 compression ratio were 400 hp at 5600 rpm and 465 lbs-ft or torque at 3800 rpm. The only transmission available was the 4-speed manual.

Obviously, an engine of this size, with hemispherical combustion chambers, dual rocker arms and huge 2.25 inch intake and 1.94 inch exhaust valves positioned on opposite sides of the combustion chambers was much stronger. At the bare minimum, 500 honest horsepower was attained by the 426 Hemi without really breathing hard.

The Hemi wasn't available for use on the street in 1964. This situation didn't sit well with NASCAR and led to the eventual pull-out of Chrysler from NASCAR competition the following year. Plymouth's hottest street machine, the 426-R engine was a detuned version of the earlier 426-S engine and shared many components such as heads, intake and exhaust manifolds, crank and rods with the old 413 engine. Its rather mild, 268° duration, cam and hydraulic lifters and 365 hp at 4800 rpm made it both a tractable and potent street engine. With a new Chrysler-built 4-speed manual transmission, it was a fine performer, reporting in with a zero to 60 mph time of 6.8 seconds plus quarter-mile marks of 95 mph and 15.2 seconds.

The 426-R package included a Hurst shifter, 11 inch brakes, plus a heavy-duty suspension system that enabled a 426-R Plymouth to substantially out-corner a normal Plymouth.

In terms of performance, 1965 was a year of status quo for Plymouth. The 365 hp, 426 cid V-8 continued as the most potent engine for street use and the Hemi continued in its two basic forms for competition purposes. In terms of the age of high performance, this was the dawn before the finest hour. Even in automotive history, the past is prelude, a preparation for greatness, the preliminary events before the main bout, a climax of evolution leading to perfection, the peak from which only decline could follow.

They called it the Satellite Street Hemi — simple and to the point. There was no need for numerical superlatives or for that matter, anything else. Some critics took it upon themselves to find fault with the less than heart throbbing appearance of the Satellite, but who cared? Plymouth sharpened up its styling the next year but the 426 Hemi would have made history even if Plymouth had stuffed i into a resurrected facsimile of a Henry J. The bottom line of the entire matter of how appropriate the lines of the Plymouth Satellite were for a performance car was simply this if it carried a little plaque on its lower front fender panel reading "426 Hemi," and if its hood sported a 426 hood ornament, then you had better look quickly because a Plymouth such as that could perform one of the fastest disappearing acts in the world. The price of the Street Hemi

was a healthy $907.60 but this didn't deter the sale of 1,826 Street Hemis during 1966.

Chrysler explained that "vehicles powered by the 426 Hemi were developed for a growing market of new car buyers — especially those who maintain an active interest in sanctioned, off-highway timed trials." A press release such as that differed little from those of other manufacturers who were in tune with the times but the power behind the words was, in this case, extra special. After all, it wasn't everyday that a true racing engine found its way into an American production automobile. There were, of course, changes necessary to make the Hemi streetable. The ram-type magnesium intake manifold was replaced by an aluminum, non-ram model with Carter 4139S and 4140S carburetors instead of the R3116 Holley racing models. The cylinder heads on both Hemis were of identical design. Those of the racing engine were aluminum, while the street version's were cast-iron. To make for a more tractable engine, a cam with less duration was used along with a drop in compression ratio to 10.25:1. All Street Hemis were assembled in "hands-on" fashion by Chrysler's Marine/ Industrial Division and were rated at 425 hp at 5000 rpm and 490 lbs-ft of torque at 4000 rpm.

Not surprisingly, it was virtually impossible to bad-mouth the Street Hemis' ability to fly down a straight line. Few American automobiles in modern times have been such an impressive performer as a 116 inch wheelbase Plymouth Satellite powered by the Hemi. *CAR AND DRIVER* (April, 1966) described it as "the best combination of brute performance and tractable street manners we've ever driven." Although Chrysler had further compromised its reputation for handling integrity in 1966 by softening the suspension of all its products, the Street Hemis were reasonably immune from the decadent results. The Hemi package included a heavy-duty suspension package of 0.92 inch diameter front torsion bars and high rate rear springs. These goodies notwithstanding, the bloom was really off the lily as far as

Above, 1966 Plymouth hemi-powered Belvedere

Plymouth handling was concerned. The Hemi put an awful lot of pounds on the Satellite's front wheels and, as *CAR LIFE* (July, 1966) noted, "Cornering briskly on a rural roadway induced a degree of body lean and tire protest out of keeping with other aspects of the car's behavior." The brakes included in the Hemi package were also disappointing. They were identical to the heavy-duty police brake option with 11 inch drums and metallic linings. Although they were the largest brakes available on any Detroit sedan, what the Hemi really needed were the Kelsey-Hayes front disc brakes available on the larger Plymouths. Acceleration of a 4-speed Street Hemi was, to put it mildly, sufficient to suitably impress both its advocates and harshest critics. *CAR AND DRIVER* (April, 1966) reported the following performance data attained with a 4-speed Satellite Hemi equipped with a 3.54 rear axle: 0-60 mph, 5.3 seconds; 0-100 mph, 12.8 seconds; standing start ¼ mile, 104 mph/ 13.8 seconds.

The shock waves emanating from the Street Hemi had barely stopped shaking the needles off seismographs around the nation when Plymouth set off another performance earthquake, the 1967 GTX. Like the Satellite, it was available with Hemi power, but its standard engine was the Super-Commando 440, a producer of 375 hp and 480 lbs-ft of torque.

The 440 wedge engine had been an option for Plymouth, Dodge and Chrysler in 1966 and was a derivative of the "B" type engine which had also been produced in 361, 383, 413 and 426 cubic inch variations. In a more mundane form, the 440 was available in the Plymouth Fury with a 350 hp rating. Both this version and the GTX's Super-Commando shared the same 10.1:1 compression, 2.08 inch intake valves and similar, but not identical, four-barrel carburetors. The GTX engine derived its additional power via a cam with higher lift, longer duration and greater overlap, larger exhaust valves (1.76 inch diameter to 1.60 inch) and stiffer valve springs that pushed the point of valve float up 200 rpm. Other enticing features of the Super Commando included a dual exhaust system devoid of resonators and an unsilenced air cleaner.

Like the Satellite Street Hemi, the GTX had high-rate torsion bars and heavy-duty shocks that moved *CAR AND DRIVER* (November, 1966) to describe the GTX as having "one of the best-handling sedan chassis we have ever driven."

Obviously, the Hemi was a stronger engine than the 440 Wedge but the Super-Commando did have several attributes that made it a very viable alternative. For one thing, it was almost $600 lower in price than the Hemi and carried a 5 year/50,000 mile warranty, whereas the Hemi came with only a 12 month/12,000 mile Chrysler back up. An acceleration match race between a GTX/Hemi and a 440/GTX was close. The Hemi was almost always the winner but, thanks to the 440's better torque at lower engine speeds, it was the leader up to about 100 mph. With TorqueFlite and a 3.23 axle, the 375 hp GTX accelerated from zero to 60 mph in 6 seconds, to 100 mph in 15.1 seconds and concluded the quarter-mile with a speed of 98 mph. "In approaching the Plymouth GTX," wrote *CAR LIFE* (March, 1967), "the car enthusiast is likely to find a great deal to appreciate. Along with the outstanding mechanical features, the car has a tailored sort of no-nonsense styling which distinctly parts it from other, more rounded members of Super Car ilk." Since 12,108 GTX's were sold during 1967, there were obviously many enthusiasts who had similar sentiments.

And there was still more to come. Plymouth callled it "The Missing Link." *MOTOR TREND* called it "the simplest, starkest, most brazenly pure, non-compromising super car in history." *CAR LIFE* considered its interior to be a carbon copy of a taxicab's. Supposedly, its initial recorded sale was to a 44-year old Midwesterner who bought it for his wife. He was the first of 44,599 people who went down to their friendly, local Plymouth dealer and said, "Make mine a Road Runner."

Necessity, it's pretty much agreed, is the mother of invention. Translated into the world of hairy-chested automobiles, that old adage reads something like this: If you want to outdo Chevrolet, build yourself a better supercar.

In essence, the rationale behind the Road Runner was so simple it's a wonder no one thought of it before. Well, actually they had, if you want to dismiss the Road Runner as just a Plain Jane, two-door sedan packing a throbbing, heart-stopping V-8 up front. But to regard the Road Runner in such simplistic terms is to miss the whole point, for it was a car with as expressive a character as any Detroit-built power machine. Like its cartoon namesake, it was homely, but on the cute side, endowed with a unique personality and very quick on the road.

Back in 1966, *CAR LIFE* had inadvertently anticipated the Road Runner when, after testing a Plymouth Satellite with a 383 V-8, it commented, "Most other models in Plymouth's Belvedere line are lower in weight, so the really ambitious enthusiast could save at least 200 lbs. by ordering a 'stripped' 2-door sedan." However, such a Plymouth would have been at best a primitive version of the real thing.

The Road Runner's standard engine was the 383 cid version of Chrysler's veteran B-engine, but it was quite different than the 383's used in other Chrysler Corporation cars. Whereas other 383's were rated at 290, 300 or 330 hp, the Road Runner's provided 335 hp at 5200 rpm. Torque was a wholesome 425 lbs-ft at a low 3400 rpm. Plymouth had reached into its parts inventory for the Road Runner 383's heads and cams. Plymouth followers were quick to recognize them as those of the 440 cid Super-Commando

V-8. Also borrowed from the Super-Commando were the Road Runners' crankcase windage tray, dual exhausts and unsilenced air cleaners. The latter piece of equipment roosted on a Carter four-barrel with 1.44 inch primaries and secondaries whose home was a large, runner-type intake manifold. *CAR AND DRIVER* (January, 1968) described this engine as being "as strong as any stock 440 we've driven." The 383 Road Runner's performance came close to supporting this slightly optimistic judgment. Standard transmission for the Road Runner was a manual 4-speed, which, with a 3.55 axle, provided zero to 60 mph times of 7.1 seconds. It was no problem at all to finish the quarter-mile in 15 seconds flat at 96 mph. The Street Hemi was available in the Road Runner, making it, said *CAR LIFE* (May, 1968), "the fastest stock machine on the strip." For day in, day out street use, however, the untemperamental 383 Road Runner engine really was a better choice. For those who had a hyper-appetite for muscle machines, the 1968 GTX with its 375 hp, 440 cid V-8 was a nice step up the ladder. Like the Road Runner, it could be had with the Hemi, but at an additional $604.75 over the price of a 440 GTX.

Maybe it was because *MOTOR TREND* wasn't sure it should take a car with "beep-beep" horns seriously that it decided to wait until 1969 to declare the Road Runner "Car of the Year." The "basic concept of simplicity and low price," said *MOTOR TREND*, "is what makes it a winner." Eric Dahlquist, *MOTOR TREND* technical editor wrote at length about the Road Runner's special atributes. "The idea of an inexpensive, high-performance car was not completely original," he noted, adding, "other manufacturers have built them before. Plymouth's master stroke was the all encompassing scope of their thrust — the cartoon character, beep-beep horn, decals, jackets, ad campaign, Sox & Martin drag clinics, all of it. It was the first time a company offered not just a car, but a mood: The Road Runner is . . . the car to have if you feel or are young."

The mood was mellowing but Plymouth's best shot came just as the curtain started to slip down on the American automobile's greatest years of performance. The 440 engine for the GTX showed up with triple Holley two-barrel carburetors in 1969. A year later the Road Runner was also offered with this 390 hp engine. The Hemi, doomed to die after 1971, was fitted with hydraulic lifters for 1970, in order, said Chrysler staff engineer Tom Hoover, to both make it a cleaner running engine and to relieve "one giant hemi headache, serviceability."

Then came the Superbird, close relative to the Dodge Charger Daytona, descendent of Furys, Road Runners and GTX's, fearless challenger of Fords and Mercurys on the NASCAR Supertracks and the winner of 38 Grand National during the 1970 NASCAR racing season. Like the Hemi the Charger Daytona/Superbird was a purebred racing design, a technical *tour de force*. Regrettably, the Super bird, like the original 426 Hemi, was too good for the NASCAR authorities who were more interested in main taining an atmosphere of keen competition than encourag ing innovation and dramatic technical advances in racing car design. Thus NASCAR effectively eliminated them as competitive cars by forcing them to run with small 305 ci engines.

Chrysler was backing away from racing in 1971 and with the demise of the Hemi after that year, the days when Plymouth offered breathtaking production cars that were just a step away from being race cars became fond memories, the best perhaps of the Golden Years.

26. Plymouth Barracuda

Somewhere, back there in all the dust kicked up by the Mustang early in 1964, was America's second pony car, the Plymouth Barracuda. Right from the start it found the going rough. Criticism came from bad mouthers who didn't like Chrysler customizing a Valiant and calling the result a "spectacular new fastback." More nasty remarks were forthcoming from those who never liked fastbacks anyway and were even less enamored by the Barracuda's 14.4 square feet rear window! The Barracuda, when bedecked with its triple black racing stripe, looked, said *CAR LIFE* (June, 1965) "not unlike a giant Easter egg . . . (it was) a near miss in the aesthetic department." *CAR AND DRIVER* (March, 1968) retrospectively joined the fishmongers by describing the Barracuda as "a car that was hurried into production and showed it, ending up looking more like a beached whale than its namesake."

Admittedly, the Barracuda was: (1), an automobile that was a stop-gap, quickly conceived response to the Mustang, and (2), from the beltline down (except for a slightly different grille) a Valiant inside and out. But, were either of these attributes exactly criminal offenses? The Valiant set the handling standard for American compact cars back in 1960 and who could ever forget that memorable day at Daytona in 1961. The ram-inducted Valiant had it all over its competition taking the top six positions in one of the early compact car races. In 1963, the first V-8 Valiant appeared and, while that in itself wasn't terribly startling, Chrysler's willingness to enter the 273 cid V-8 Valiants in that year's Monte Carlo was, at the least, commendable. The Valiant didn't win but one driven by Scott Harvey did earn a third place class ribbon, setting fastest time in one of the speed tests around the Grand Prix circuit. Now maybe none of this put the Valiant into the Mercedes class but it certainly wasn't a heritage the Barracuda had to hide under a bushel. Similarly, while it would have been more to Chrysler's credit to have parted with the pennies and dolled up the Barracuda with a spiffier set of metal work, it was hardly unique among the pony cars in sharing much in common with a far more mundane family compact car.

After taking a look at the base Mustang's $2,368 sticker, Chrysler chose to undersell the Ford sporty car by the grand total of $3. This pricing strategy was interesting. A Valiant Signet hardtop was priced $109 less than the basic six-cylinder Barracuda but the Barracuda had many items as standard equipment that were optional on the Valiant. Thus, Plymouth was probably forced by Ford into either accepting a lower profit margin on each Barracuda or be faced with an unfavorable pricing position vis-a-vis the Mustang.

The first Barracudas started appearing in Plymouth showrooms early in May, 1964, and even the strongest Mopar advocate went away just a little disappointed after giving them the once-over. Neither the standard 170 cid, 101 hp or the larger 225 cid, 145 hp slant six offered sufficient power to move the Barracuda at an acceleration rate acceptable for admission into the school of high performance. Things appeared more hopeful for Barracudas powered by the 180 hp, 273 cid V-8 and fitted with the $179.20, 4-speed transmission featuring a Hurst linkage. Chrysler had derived the 273 engine from the larger, 318 cid V-8 and had first offered it in the spring of 1963. One of its

best features, aside from untemperamental behavior, was the 273's low weight, some 55 pounds less than the 318 and only 50 pounds more than the less powerful 225 six. The V-8 Barracuda provided modest performance of zero to 60 mph in 11 seconds. Not enough, obviously, to inspire a Beach Boys top-forty song but enough, along with decent handling, to serve as a springboard into better times.

Anyone who got seasick looking at the Barracuda would suffer for another two years but even its harshest critics had to recognize the 1965 and 1966 Barracudas as vastly improved over the first model. "It handles like a champ," said *MOTOR TREND* (January, 1965). *CAR LIFE* (June, 1965) cast its vote the same way, declaring that the Barracuda "can be flailed through corners as quickly as most out-and-out sports cars."

The key to these magazines' hearts was the "Rallye Suspension" portion of the Barracuda's "S" performance package. To say the Barracuda benefited from this option was classic understatement at its best. Plymouth engineers claimed a Barracuda S would experience less than 3 degrees of roll in a 0.3 G turn thanks to larger, 0.87 inch front torsion bars and anti-sway bars plus 6, instead of the normal 4.5, rear leaf springs. Also contributing to the Barracuda's surefootedness were Goodyear's Blue Streak racing tires mounted on 14 x 5.5 J rims.

The effectiveness of this suspension was attested to both by motoring publications and Barracuda owners. *POPULAR MECHANICS* (April, 1966) noted in its Barracuda Owner's Report, "Many with the Formula S package were especially pleased with handling." *MOTOR TREND* (February, 1966) added to the chorus of enthusiasm about the Barracuda's road manners, reporting, "Cornering is the 'Cuda's' forte." Certainly leaving no doubt about the Barracuda's strength in this category was Scott Harvey's successful quest of the 1966 SCCA National Rally Championship with the Team STAR-FISH Barracuda.

After having been dusted off by a Barracuda S in the turns, drivers of ye olde and out of date British-built two-seaters seldom had a chance to focus their eyes on its backside. The explanation for the Barracuda's rapid straight line action was its worked over and warmed up 273 V-8. By virtue of a high-lift cam, dome shaped 10.5:1 pistons, solid lifters, dual breaker points and a Carter AFB four-barrel carburetor, the Barracuda now had 235 horsepower at 5200 rpm. Moreover, the 273 V-8 didn't run out of breath as it reached its power peak, happily revving instead up to 6000 rpm. The Barracuda, with this engine, achieved a zero to 60 mph time of 8.0 seconds.

Included in the $258 S-pack were larger, 10 inch drum brakes instead of the smaller 9 inch versions used on the six-cylinder Barracudas. Availability of these brakes was a step in the right direction but an even better choice were the front disc brakes provided as a dealer installed option. Incidentally, Scott Harvey not only contributed to the Barracuda's development through his rally successes but assisted in the creation of the S-package which was first tested on a Valiant known as the "Red Snapper" in 1962.

One of the most memorable features of the Formula S Barracuda was its low back pressure exhaust system with super-sized outlets. "What must be the loudest muffler

system on any production car,'' said a suitably impressed *CAR LIFE* (June, 1965), ''produces a rumbling reminiscent of a runabout and a Rice Krispies overrun: Snap, Crackle and Pop!'' Alas, this system was soon toned down to a decibel level somewhat less likely to arouse the interests of the highway patrol.

Thanks to the S type suspension and the vitality of Chrysler's 273 V-8, the Barracuda had quickly moved away from the status of just another cutesy, little hardtop into an automobile without any American counterpart. This is not to say that comparison with the 271 hp Mustang was not valid. Obviously, their prices and general similarities made tire-to-tire reviews inevitable, but the Barracuda's greater length and wheelbase, plus fastback design, made it one of the very first sports-station wagons, and suggested that, rather than being regarded as a Mopar-Mustang, the Barracuda deserved recognition as a car with its own unique character. In other words, it was inferior to the Mustang on some points but scored higher in other areas. *CAR LIFE* (June, 1965) hit on this spot, describing the Formula S Barracuda as ''more nearly a sports sedan than others being built in Detroit today.''

From this viewpoint, the only major weakness of the Barracuda was its appearance. Marginally attractive to begin with, it had pretty much shot its bolt by the end of the 1966 model year, but relief arrived in super fashion the following year. As it had done on previous occasions, Chrysler with the 1967 Barracuda aptly demonstrated it could — when moved by the spirit — match the best efforts of the Ford and GM styling studios. If the first Barracudas invited comparisons with super-sized Easter eggs, their replacements suffered no such humiliations. Chrysler was quick to point out that, ''It doesn't look like the others. If anything, Barracuda was styled after cars like Ferrari and Aston Martin (which is hardly a bad tradition to follow).'' Indeed, it wasn't and, in the Barracuda's appearance, overtones of the Ferrari 250GT 2+2 and the Aston Martin DB4 were subtly blended with a degree of good taste that pleased almost everyone. Chrysler still didn't envision the

Barracuda outselling the Mustang but, with convertible and notchback models joining the fastback version in 1967, it was apparent that it intended to pump up Barracuda's sales. (Although the Barracuda now matched the Mustang in body styles, its longer, 108 inch wheelbase, and 2 inch wider body actually extended the design distance between the two cars. At 192.8 inches the Barracuda was the longest of the pony cars. More than ever, the Barracuda was a sports sedan, a true American grand tourer. By moving its front wheels forward 2 inches, Plymouth's engineers improved the Barracuda's weight distribution. The wider body and chassis also brought with it a 2 inch wider front tread.)

All the good things from the earlier model such as the S package (which now included front disc brakes and, in place of the Goodyear Blue Streak tires, used Firestone D70-14 wide oval super sports) and the great 235 hp, 273 V-8 were carried over into 1967. Joining the engine lineup was a 280 hp version of Chrysler's long-lived 383 V-8. This engine, with TorqueFlite, increased the Barracuda's road-weight by 265 pounds. When a 4-speed manual trans-mission was used, the weight penalty was reduced to just 140 pounds. In either case, the impact upon the Barracuda's handling was minimal. Due to the 1967's longer wheelbase, use of the 650 pound 383 V-8 altered front-rear weight distribution by just 0.2% as compared to a 1966 model with the 273 V-8.

Be this as it may, use of the 383 engine as a Barracuda powerplant made little sense after 1968 when the 340 cid V-8 became available. Along with the various configura-tions of Chevrolet's 265 V-8 and the Mustang Boss 302 V-8, this engine ranks as one of the great medium dis-placement V-8's of the performance age. *MOTOR TREND* (January, 1968) saw it as ''Unquestionably one of the more exciting engines tested this year. There are few praises in the latest generation of cars, and this engine is one of them.''

Compared to the 273 V-8, the new 340 engine weighed

Above, 1966 Plymouth Barracuda

virtually the same but developed 275 hp to the older engine's 235. Both engines had the same 3.31 inch stroke with the 340 gaining its extra cubes via a 0.64 inch bore increase to 4.04 inches. Adding vitality to the 340 were new cylinder heads with more port area and room for healthy-sized, 2.02 inch intake and 1.60 inch exhaust valves. Respective valve sizes for the 273 engines were 1.78 inches and 1.50 inches. Hotter cams with more duration and greater lift were also developed for 340 engines with either automatic or manual transmissions.

Whereas Barracudas with the 383 engine left the starting gate amidst great billows of smoke from their rear tires only to run out of breath at the quarter-mile mark, the 340 Barracuda S started strong and finished stronger. Its peak horsepower came on at 5000 rpm and didn't drop off substantially as revs reached the 6000 rpm mark. This type of lusty, straight line manners was joined by excellent handling since a 1968 340-S Barracuda weighed 100 lbs less than a year older Barracuda with the 383 V-8.

"The 1968 Barracuda 340-S," said CAR LIFE (December, 1967) "is a good example of the better Grand Touring automobiles available on the domestic market." Scott Harvey, Barracuda expert No. 1, wrote in SPORTS CAR GRAPHIC (December, 1967), "This one comes as close to race car handling as anything you can buy straight out of an American dealer's showroom."

Tuned to the teeth, a 340-S Barracuda could accelerate from zero to 60 mph in under 6 seconds. However, a more typical and realistic time for a TorqueFlite 340-S with a 3.23:1 rear axle was 7 seconds.

For those who couldn't find satisfaction in the Barracuda's 95 mph speed in the quarter-mile, Chrysler offered up the Hemicuda in early 1968. This machine, with no emission control equipment, was illegal for street use and intended only for the serious drag racer. Its engine was of course the great Hemi 426.

The major Barracuda marketing/performance innovation for 1969 was the new 'Cuda series, described by CAR & DRIVER (October, 1968) as a "kind of low line Barracuda fastback in the Road Runner idiom." For visual identification purposes, the 'Cuda featured its own special paint scheme and non-functional hoodscoops. For purposes of sport, its standard engine was the 275 hp, 340 cid V-8. Also available was a 383, four-barrel V-8 which, with a cam from a 440 GTX engine, turned out 300 hp. CAR AND DRIVER (October, 1968) had this to say regarding the 'Cuda 340 and Formula S Barracuda: "They handle, brake and feel like a sports car ought to handle, brake and feel." The 'Cuda 340 was originally scheduled to be called the Barracuda MoPar 340 but, regardless of what name was attached to it, this new model with 4-speed manual gearbox and 3.55:1 axle accelerated in rapid fashion: zero to 60 mph in 6.3 seconds, the quarter-mile in 14.22 seconds.

The then normal three year styling cycle came up for renewal in 1970 for the Barracuda and, this time around, Plymouth chose to reshape it into more of a pony car and less of a sports sedan. Overall length was reduced 4 inches down to 186.6 inches. Since most of this was taken from the rear deck, the new Barracuda's trunk space was on the sparse side. After sticking with fastback styling since 1964, Plymouth decided enough was enough and sent the 1970 Barracuda out to play in just convertible and notchback styles. The Barracuda's new look was contemporary and distinctive, a tribute to its designers who managed to move it closer to the mainstream of pony car styling while not giving the Barracuda a look-alike complex. If the customer

was interested just in acceleration, the new 'Cuda was his cup of tea. Its standard engine was the 330 hp, 383 V-8 and optional engines included a 335 hp, High-Performance 383, the 426 Hemi with two four-barrels and the 440 V-8 with either 375 hp or 390 hp. These variations were, however, actually mutations of the Barracuda's heritage, which was summed up in the word "balance." Sure, those big-engined 'Cudas were fearsome creatures down straight line row but, like the other big-engined pony cars, this expression of power took away most of the unique driving features that had made the 340-S Barracuda, to cite one example, such an attractive automobile.

But all was not lost! The Barracuda was destined to finish out 1970 in style. The son of 340-S was not stillborn but alive and well as the AAR 'Cuda. Prior to 1970 model introduction time, Chrysler had tested the new Barracuda at Mid-Ohio raceway. The intent was to see if a 305 cid version of the 340 engine, which was race-legal for the 1970 Trans-Am season, could cut the mustard. Chrysler, unhappily, learned the Barricuda was some five seconds away from a competitive lap speed. This did not discourage Dan Gurney and his All American Racers from having a go at Trans-Am with the Barracuda during the 1970 season. No doubt the basic ingredients were there. Gurney and Swede Savage were a near perfect blend of veteran and young chargers and the AAR organization itself was spearheaded by Phil Remington, but one season just wasn't long enough for AAR to learn and win at the same time. As SPORTS CAR GRAPHIC (March, 1970) observed, "The cars . . . are completely new to the series, and will probably have to spend the season learning. By mid-season they may begin to show they're competitive, but they've got a tremendous amount of sciencing to do in the meantime to catch up." SPORTS CAR GRAPHIC was, indeed, right on target. The early season races saw the 'Cuda far back at the finish, often listed as DNF but, gradually, things improved and by July, at Lime Rock, Swede Savage was finishing second to Mark Donohue's Javelin. There's little doubt that if another season had been made available to Gurney he would have turned out a winner. That, of course, was denied him as the 1971 Trans Am became virtually a one factory (Javelin) show.

The all-important by-product of this much too brief Barracuda foray into Trans-Am racing was by far the AAR 'Cuda. It relied upon the great 340 V-8 for its power and, with an Edelbrock aluminum intake manifold and triple, two-barrel Holleys, its rated horsepower was 290 at 5000. In many ways the AAR 'Cuda was akin to the first generation Shelby Mustangs. A man's car, described by SPORTS CAR GRAPHIC (June, 1970) as "a mean brute that has to be mastered. It has to be driven, because that's what it was designed for."

And, that's the way the Barracuda ended the Great Decade, a car capable of zero to 60 mph in 6 seconds and touching a top speed of nearly 140 mph. Indeed, that's also the way it greeted 1971. But the following year the Barracuda was reduced to just one body style, the two-door hardtop and three engines. One was still great, the 340 V-8. The end of the road was just a model year or two away, however. There was a 1974 Barracuda but neither of its two engines (a 318 cid, two-barrel rated at 170 net hp and a 360 V-8 with four-barrel carburetor and 245 net hp) provoked the sensations that were there for the taking back in the early days. Midway during the model run, Plymouth bowed to the inevitable and ceased production of the Barracuda and another great car became just a great memory.

It's The Talk of the Test Drivers!

THE FABULOUS '56 PONTIAC WITH A BIG AND VITAL GENERAL MOTORS "AUTOMOTIVE FIRST"!

Believe us—it isn't easy to impress a test driver!

But they're cheering Pontiac in a big way. What's set them buzzing is that big and vital General Motors "First" combining:

Pontiac's new big-bore Strato-Streak V-8 with the terrific thrust of 227 horsepower.

General Motors' new Strato-Flight Hydra-Matic* that gentles this mighty "go" to smoothness beyond belief.

You don't need a test track to prove that here is the lift of a lifetime.

Traffic tells you. Here's "stop-and-go" response as fast as thought itself. *A hill helps.* High or low, it's left behind without a sign of effort. *And passing definitely pins it down.*

Gun it and instant, flashing power sweeps you swiftly by the loitering car ahead. No drag, no lag—just safe and certain "go"!

There's plenty more to charm you. The safety of big new brakes, a steady ride, advanced controls. Glamorous new beauty.

But, above all, it's that fabulous new "go" that gets you!

Drive a Pontiac today for a glorious double thrill. There'll be pride in your heart, a torrent at your toe-tip. What more could anyone want?

*An extra cost option

'56 PONTIAC

PONTIAC MOTOR DIVISION OF GENERAL MOTORS CORPORATION

27. Pontiac

The first Pontiac, touted as the "Chief of the Sixes," made its debut in January, 1926, at the New York Auto Show. Although it was described prior to production as a companion car to the Oakland, it soon became the dominant member of this partnership and, in 1932, the Oakland was discontinued. Throughout the thirties and forties the Pontiac was a popular but certainly uncontroversial car. Fifth in sales in 1941, Pontiac resumed production in 1945 with cars that were a continuation of its conservative tradition.

The old way of doing business at Pontiac began to give way to a new era with the arrival of the 1955 models. They were not the first to be equipped with V-8's (the 1932 model enjoys that honor) and, amidst all the excitement greeting Chevrolet's sensational 265 cid V-8, the potential of the new Pontiac V-8 was not highly publicized.

Pontiac's 287 cid V-8 with wedge shaped combustion chambers and stamped rocker arms was easily mistaken for an up-sized Chevrolet V-8. There were design similarities between the two but they were totally different units and the Pontiac V-8 was somewhat more expensive to produce.

A 1955 Pontiac with Dual-Range Hydra-Matic and 180 hp (Pontiacs with the 3-speed manual transmission were rated at 173 hp) was still a modest performer. Zero to 60 mph required 13.8 seconds and the standing start quarter-mile, 19.7 seconds. The Pontiac's top speed stood at 102 mph. In effect, the 1955 Pontiac had performance that matched its appearance: nice but not super-exciting. This situation wasn't altered substantially with the introduction of a $35 power-pack option consisting of a four-barrel carburetor boosting horsepower output to 200, but it, at least, indicated that Pontiac wasn't ignorant of changes taking place in the market.

Below, 1957 Pontiac Bonneville

This effort to shake off the dead hand of the past received a major shot of adrenalin when Semon (Bunkie) Knudsen took over as Pontiac general manager in July, 1956. The most dramatic example of his bold leadership came with the 1959 models but, even before his arrival, Pontiac was making some forays into the high-performance arena. The 1956 models were given boosts in displacement to 316.6 cubic inches and even the humblest Pontiac was delivered with a 205 hp engine. Moving up the scale was a 227 hp option with a new four-barrel carburetor and higher lift cam. Later in the year came the Strato Streak engine with dual four-barrel carburetors and a rating of 285 hp. In June, 1956, Ab Jenkins, the 73 year old veteran of innumerable speed runs at Bonneville, and his son averaged 118.337 mph for 24-hours with a 285 hp Pontiac on the Utah salt flats. In the course of this NASCAR supervised venture the Pontiac also completed 100 miles at a speed of 126.02 mph.

Knudsen fought successfully for Pontiac, like Chevrolet, to have a fuel-injected model for 1957. The outcome, the Bonneville convertible, was not a particularly exciting performer. Even with 310 hp, its 4,175 pound weight seriously hampered its acceleration ability. The Bonneville's quarter-mile time, for example, was an unimpressive 18.0 seconds. This, fortunately, did not have an effect upon Pontiac's growing performance reputation since only 630 Bonnevilles were produced.

Receiving far more publicity, and all of it favorable, was the Pontiac's strong showing in the 1957 Daytona Speed Week. With the same 3.94 inch bore and a larger 3.56 inch stroke (up from 3.25 inches), the Pontiac V-8 now displaced 347 cubic inches and was available in several potent versions. With dual four-barrel carburetors, high lift cam and 10.25:1 compression ratio it developed 270 hp at 4800 rpm. In time for Daytona, Pontiac offered a triple two-

barrel carburetor version with 290 hp, for $170. In very limited supply and not readily available to the public was a 317 hp version with Tri-Power, special cam, heavy valve springs and solid lifters. A Pontiac with this 317 hp engine was clocked at a 131.747 mph, two-way average across the measured mile. Another 317 Pontiac, driven by John Zink, Jr., was even faster with a 136 mph average but his car was disqualified after officials discovered one cylinder had a higher than standard compression ratio.

All Pontiac engines for 1958 were identified as "Tempest 395's" due to their torque output of 395 lbs-ft at 2800 rpm. The really interesting performance versions arrived after the traditional fall new model introduction. Just in time for the Daytona slugfest were two "Super Tempest 395-A" engines, either in PK (single four-barrel, 315 hp) or PM (triple two-barrel carburetors, 330 hp) form. Both engines were available with Hydra-Matic, or standard or heavy-duty Borg-Warner 3-speed manual transmissions. At Daytona, the 330 hp Pontiacs streaked across the sand at speeds ranging from 131 mph to 146.045 mph. Although Pontiac won only 3 of 45 NASCAR sponsored Grand Nationals during 1958, one of its victories was the highly visible Daytona event won by Paul Goldsmith at a speed of 101.18 mph. The following year, Vicki Wood drove Norm Latham's 1958 Pontiac with a Latham supercharger to a speed through the measured mile of 147.42 mph. This was, with the exception of the Indianapolis type racers, the fastest car at Daytona in 1959. Another Latham-blown 1958 Pontiac won first place in the experimental class with a speed of 140.186 mph.

Pontiacs of this vintage are not remembered for their styling which, particularly in the Bonneville line, was heavily overladen with chrome trim, but even their strongest critics conceded it was an appearance that was performance oriented and clearly reflected Knudsen's belief that "You can sell a young man's car to old people, but you can't sell an old car to young people."

The Pontiacs for 1959 were very much "young cars." This was the age of the 80 inch wide GM cars with complex-curved, panoramic windshields that would soon be for-

gotten, but these deviations from common sense were, in Pontiac's case, more than compensated for by some real engineering advances. The most apparent was Pontiac's new widetrack stance. With tread increased by nearly five inches, Pontiac, at least, took advantage of its width to give its cars substantially improved handling. There was also a substantial boost in Pontiac power for 1959. All Pontiac V-8's displaced 389 cubic inches and three performance engines were available, all with 10.5:1 compression ratios. The first, with Tri-Power, was rated at 315 hp at 4600 rpm. Next in line was a 330 hp, single four-barrel carburetor model followed by a Tri-Powered version with a highlift cam and 348 horsepower.

In awarding Pontiac its "Car of the Year" award, *MOTOR TREND* described Pontiac as "the best balanced passenger car in America," citing it as "making the most significant engineering advances . . . with its wider track and the year's best combination of handling, ride and performance." Pontiac certainly had that last commodity in abundance but was still able to win only a single Grand National during the 1959 NASCAR season. Nonetheless, the sight and sound of Fireball Roberts' Bonneville lapping Daytona at nearly 150 mph, plus his victory at Daytona in the first Firecracker 250, helped maintain Pontiac's new image.

The American supercar is best noted for its stunning power, top speed and acceleration. America was the land of the big V-8 and thus it is not surprising its cars earned such a reputation, but there's more to the story of American performance than just straight line get up and go. The 1960 Pontiacs were prime examples that Detroit was also paying attention to advancing the handling and braking of its products to keep pace with all the power that was inside those big V-8's.

As before, the Tempest 425A engines were available with Tri-Power and up to 348 hp. This allowed a Pontiac with a 2.69 axle to reach a top speed near 150 mph. For

Above, 1959 Pontiac Bonneville

maximum acceleration, a 3.64 axle was also offered. For an additional $225, the purchaser of a 425-A Pontiac could opt for a dealer installed cam and solid lifter kit that officially left its horsepower and torque output unchanged but allowed for higher rpm operation without valve float. Pontiac dealers could also perform factory approved "economy operations" that included porting cylinder heads, polishing combustion chambers, increasing bearing clearances and installing Forged-true pistons that provided a 14:1 compression ratio. Such an "economy tuned" Pontiac was, of course, nothing less than an out and out racing car with at least 400 hp available.

Keeping pace with the Pontiac's power were a number of regular production and special order wheel and brake options including 15 inch wheels with 6 inch rims and heavy-duty, Moraine brake linings. Attractive, as well as functional, were the optional cast aluminum brake drums with special rims that were attached to the integral bearing hub and wheel by eight chromed nuts.

Victories in the preliminary 100 mile races prior to the running of the 1960 Daytona 500 made the new Pontiacs odds-on favorites to win that important NASCAR event. Fireball Roberts underscored Pontiac's potential with the fastest qualifying time of 151.566 mph with his 1960 Bonneville. Nonetheless, it was Junior Johnson's Chevrolet that took the checkered flag after Robert's car dropped out with engine failure.

Pontiacs did far better in the 1960 National Hot Rod Association's Drag Championships. Jim Wanger, with a Pontiac prepared by the performance-oriented Royal Pontiac dealership of Royal Oak, Michigan, won the SS/S (Super Stock-Stick Shift class) with a 14.14 second, 102.04 mph run. Another Pontiac finished second in the Super Stock-Automatic class. Earlier in the year, Wanger's Pontiac had also emerged as the top Stock Eliminator at the NHRA/NASCAR Winternationals.

The 1961 Pontiacs, and all the GM automobiles for that matter, provided a refreshing respite from the wider and longer syndrome that detracted from the attractiveness of the 1959 and 1960 models. The new Pontiac bodies were an inch lower but they were also 2.5 inches narrower and 4 inches shorter. More extensive use of aluminum alloy in

Below, 1961 Pontiac Ventura

their engines and transmissions also helped reduce the weight of the new Pontiacs. Although their horsepower ratings remained unchanged from the previous year, a dealer installed package was available that provided for an output of 363 hp at 5600 rpm. Its major features included, in addition to the performance components of the 348 hp engine, cylinder heads with room for 2 inch intake valves, a solid lifter cam and forged pistons. Pontiacs with this engine and the heavy-duty 3-speed manual transmission were capable of 105 mph in the quarter-mile. By comparison, a 348 hp Tri-Power Pontiac reached a quarter-mile speed of 95 mph. This speed could be improved upon by ordering the triple carburetor setup with the available mechanical, rather than vacuum, progressive linkage. For serious competition, Pontiac also provided numerous heavy-duty chassis items, a floor-shift conversion for the 3-speed manual transmission, plus weight-saving aluminum front and rear bumpers.

Although it was a 1960 model, it was a Smokey Yunick prepared Pontiac that Marvin Panch drove to victory in the 1961 Daytona 500 at a new record of 149.6 mph. At one point during the season, Pontiac had twice as many NASCAR victories as any of its competitors. Among its many successes were wins in the Firecracker 250 and the Charlotte World 600-mile race, where Pontiacs finished 1, 2, 7, 8, 9, and 10.

Late in 1961, Pontiac built the first of what was destined to become one of the classics of the performance era, the 421 Heavy Duty engine. Due to a new NHRA ruling that any cars competing in the stock class had to be factory built, Pontiac abandoned its previous policy of providing competition components as over the counter dealer options. In its drag racing form the 421, which was available only as a Catalina hardtop or two-door sedan, was joined to a close-ratio 4-speed transmission with a Hurst Shifter. Carburetion was by dual, four-barrel Carter AFB units. A No. 10 McKellar cam (named for and created by the engineering genius of the same name), solid lifters and 11.0:1 Mickey Thompson forged pistons were its most noteworthy features. For $342.85 the customer was receiving a car with a laughably low 405 hp rating at 5600 rpm. During its development, an output of 432 hp had easily been attained and its true potential was actually closer to 465 horsepower, as evidenced by its ability to propel a full-sized

Pontiac to a zero to 60 mph time of under six seconds. Quarter-mile runs yielded results of 13.9 seconds and 107 mph. During 1962, Pontiac put its racing cars on a weight reduction program that included, in addition to the previously noted aluminum bumpers, thin-gauge aluminum front fenders, inner fender wells, hood and radiator brackets. These changes lopped 159 pounds from the Pontiac's ready-to-race form. For NASCAR racing, Pontiacs also were fitted with aluminum rear fenders and trunk lids that put them under the weight of competing Fords and Chevrolets. In spite of increasingly stiff competition from Ford, the Pontiacs won both the USAC and NASCAR Championships in 1962.

Figuring prominently in the Pontiac performance picture during 1962 was Mickey Thompson whose Pontiac-powered Challenger I had earlier been clocked at 406 mph at Bonneville. In July, he broke numerous American Class B and unlimited records on the Utah salt flats with a 421-engined Pontiac Catalina, including a new flying mile mark of 153.67 mph. Thompson returned to Utah in September with his Pontiac sporting twin turbochargers that were developed by Thompson-Ramo-Woolridge and supplied to him by the Pontiac factory. This very interesting engine was stock except for a reduced 8.5:1 compression ratio. The turbochargers delivered a healthy 30 psi boost and the 421's estimated output was 550 hp. Unfortunately, its true potential was never reached since, on its first run, pressure from the turbochargers blew a head gasket. Thompson did estimate that just before that mishap he was traveling at 190 mph.

The 1963 racing season promised to be the most competitive since the old 1957 anti-racing edict had either been publicly or tacitly revoked by the American automobile industry. Pontiac was more than just the reigning USAC/NASCAR Champion; it was also one of the best examples that winning on Sunday sells cars on Monday. Not everyone who liked high performance cars could afford them, but they were prime influences upon those who could.

In 1956, Pontiac was sixth in sales, having manufactured just over 400,000 cars. By 1962, by virtue of producing 521,933 cars, Pontiac had solidified the hold on third place that it had seized the previous year. Pontiac's performance prowess was virtually universally respected and it had no apparent intentions of stepping away from a position of superiority in 1963.

Its production "421 High Output" models used the same block as the competition engines with cylinder heads from the 1960-61 racing models. With hydraulic lifters and 10.75:1, flat top cast aluminum pistons they were rated at 370 hp in Tri-Power form and at 353 hp with a single Carter AFB four-barrel carburetor. A 4,500 pound Grand Prix with the 370 hp engine and 4-speed transmission turned an impressive zero to 60 mph time of 6.6 seconds.

For competition use, Pontiac offered three versions of its 421 Heavy Duty V-8. A single four-barrel carburetor version with a 12:1 compression ratio and 390 hp was intended for NASCAR and USAC racing. For drag racing and limited street use, the 405 hp engine was recommended. Finally, strictly for drag racing and with "full throttle bursts limited to relatively short bursts" was a 410 horsepower block buster with dual four-barrel carburetors and 13.0:1 compression ratio. In actuality, this engine, like the other Pontiac competition V-8's, was grossly underrated. Its true potential exceeded the 500 hp mark at 5500 rpm.

The chassis components that accompanied either this or the 405 hp version were described by *CAR LIFE* (July, 1963) as "the most complete and carefully engineered dragstrip package coming out of Detroit this year." Cast aluminum, split-flow headers that would literally melt if full throttle runs went much beyond the quarter-mile mark saved forty-five pounds. Aluminum bell housings and a frames with holes cut in the side panels and sans the bottom sides of their box sections were other key elements of the lightweight dragstrip Pontiacs. With all insulation removed and plexiglass side windows installed, the Pontiac weighed less than 3,300 pounds. Some interesting changes were also made in the standard Pontiac suspension to render it more efficient for drag racing. In order to obtain the maximum amount of front-to-rear weight transfer on take off, the Pontiac's rear coil springs were much softer than stock. The rear shocks had no resistance on the down stroke and those in front had no rebound control.

Then came that infamous edict from the inner sanctum of the Fourteenth Floor of the General Motors Building: all GM divisions were to cease and desist in their competition and performance activities. The men of Pontiac, along with their compatriots at Chevrolet, who loved the sights and sounds of a race bred American V-8 at full throttle would prove to be remarkably adept at partially circumventing this command, but, early in 1963, it spelled the end both of Pontiac's supremacy and competitiveness in NASCAR racing.

Early in March, 1963, came the announcement that really made it official: Fireball Roberts, who had raced Pontiacs with the number 22 on their sides since 1959, announced he was switching brands and joining the Ford ranks. "It was something I'd been actually thinking about for a long time," he said, "Pontiac and General Motors seemed to be de-emphasizing performance and Ford was pushing it hard and building a terrific racing car at the same time. Also, Ford seemed interested in having me make appearances for them and things of that nature. It was an attractive picture. I got the chance to make the move and made it."

There's little doubt that if Pontiac had been allowed to remain in racing it would have responded in double barrel fashion to the mounting pressure from Ford. For example, the development work Pontiac was lavishing on a dual overhead cam version of its 389 V-8 with four valves per cylinder very likely would have led to a new generation of racing engines.

In spite of reaching the end of the racing road, things weren't really all that bad for Pontiac in 1963. Pontiac's youth-oriented stance, first created by Bunkie Knudsen in the late fifties and adhered to by his successors, enabled it to sail right on by this setback. Pontiac's management was aware that young car enthusiasts both influenced the car-buying habits of older adults and were, thanks to their own affluence, becoming a major force in the marketplace. What was needed to exploit this condition was an automobile tailored to their taste, priced within their economic reach. Such a car would very likely make automotive history. Ford certainly made it with the Mustang but so did Pontiac and, in the process, rather than having its performance reputation decline saw it flourish as never before. That car, the fabled GTO, will be covered in Chapter 29.

Right, Top, 1964 Pontiac Catalina 2+2
Right, Middle, 1965 Pontiac Catalina 2+2
Right, Bottom, 1967 Pontiac Catalina 2+2

Isn't it interesting how America's most exciting new automobiles always end up in Pontiac dealers' showrooms.

This time it's the all-new Firebirds.

1970

28. Pontiac Firebird

The Firebird, as supercar or pony car, invited comparison. In the marketplace, its obvious rival was Mercury's Cougar. Both cars touted their European-ish features but, of the two, the Firebird contained more "Old World" features. At least one major publication, for example, depicted its handling and ride as "vintage." In other words, it rode and cornered with the stiffness found in such British sports cars as the Austin-Healey 3000 and MG-B. A more contemporary development that clearly reflected an awareness among the Firebird creators of how they did things "across the pond" was represented by the Sprint version of the Firebird. Most of the pony cars offering six-cylinder engines did so with almost a complete absence of innovation. For the most part, they were bottom line paper tigers with little to interest the performance purist. This wasn't the way Pontiac tended to its business. A bargain basement 165 hp six was there for the asking but the ohc, 230 cubic inch six in 215 hp Sprint form was a viable performance alternative to a big bore V-8. By virtue of weighing 180 pounds less than the 400 cid Pontiac V-8, the Sprint six reduced the Firebird's understeering tendency to a discernible degree. This handling bonus did not come at the expense of acceleration, either. Granted, no six-cylinder engine built in the U.S. during the sixties could trade punches with the mighty V-8, but the Sprint's zero to 60 mph time of approximately 10.5 seconds wasn't a source

Below, 1967 Pontiac Firebird

of embarrassment to Pontiac, either.

The idea of a six-cylinder supercar wasn't part of the scheme of things during the late sixties and this, as much as anything else, doomed the Sprint to a short three year life span. Still, the point has to be made; the potential was there to create an automobile with no American counterpart. Pontiac illustrated this capability with its Pontiac Firebird Sprint Turisimo (PFST). With a nice, tight suspension using nylon and steel rather than rubber in the roll bar links plus a larger roll bar and 8.5 inch wheels sporting 10 inch wide Firestone racing tires, this Firebird was an exquisite handler. *CAR LIFE* (April, 1968) reported, "The PFST became almost free from body roll even in rapid transient conditions." Under its shaker-type hood, the PFST sported an engine with triple Weber downdrafts, so it obviously wasn't lacking in the power department.

The real source of power in the 1967-69 Firebird, however, was its 325 hp, 400 cid V-8. This engine was also used in the GTO and differed only by having a throttle linkage that prevented the secondary carburetor barrels from opening beyond the 90% mark. The Firebird's 400 cid V-8 was also available with Ram Air and, in either form, it delivered the goods in true supercar style. Indeed, *CAR LIFE* (August, 1967) considered it simply a supercar of somewhat diminutive proportions. Its 6.5 second time from zero to 60 mph with a 4-speed Firebird 400 was bettered only by those of the 427 cid Corvette and the Mopar Hemis.

Pontiac rated the Ram Air 400 at 325 hp but, with a hotter

cam and stiffer valve springs, it undoubtedly deserved higher numerals. Certainly its zero to 60 mph time of 6.4 seconds and quarter-mile speed of 100.3 mph, as reported by *MOTOR TREND* (May, 1967), supports that contention. Also backing up that conclusion is the 360 hp quoted by Pontiac for the same engine (without the throttle restriction) when installed in the GTO. The Ram Air option was not inexpensive. It retailed at $263.30 above the price of the 400 engine which itself carried a sticker of $274.00.

Pontiac had virtually no input in the basic design of the Camaro, which, of course, was the starting point for the Firebird. This situation meant that the 1967 Firebird was afflicted with the dreaded plague of the single leaf rear springs. Thanks to dual rear traction bars that were used on the most powerful Firebirds, they were far less prone to axle windup and wheel hop. Although withdrawn in mid-1969, Pontiac's offering of Koni shocks as a Firebird option shortly after it went on sale also was a positive move in this regard. Incidentally, the heavy-duty suspension that was included in the 400 V-8 package was available on any Firebird for only $9.32!

One of the most memorable demonstrations of the capability of the first series Firebird was reported by *CAR AND DRIVER* (March, 1968). There was no question about *CAR AND DRIVER's* enthusiasm for the Pontiac pony car. "What Pontiac has done is to have seized on the 'personal car' concept with more enthusiasm than anyone else since the first Mustangs and developed the Firebird/Camaro body into a real driver's car." Having said this, *CAR AND DRIVER* then credited the 400 High Output Firebird with 4-speed manual transmission and 3.55:1 rear axle with a

zero to 60 mph time of 5.5 seconds.

Not every car buff magazine shared the enthusiasm of *CAR AND DRIVER*, however. *CAR LIFE* (October, 1968), for example, contended "For 1969, this entrant continues to miss the American GT bull's-eye by a wider margin than its competitors." This really wasn't a fair shot at the Firebird. There's no question Pontiac would have been happier if the Firebird didn't have to be the Camaro's kissing cousin but, that's corporate life. Matched against the big engined Camaros, it always seemed the 400 Firebird came away looking stronger, acting stronger, and with just a little more class.

When it came to Trans-Am racing, the Firebird had precious few shining moments and the tragic and untimely death of Jerry Titus at Road America in 1970 removed from the Firebird's racing program one of its great, and certainly most talented, contributors. The ultimate irony concerning the Firebird's venture into SCCA racing and its maturing into a truly outstanding American car, comparable on many counts to far more expensive European models, is two-fold. First, in spite of its lackluster Trans-Am record, Pontiac saw the magic of the name (remember this was the same company that brought you Bonneville, Grand Prix, 2+2, Le Mans and GTO) and before anyone else opened their eyes, had secured the right to its use from the SCCA. Secondly, and surely more important, unlike its contemporaries, the Firebird didn't turn turtle in the early '70's. Granted, the latter years of that decade saw Firebirds of sharply reduced power being produced but, in 1973 and

Above, 1969 Pontiac Firebird Trans Am

1974, the Great Super Duty 455 engine had its share of the glory. Only about 1200 were built, but what machines they were! According to *CAR LIFE,* the 455-SD with Turbo Hydra-Matic turned the quarter-mile in 13.8 seconds and 103.6 mph.

Pontiac's venture into Trans-Am racing didn't get off on the best footing. Since it didn't have a competitive engine under 305 cid, it had to operate semi-sub rosa via racing a Canadian-built Firebird that was nothing less than a Chevrolet Z-28 masquerading as a Firebird. Pontiac considered going the tunnelport route with its own 303 V-8 but this plan never became operational and the few engines that were built ended up in Firebirds destined for Grand National NASCAR competition.

The frustrations that abounded in its Trans-Am effort didn't prevent Pontiac from bringing forth a production model Trans Am that, in both its 1969 and new look 1970 versions, was an excellent super/pony car. Furthermore, it wasn't, at least in public anyway, burdened with any guilt about the inconsistency of marketing a car known as the Trans Am with engine some 95 cubic inches above the legal class limit. Many motoring journals didn't let Pontiac get away with this without a jab or two, but at least *CAR LIFE* (April, 1969) tempered criticism with perspective. Its unhappiness with the Trans Am, explained *CAR LIFE,* was "Simply because a Ponycar named the 'Trans-Am' (sic), riding on the fame of the road racing circuit, and styled and powered for performance should handle better."

Well, *CAR LIFE did* have a point, but take away the name and what was left? A pretty fine automobile. Sure, it

Below, 1979 Pontiac 10th Anniversary Trans Am

was nose heavy and had plenty of understeer, but, with optional, 7 inch wheels and its new 1 inch diameter front roll bar, the Trans am didn't embarrass its owners in the turns. Even *CAR LIFE* had to admit, "The Trans Am (sic) stuck like glue, but once it had reached the limit of adhesion, there was no getting it back." At least getting there was fun, though.

Advocates of a Z-28-ized Pontiac Trans Am would have been happier if Pontiac had followed John Fitch's lead, back in 1968, with his Fitchbird. The styling modifications Fitch adopted for this car weren't terribly exciting; a mesh grille up front that enclosed the headlights and not-too-pretty C-pillar extensions, But Fitch carefully retuned the Pontiac's suspension, adding Engelbert steel-cord, radial-ply tires, and Koni shocks to provide Firebirds with very competent handling. For approximately $1,000 beyond the price of a 400 cid Firebird, Fitch also installed a high performance cam and free-flowing exhaust system that he claimed raised its horsepower to 365 hp. Sprint-based versions of the Fitchbird were also built and sold in small numbers.

But, who can quarrel with success? The 1970½ Trans Am's standard engine was the 400 cid, 335 hp Ram Air and, if this wasn't enough, the Ram Air IV version, with its 345 hp underrating was there for the asking.

In the new form, the Firebird was available in four flavors (Base, Esprit, Formula, and Trans Am) ranging in performance from mild to wild. The Trans Am, with its front air jam, rear spoiler and neat front fenders air extractors, had the looks, the class, the handling and the straight line performance that made the purists' complaints about the legitimacy of its name look like a lot of silly gobbledygook.

I wouldn't stand in the middle of the page if I were you...
It's a Pontiac GTO!

If you insist on reading at a time like this—that's a 6.5 litre Gran Turismo Omologato aimed right at you, 325 bhp @ 4800 rpm with 1-4BBL. It may have an optional 3-2BBL setup with 348 bhp, look lively! As it goes by, notice the nylon red-circle tires and dual exhausts. Listen to the standard 3-speed transmission with Hurst shifter going through the motions. Or, the fully synchronized 4-speed on the floor*. Or, the automatic* transmission with column shift—you can't tell from here. It may even have a console*. Like every GTO, it has heavy-duty springs, shocks and stabilizer. Quick, get off the page!   *Optional at extra cost.

the GTO makers—Pontiac
PONTIAC MOTOR DIVISION • GENERAL MOTORS CORPORATION

29. Pontiac GTO

Oh, how the purists wailed when Pontiac announced the GTO back in 1964. To label any American car a GTO seemed to be the worst kind of name stealing. In the view of *ROAD AND TRACK,* it was "an unforgiveable dishonesty." Yet, the men from Pontiac never flinched, not even once.

For the record, Pontiac had as much right as Ferrari or anyone else to use the GTO name. The F.I.A. had established the Gran Turismo Omologato classification in the hope of spurring the racing of true, high speed road cars. In order to qualify for international competition, at least 100 were to be built. Production of Ferrari's GTO never even came close. Pontiac, on the other hand sold over 32,000 of its GTO's during 1964. Granted, the two cars weren't directly comparable on many points, (although *CAR AND DRIVER* felt otherwise, tested the two side by side and concluded Pontiac's was better) but both were true high performance cars regardless of what they were called.

Pontiac had been riding high, wide and handsome down the performance road since 1956, when Bunky Knudsen became its general manager. Until General Motors put the hammer down on the performance activities of its automotive divisions early in 1963, Pontiac was the car to be reckoned with, both on the NASCAR supertracks and the NHRA dragstrips, not to mention the local boulevard.

A year before the GTO debuted, Estes, at least it seems in retrospect, gave the nation a peek at his strategy to outflank GM's anti-performance mandate. The 1963 Tempest, while still retaining the curved driveshaft and transaxle of earlier model Tempests, was far different under the hood than its predecessor. Instead of again offering as optional equipment the Buick 215 cid aluminum V-8 (which only 2% of 1962 Tempest customers selected anyway), Pontiac took a different route for 1963. This time around a downsized 326 cid version of Pontiac's neo-classic 389 V-8 became the V-8 option. This engine had the same weight and external measurements as its big brother. The two engines differed only in their bore. That of the 326 was 3.71875 inches, the 389's was 4.0625 inches. It seemed on the surface that Pontiac should have slipped the 389 V-8 into the Tempest and not have gone to the trouble of shrinking its displacement. A couple of spirited miles behind the wheel of a 280 hp, 326 cid Lemans provided a vivid explanation, however. That squirrelly independent rear suspension made for some interesting moments when the macadam got twisty and, to be frank, was put to its outer limits of control behind 280 hp. Pontiac's move was the right one. Any additional power in that chassis would have been almost totally unusable.

The next year a new A-body chassis and suspension with conventional perimeter frame, coil springs and solid rear axle took the place of the old Tempest's unit body, swing axle and transaxle. Advocates of the Tempest's European-like design philosophy lamented its demise, but on every conceivable point relative to performance in its broadest sense, the GTO was a far superior automobile.

It's generally recognized that John Z. DeLorean, then Pontiac's chief engineer, was one of the men most involved in the birth of the GTO. However, plaudits are also in order for its general manager back in 1964, Pete Estes. He sanctioned the GTO's secret development and then OK'd its announcement before The Big Boys at the helm had a chance to torpedo its maiden voyage. Even so, it was a close call since, as *MOTOR TREND* reported (March, 1964), "word is that GM top brass were pretty upset about this— and the car was almost cancelled after it was introduced." The anti-performance gang did inflict a form of revenge upon the GTO by not allowing the 3-speed Hydra-Matic to be part of its option list. For a time, a plan also was considered limiting all A-bodied GM intermediates to engines no larger than 330 cubic inches. No division chief was happy about that bit of nonsense, particularly after the GTO scored its original sales successes and everyone at GM was champing at the bit to build his own type of GTO automobile.

An early Pontiac ad for the GTO described it as an automobile "For the man who wouldn't mind riding a tiger if someone'd only put wheels on it." Thus, right from the beginning, "tiger" became synonymous with GTO, a relationship which became a key element in its promotion as a car without a domestic peer.

Estes characterized the GTO as "a significant addition to Pontiac's list of high performance and individualized sports car developments." Some grumbling was in order over Estes' somewhat loose use of the term "sports car," but no one could dispute his linking of high performance to the GTO.

The GTO began its decade plus one career as a $295 special option for the Le Mans two-door coupes or convertible, but what an option it was! From the outside, the Tempest GTO was identified by special "GTO 6.5 litre" labels and a hood with (unfortunately) false twin air scoops. Far more interesting was the performance derived by mating Pontiac's untempermental 389 cid V-8 (carrying the heads from the 421 HO engine) with the relatively light Tempest body and chassis. Pontiac claimed that it was "the first manufacturer aside from racing and sports car makers to offer the small car/big engine combination."

The base GTO engine was a single carburetor job rated at 325 hp. The neo-classic three two-barrel Rochester Tri-Power setup with a fully mechanical linkage was also available and boosted the GTO's output to 348 hp. All GTO's were equipped with a seven-blade, 18 inch fan joined to a cut-out clutch, dual exhausts, special, 14 inch wheels with 6 inch rims on which were mounted, depending on the customer's preference, either U.S. Royal SS-800 Red streak tires or premium quality white walls. A 10.4 Belleville clutch with a grey-iron pressure plate was also fitted to the GTO. The standard GTO 3-speed manual transmission offered synchromesh only on the top two speeds, but the excellent all-synchromesh 4-speed Muncie gearbox was optional, as was a 2-speed automatic transmission. The base GTO was equipped with heavy-duty springs and shocks, but customers could order a suspension option with even stiffer shocks or, it they were more interested in a smooth ride than optimum handling, they could select a softer suspension for smooth, boulevard ride.

As expected, GTO performance was stunning. The 325 hp, 4-speed version, even with the heavier convertible chassis, turned zero to 60 mph in well under 8 seconds and a

coupe with Tri-Power, and tuned for drag racing, ran the quarter-mile in 107 mph and 13.29 seconds. A normal GTO with 348 hp, 4-speed, 3.23 rear axle and the optional metallic brake lining could turn the zero to 100 mph to zero run in under 20 seconds.

The officialdom of General Motors might have been displeased by Estes' development of the GTO but there was no real arguing with success. The original production game plan for the GTO called for only 5,000 to be built to test the market, but by the end of January, 1964, some 10,000 had been sold and for the total model year 32,450 were purchased. The following year, which saw the GTO's Tri-Power engine boosted to 360 hp, 75,352 were sold.

The success of the GTO as a Tempest option package paved the way, in 1966, for the creation of the GTO as a separate Pontiac series. This shift gave the GTO greater visual distinction from the lesser Tempest models in the form of its own grille, parking lights, hood and tail light design. Early in the model run, the GTO became available with the Ram-Air kit. Its key feature was a functional hood scoop with a thick foam rubber lip that provided a tight under-hood seal with the carburetor intakes. The Ram-Air option required the purchase of the 4-speed, close ratio transmission, heavy-duty fan, metalic brake linings and the "Safe-T-Track," non-slip differential. Performance of a Ram-Air GTO was impressive. With a blue-printed engine it ran the quarter-mile in 12.84 seconds.

The specification charts for the 1967 GTO certainly vindicated the view that Pontiac was still pursuing the development of the GTO as a pure, high performance automobile. The 389 engine was replaced by a slightly larger, 400 cid version, but, in the standard, four-barrel carburetor form, the GTO's rating remained unchanged at 335 hp. A new Quadrajet four-barrel carburetor replaced the vintage Tri-Power setup as the "hot" GTO setup. The Ram-Air induction system was continued as an option.

Pontiac was obviously aware of the impact upon insurance rates of ultra high horsepower ratings and thus claimed only 360 hp for its Ram-Air and High Output GTO engines. It quoted the HO and Ram-Air engines as reaching their peak horsepower at 5100 and 5400 rpm respectively.

There was, however, yet another engine whose mere availability in a GTO suggested decadence to the GTO performance purist. This was the 400 cid V-8 engine with an 8.6:1 compression ratio (all other GTO engines had 10.75:1 compression ratios), a mild two-barrel carburetor and 255 hp at 4400 rpm. This wrapping of a sheep in wolfs' clothing seemed to be nothing less than a crass cheapening of the original GTO small car/big engine/super performance concept. Nonetheless, the 1967 GTO finished second only to the Chevrolet SS396 in muscle car sales.

With sensational new styling, featuring an Endura front bumper that endowed the GTO with one of the cleanest front end designs ever to appear on an American automobile, plus new performance features, the 1968 GTO fully deserved *MOTOR TREND* magazine's designation as the *"Car of the Year."* In presenting this award to Pontiac general manager John Z. DeLorean, *MOTOR TREND* publisher Walt Woron remarked that, "Pontiac has established new design standards and supplied the entire industry with a method for accomplishing them. Never before," Woren continued, "has an automobile been so successful in confirming the correlations between safety, styling and performance as the 1968 GTO."

The visual appearance of the new GTO when compared to Pontiacs of a decade earlier provided dramatic evidence of just how rapidly the state of the art of American automobile styling had progressed. Whereas the late fifties Pontiac was bedecked and bedazzled with chrome, the 1968 GTO's bright work was minimal. Its imposing visual

Above, 1966 Pontiac GTO

impact was due entirely to its gracefully molded, flowing body lines and lack of gimmicks. It was indeed one of the finest styled American cars of the post-war years.

In the engine department, the GTO was still offered with the regular fuel, low compression (8.6:1) engine now developing 265 hp, but there were substantial performance advancements that helped mitigate the pain caused by this engine's availability in a GTO. The true standard GTO engine with a single Rochester four-barrel pumped out 350 hp. With a hotter cam, this rating was boosted to 360 hp. Midway through the model run, the Ram-Air package originally rated at an artificially low 360 hp at 5400 rpm was replaced with an improved "68½ Ram-Air" package with a hotter cam, lighter, better breathing valves and new cylinder heads. All these new goodies officially provided only a 10 horsepower boost to 370 but, as before, this was an unrealistic, for-insurance-company-consumption-only rating.

The twin hood scoop Ram-Air setup (which the driver could either open or close via an interior mounted lever) of the 1968 GTO was continued over into 1969. For $343, a new Ram-Air IV setup, which added another air scoop system located in the GTO's grille, joined the GTO performance option list.

In January, 1969, Pontiac offered what it described as a car that "goes one performance step further in the popular muscle car field." This was The Judge version of the GTO, of which 6,833 were produced during the 1969 model run. As coupe or convertible, The Judge, with its unique black grille, exposed headlights, special tri-color side stripes and

Below, 1969 Pontiac GTO Judge

"The Judge" decals, had instant identification built into its appearance. If there was any doubt, however, its 60-inch wide "floating deck air foil" dismissed them with ease.

These styling changes subjected The Judge to a fair amount of criticism as an example of Pontiac's willingness to dilute the GTO formula for the sake of sales. In fairness to Pontiac, however, it should be remembered that The Judge's base engine was the 366 hp Ram-Air, 400 cid V-8 and, as an option, the 370 hp Ram-Air IV setup was available.

Alas, even The Great One, the founder of the breed, began to lose its vitality during the 1970 model run. The same engine lineup as offered in 1969 was continued in 1970 along with the addition of a 455 cid, 360 hp opiton, but before the end of the year both Ram-Air options were dropped. This was enough bad news, but a potent new engine, the Ram-Air V, a bruiser with round intake and exhaust ports, an aluminum, high rise manifold, solid lifters and large Holley four-barrel, 780 cfm carburetor, never made it into a factory-produced GTO.

From this point, the GTO degenerated rapidly. The year 1971 saw the first low compression GM engines with their new net horsepower ratings. The most potent GTO with the optional 455 cid, 335 hp still had "It," but the following year the 455 HO engine's output dropped to 300 hp. In 1972 and 1973, GTO represented only an option package for the Le Mans series and the following year it became an option on the Ventura two-door coupe and hatchback. There were still such items as a fresh air shaker hood and heavy-duty suspension included in the GTO package, but, with the 350 cid V-8s developing 200 hp at 4400 rpm, the 7,058 GTO's built in 1974 were an anemic end.

VERSATILE!

The COBRA glides along in 15 mile per hour traffic in fourth gear as effortlessly as it tows a ski boat at 70. (Try that with your present sports car!) We really hesitate to brag for fear the so called "purists" will condemn·us but... this remarkable high gear flexibility displayed by the COBRA is almost like having an automatic transmission! And...with Ford's revolutionary 289 cubic inch V-8 under the hood the COBRA will run comfortably with any company you wish to keep...or leave! COBRA's versatility is truly TOTAL PERFORMANCE, try it!

COBRA
POWERED BY FORD

SHELBY AMERICAN, INC. 1042 PRINCETON DRIVE, VENICE, CALIFORNIA

MOTOR TREND/NOVEMBER 1963 **13**

30. Shelby Cobra

When George Stirrat, in March, 1960, began work on Ford's 221 cid V-8 (initially identified as the "Canadian X Project"), it's doubtful he envisioned its use in one of the great performance two-seaters. Along similar lines, FoMoCo fans who savored the sight of a 427 cid NASCAR Ford flat out at Daytona understandably may not have anticipated that engine powering the most awesome two-seater of the performance age.

No one needs to suffer recriminations for lacking clairvoyant powers in this regard but, looking back at the early sixties, it's fascinating to see the key elements that in combination strengthened and fortified each other, and, thus, made the Cobra a car greater in performance brilliance than the sum total of its parts.

A list of the men contributing their talents and skills, not to mention a tidal wave of limitless enthusiasm, to the Cobra's genesis, development and maturation reads like a who-was-who of the sixties performance scene. Ken Miles, Dave MacDonald, Dan Gurney, Pete Brock and Phil Remington personified both "the seat of my pants tells me the car isn't right" approach and some of the best technological approaches to the design of a sports car. But, at the top of this mountain of top notch motoring mentality was the man himself, Carroll Shelby. We've already briefly met Shelby in the Shelby-Mustang chapter, but a few points about his career, germaine to the Cobra's evolution, still need to be made.

Shelby emerged from relative obscurity as a sports car driver in 1956 when he became the SCCA's National Champion, a title he also won the following year. These successes in the United States were followed by a win along with Ray Salvadori in 1959 at LeMans in an Aston Martin. Shelby's last driving season was in 1960 and he went out in style as the USAC Road Racing Champion. As early as 1954, Shelby had spent time in Europe as an Aston Martin team member, an experience that not only brought him into contact with Europe's positive attitude towards the true, dual purpose sports car but also kindled his desire to someday build an automobile that would meet or exceed anyone's measure for a sports car.

Just about everyone who was touched by those magical, often raucous, always exciting, and never boring, sports cars of the fifties had at one time or another similar dreams. Some, like Harley Earl, worked for giant corporations and could make it happen. Others like Bob Carnes (whose Bocar was a moderate, brief success in American racing) got to first base and produced a few cars before the flood of red ink from their ledgers drowned their efforts. Then, for every Carnes, there were dozens of others whose dreams never got beyond the castle-in-the-sand stage.

Then, there was Shelby. Call it luck, pluck, the smiling of the Gods upon a favored earthling or something else, but whatever the reason, Shelby made it big in a big way. At a time when his racing career was brought to an end for health reasons, and Shelby was shopping for the bits and pieces needed to build his dream sports car, two manufacturers, one small, the other large, were facing business crossroads. For the old line English AC firm, it was more of a dead end than a road offering a choice of directions to follow. Since 1957, its Ace roadster had been available with the Bristol

two liter engine whose ancestry included the pre-war BMW 328. Long in the tooth, but vibrant, this two liter engine had made the Ace-Bristol one of the top performing small-engined sports cars in the world. It was also one of the best looking, but all good and bad times run their course and, in the early sixties, Bristol decided to end production of its venerable two liter six. This put AC in a bit of a twiddle. Its own two liter six was even older than Bristol's and lacked the needed power output to fill the resulting void. A reasonable alternative was use of a 2.6 liter English Ford Zephyr engine which, in tuned form, could be coaxed into the 170 hp range. A far more attractive alternative came from Shelby, who proposed mating the Ace with Ford's light weight 221 cid V-8 which, even in its most modest form, was good for 143 hp and was lighter than the Zephyr six. The actual technique used by Shelby to seduce Ford into going along with this plan required a great degree of verbal dexterity on Shelby's part, but he pulled it off. Ironically, especially in view of what the Cobra eventually did to the Corvette's racing status, GM refused to go along with Shelby's plan back in 1957 to market a sports car with a European body and chassis and a Chevrolet V-8. They had their chance and passed it by. Ford didn't, and that made all the difference. Ford provided Shelby with a 221 V-8 which he promptly dispatched to AC who made some extensive modifications to a car destined to be the first of the Cobras. This prototype was sent, engineless, to the U.S. in time to receive an early 260 cid V-8. Ford was obviously eager to see Shelby succeed and, to send him off, they saw to it that the 260 V-8's Shelby received were capable of a healthy output. With 9.2:1 compression ratio heads, a small Holley four-barrel carburetor, large valves and ports plus a hot cam and mechanical lifters, they were rated at 260 hp. With the exception of steel tubing headers, Shelby installed these engines in his Cobras as delivered from Ford.

In its prototype form, the Cobra manifested two very important attributes contributing greatly to its future success. The first was obvious to anyone who got down on his knees and took a close look at its assembly. The Cobra was not just an Ace with an American V-8. Virtually every important component that was to carry additional stress due to the doubling of the AC's power had either been strengthened or replaced with a stronger unit. This "do it the right way from the beginning" philosophy elevated the Cobra far above the backyard bomb variety of sports car

The Cobra's second great virtue was rooted both in Shelby's past experiences and in his dreams. He knew from his European adventures what was needed to win world class races and his dream was to produce a car with that level of performance. In a world populated by ultra-quick, race-bred Ferraris, Jaguars and Corvettes, the chances that a newcomer could break their monopoly weren't good, but that never really crossed Shelby's mind. Instead, his car very quickly forced every major European and American publication to revise their measurements of sports car performance. Virtually overnight, the Cobra became the new bench mark, the new yard stick, the new standrd of excellence.

An early Cobra brochure was direct and to the point, "Buy it or watch it go by." The prototype, tested both in bare aluminum and a variety of body colors, consistently turned in zero to 60 mph times bordering around 4.2 seconds. Quarter-mile runs were completed in approximately 13 seconds and, with a 3.54:1 axle, the Cobra's top speed was in excess of 150 mph. With an under $6,000 price tag, there was simply no other car in the world that was quite like the Cobra or that could match its performance. Its suspension, with front and rear transverse leaf springs, wasn't, however, the latest or the greatest design. Etched into the memory of many race goers of the mid-fifties were scenes of Ace-Bristols rounding corners with a good deal of body roll. Some of this misbehavior was missing from the Cobra due to the use of larger and stronger chassis tubing. Thus, on most long and smooth race tracks, the early Cobra's handling fell within the accepted standards for front-engined sports cars.

Late in 1962, the Cobra, driven by Bill Krause, made its racing debut at Riverside Raceway in California. It didn't make it to the finish line due to a broken stub axle, (this component was strengthened on subsequent cars) but, while it raced, the Cobra had no difficulty in keeping the new Sting Ray off its tail.

After only 75 Cobras had been constructed, Ford's 289 cid V-8, identical to the 260 V-8 except for its 4.0 inch bore, became available. With solid lifters, high-lift cam and a 460 cfm Autolite carburetor, the basic 289 Cobra with 271 hp was turned over to its sweaty palmed owner. It should also be noted that, after the first 125 cars had been built, a switch was made from cam gear steering to a rack and pinion system.

In order that Cobras could compete successfully anywhere in the world, in virtually every imaginable form of automotive competition, Shelby offered a wide variety of options. Beyond the base 271 hp engine were versions with 300 hp and two four-barrel carbs, a 325 hp unit with four Weber, 48 mm IDA carburetors and the top of the line 380 hp, 289 cid with these Webers plus reworked heads and a very wild cam. Any of these engines were available in special drag racing, "Dragonsnake" Cobras. Shelby of course, also offered roadsters for road race use that enabled Cobras to win the SCCA's A-Production National Championship in '63, '64, '65, '66, '67 and '68.

The Cobra's first Sebring venture, in 1963, wasn't memorable. Five began the 12-hour trek, but only two went the distance to finish in 11th and 29th place. At this point, the Cobras were still in the sorting out stage, whereas their Ferrari GTO rivals were enjoying both great speed and reliability. The following year it proved to be a far more interesting encounter. Earlier in February, at the Daytona 12-Hours, the first of an eventual "production run" of six Cobra Daytona Coupes appeared. The Coupe's mission was to wrest the Manufacturers' World championship for Grand Touring Cars from Ferrari. Contemporary F.I.A. competition regulations allowed the substitution of one body for another as long as no chassis or engine variations took place. Both Ferrari and Aston Martin had taken advantage of this rule to develop coupe versions for competition. Faced off against these cars, the Cobra roadster was at a severe aerodynamic handicap and the Daytona Coupe, designed by Pete Brock, gained virtual parity for Cobra in this area. In its first race at Daytona, the coupe very nearly came away a winner. Driven by Bob Holbert and Dave McDonald, the Cobra held a six lap lead over the fastest

GTO Ferrari when a refueling fire put it out of the running. At Sebring, the repaired Coupe, with the same driving team, finished fourth overall, behind three Ferraris running in the prototype class. This finish gave Cobra important points toward the GT Championship. Other Cobra roadsters finished in fifth and sixth places, convincingly demonstrating their superiority over "production model" GTO Ferraris.

Sebring, 1964, also provided a glimpse into a "what could have been" Cobra/Corvette confrontation. For the first five hours, the Grand Sport Corvette of Roger Penske and Jim Hall had battled with the Cobra Coupe for the top position behind the trio of rear-engined Ferraris. The Corvette's ability to do so was a clear indication of Chevrolet's capability to compete if not hampered by a corporate animosity towards racing.

Over the season, the Cobras weren't quite strong enough to break Ferrari's hold on the GT Championship, but it was close. Ferrari ended the year with 84.6 points, Cobra with 78.3 points. This, obviously, was a disappointment for the Shelby men, yet the season had provided, aside from the Sebring success, many Cobra achievements. At LeMans, Dan Gurney and Bob Bondurant placed the Coupe fourth overall and first in the GT class. In practice, Gurney's best lap of 3 minutes, 58.6 seconds was over six seconds faster than the best GTO Ferrari's. In the process, the Cobra was clocked at over 182 mph.

The Coupe's success was more than just the first ever GT victory at LeMans by an American-engined car. Bernard Cahier (SPORTS CAR GRAPHIC, September, 1964) said it best, "The Cobra-Ford engine, basically a production push-rod engine which can be brought by anyone, has been strikingly improved by racing to the point where it had become a reliable, winning power plant capable of pulling a big GT car at an average of over 120 mph for 24 hours . . . This convincing demonstration by the 4.7 liter push-rod Ford engine is particularly interesting to those who are fond of, and convinced of, the usefulness of motor racing. It is also a striking answer to the recent statement of Mr. Donner of General Motors stating that racing does not improve production automobiles."

Mr. Donner, of course, was entitled to his view, and, at GM, his view was law. It was not, however, the way Carroll Shelby saw things and, at Sebring '64, Ken Miles was doing a little improving of the breed on his own out on the track. Pinched into his car's 289 chassis was a 427 Ford NASCAR engine with some 480 hp on tap. Just about every Sebring '64 report details how Miles collided with the only tree in a 3 or 5 acre field during practice, but this didn't hold him back very long. Working virtually as his own pit crew, he got the car back in shape for the race's 10 a.m. starting time. The sight and sound of Miles' car was memorable. He spent a lot of time in the pits sorting out a myriad of problems, but he also put on quite a show until he retired for good during the twelfth hour. Those who knew better weren't turned off by the 427 Cobra's lack of traction and less than precise handling. Instead, they saw the potential of linking a big, untempermental V-8 with a suitably modified lightweight chassis and suspension.

Later, in December, 1964, the upsized Cobra appeared at Nassau, first with a 390 cid aluminum block V-8 and then with the 427. Its suspension was still of the familiar leaf spring variety but its frame was further lightened and, with a super-thin aluminum body, it weighed in at approximately 1,600 pounds, some 400 less than a production 289 Cobra. It didn't finish at Nassau but, said SPORTS CAR GRAPHIC

(November, 1964) "It went like the hammer and was only beaten, and just, by a lightweight GS Sting Ray in the hands of Roger Penske and then only because some chassis bits broke up and Ken [Miles] had to slow down."

At this point in time, a pair of 427 Cobra prototypes with fully independent, coil spring suspensions were nearing competition and on January 27, 1965, the 427 Cobra made its press debut at Riverside. Visually, the new Cobra was obviously related to the 289 version, but, at the same time, there was no mistaking it for anything else but a 427 Cobra. Its approximately 7 inch wider body, larger grille with no grid work, flared-out fenders and 7½ inch wide Halibrand knockoffs left no room for doubt. With its "out-of-the-box" Ford Grand National 427 V-8 (equipped with dual AFB Holleys) and street tires, the Cobra was capable of "Heaven Can Wait" performance. Ken Miles provided the most memorable testimony: zero to 100 mph and back to zero in 13.8 seconds. As a famous Cobra ad noted, "Owning a new '427' Cobra isn't quite like your first sports car."

Total Cobra production amounted to just 1,011 cars, of which 356 were of the 427 variety. Some 427 Cobras were

The Continuing popularity of the Shelby Cobra is amply illustrated by the fact that several replicars have recently been made available to the public, including the Contemporary Cobra models illustrated below (427, top; 289, bottom).

actually not powered by the 427 engine but by the more civilized 428 street V-8. These were slightly less powerful but hardly anyone really noticed the difference. For competition purposes, the 427 Cobra came with the high riser version of the 427 attached to a single Holley 780 cfm four-barrel. If desired, cast aluminum heads, intake manifold and timing chain cover were also available, as were numerous competition bits and pieces. Typically, such cars ran the quarter-mile in 12.3 seconds and 121 mph. In between the street and all but competition 427's, an S/C (semi/competition or street/competition) 427 Cobra was offered combining the best features of both. A typical S/C Cobra had a lightweight competition body, medium-riser 427 engine with two four-barrels and side exhaust cutoff among its more notable features.

The Cobras did far more than just bring the United States the World Manufacturers' Championship for Grand Touring cars in 1965. They were performance giants and the ultimate refinement not only of the front engined sports car but also of the classic dual-purpose sports roadster. Unlike the Corvette, which blended creature comforts with stimulating performance, the Cobra was always built for one purpose and one purpose only: to out perform any other production sports car in the world. When you do that well and with class, then you do, indeed, create a legend. What more can be said about Carroll Shelby's effort except, "well done, mission accomplished"?

31. Shelby Mustang

The 271 hp Mustang certainly was a heart throbber. Neither its performance or appearance needed excuses and, as an image builder, it played a major role in the Mustang success story, but a more potent automobile was needed to fulfill Ford's desire to send the Mustang into the S.C.C.A.'s very competitive Class B production sports car racing. Lee Iacocca needed no soothsayer, crystal ball or executive committee to help him select the man to create such an automobile. There was only one possible choice, that homegrown, honest to gosh American sports car hero, national champion, Mr. "Oh shucks it was nothing" in his bib coveralls driving a big 4.9 Ferrari, superb businessman and racing genius extraordinary wrapped up in one delightfully human package: Carroll Shelby. By late 1964, Shelby's 289 Cobra had dealt the Sting Rays a stunning setback in competition and he was in the early stages of developing Ford's GT-40 into a world class racing/sports car. For Shelby to revamp the Mustang into a car that would sock it to the small block Corvettes and the British Jaguars in S.C.C.A. racing would simply be a case of doing what came naturally.

The little detail of fulfilling the S.C.C.A.'s dictum that 100 models of *any* production car had to be built by January 1, 1965, in order to be eligible for the season's racing was taken care of at the Mustang San Jose, California, assembly plant. In one fell swoop they built the required number of Mustangs with 271 hp engines and delivered them to Shelby's facility at the Los Angeles International Airport.

Thus began the Shelby segment of the Mustang performance story. The small matter of what to call the Shelby-ized two-seater was, legend has it, decided by Shelby who decreed it would be labeled the GT-350 in recognition of the 350-odd feet separating Shelby's office in Venice, California, from a building across the street.

As delivered to Shelby, the soon-to-be GT-350's had already been spruced up by Ford in anticipation of what their future held. All were fastback models powered by the 271 hp engine. Lacking were such items as engine hoods, rear seats, grille bars and exhaust systems. Included in their assembly was a one-piece "export brace" for the front shock absorbers, a shortened heavy-duty Galaxie rear axle with a Detroit Automotive split differential, Borg-Warner T-10, close-ratio 4-speed transmission with an aluminum casing, and Koni, Dutch-built adjustable shock absorbers. Ford also saw to it that the GT-350 would have first class braking. At the front were 11.3 inch Kelsey Hayes ventilated disc brakes with heavy-duty pads. Stopping power out back was handled by drum brakes (fitted with sintered metallic linings) from the largest Ford station wagon that were ½ inch wider than the stock Mustang's. The station wagon also provided the GT-350's 15 inch x 5½ inch wheels on which were mounted Goodyear 130 mph Blue Dot 7.75 inch 13 inch tires.

Being well acquainted with sports car racing, the Shelby crew knew what additional features the GT-350 needed to stun the Sting Rays. At the front, a one inch sway bar was installed along with longer idler and Pitman arms that reduced the car's overall steering ratio from 21:1 to 19:1. This also lowered the steering wheel turns lock-to-lock to 3½ from 3¾. The upper control arms were also lower by

one inch. At the rear, trailing arm, radius rods were welded to the frame and to the rear end housing. This setup virtually eliminated axle hop and rear spring windup.

To bring the GT-350 engine up to 306 hp at 6000 rpm and 329 lbs-ft at 4200 rpm, several items developed from the Cobra program were used, including an aluminum high rise intake manifold, finned valve covers and 6.5 quart capacity oil pan. A Holley 715 cfm carburetor was also installed as were steel tubing exhaust headers and low restriction, dual, fiberglass packed mufflers.

With its Wimbleton white finish and optional Guardsman Blue down-the-body racing stripe, the street version of the GT-350 had an imposing "don't mess around with me" appearance. Shelby's official GT-350 performance figures were not likely to disappoint anyone. With a 3.89 rear axle, Shelby reported the following times: 0-60 mph - 5.7 sec.; 0-100 mph - 14.9 sec.; standing start ¼-mile - 14.5 seconds/98 mph; top speed - 133 mph.

Most published road tests of the GT-350 didn't quite come up to these standards but virtually no driver walked away from a GT-350 disappointed after putting it through its paces. *CAR AND DRIVER* (May, 1965) concluded, "In all honesty it cannot be said that the Mustang 350 GT (sic) is the sort of car a sane man would enjoy driving at all times and under all conditions . . . The journey and all the chuff and bang from the side exhaust pipes, is simply part of the fun. Not a lady's car by any stretch of the imagination; probably not even a gentleman's car for that matter; but surely a man's car, in the tradition of the Blower Bentley or the Cad-Allard." Less flamboyant, but certainly to the point, was *MOTOR TREND* magazine's opinion: "The GT-350 is one car that'll never put you to sleep at the wheel."

The GT-350R, as the "Competition Prepared Version" was labeled, made its racing debut at Green Valley Raceway, Texas, early in 1965. Driven by Ken Miles, it won a preliminary race and finished second in two subsequent heats. During 1965, the very first GT-350R constructed made Shelby, Iacocca, and all friends of Ford quite happy by winning the SCCA B/Production titles. The GT-350R went on to remain the champ both in 1966 and 1967.

The out-the-door price of the GT-350R was $5,950, whereas a GT-350 was ticketed at $4,547. For those extra dollars, the GT-350R purchaser obviously acquired a winner. Each car was given a track test at Willow Springs Raceway to assure all was in working order. The changes made to the GT-350 to move it up to "R" status were extensive but well within both the spirit and letter of the S.C.C.A. regulations. The engine was blueprinted and balanced, its ports enlarged and polished and a racing cam was installed. A cold air plenum chamber connected the 715 cfm Holley to the hoodscoop and larger, straight-through mufflers plus an oil cooler was also added. The Shelby American Automobile Club credits this engine with 325-350 horsepower.

There were quite a few visual features unique to the GT-350R. By removing the rear quarter panel vents and covering over the opening that remained with aluminum sheeting, car weight dropped approximately 50 pounds. The front bumper and gravel pan were removed and their place taken by a single piece fiberglas front apron. At the rear, the bumper was banished, again in the interest of weight reduction (which totalled approximately 250 pounds).

Sales of the 1965 GT-350 were modest, totalling just 562, along with approximately 25 R models. Obviously, the market for these highly specialized two-seaters was limited but, equally obvious, their impact upon the performance scene was not. Their successes reflected very favorably both upon the basic design of the Mustang and the competence of Shelby American, Inc.

_1967_

Changes in the GT-350 (it was now officially the Shelby GT-350 rather than Mustang GT-350) for 1966 were not substantial. Actually, the first 250 cars built were based upon 1965 Mustangs. After that point, pressure from Ford to reduce production costs led to the deletion of the Koni shocks, lowered front A arm and the rear traction bars.

An interesting marketing success by Shelby was the sale of 916 cars to Hertz for rental to drivers age 25 or older belonging to their Hertz Sports Car Club. Identified as GT-350H's they were essentially standard GT-350's equipped with C-4 automatic transmissions.

More interesting than this development to devotees of horsepower was the mid-April, 1966, debut of a Paxton Supercharger option for the GT-350. Shelby suggested a retail price of $670 for this item which, it claimed, would boost horsepower by up to 46%. No more than 150 GT-350S models, as the supercharged GT-350 was labeled, were built. To this total must also be added a very small number of 1965 models that were also supercharged.

Joe Granatelli of the Paxton company pegged the GT-350S at over 400 hp and claimed such a car with a C-4 automatic (this transmission was also offered on the 1966 GT-350) transmission would accelerate from zero to 60 mph in 5 seconds. *MOTOR TREND's* test of such a machine yielded a time of 6 seconds for the same run while *CAR LIFE* reported a 6.2 second figure.

Both in 1965 and 1966, a small number of GT-350's were prepared for drag racing. Their engines were the standard, 306 hp versions but customers were given access to a full list of options that enabled the "Shelby GT-350 Drag Mustang" to be a consistent class winner.

The best sales year yet for the Shelby Mustangs was 1967. However, if you regarded the 1965 and 1966 models as the only proper form of a sports car, then you were a trifle disappointed in the new models. The reason for this apparent inconsistency is simple. The new Shelby Mustangs, yes, there were two of them, were less raucous and more civilized than before. Thus, they lost a few admirers but also appealed to a much broader spectrum of the performance market. Some critics saw the new cars as positioned between the early, starkly uncompromising cars and the luxury oriented, yet lively, GT cars that were yet to come. The 1967 GT-350 still was rated at 306 hp but, since it lacked the steel tubing exhaust headers that Shelby-American earlier claimed increased horsepower, the 1967 engine was almost certainly less powerful than the earlier versions. The GT-350 suspension was essentially the special handling package available on the production Mustang. However, a thicker, 0.94 inch diameter front antiroll bar was used along with Gabriel adjustable shocks (Koni models were optional).

With Ford going the big engine route with the Mustang, it was both obvious and proper for Shelby to do likewise. The result was the Shelby GT-500 powered by the 428 "Cobra LeMans" engine. It didn't take much talent to be suspicious of its 335 hp rating. With dual four-barrel 600 cfm Holleys, aluminum, high rise intake manifold plus "high-rev" hydraulic valve train and special cam, it was very, very strong. An early GT-500 engineering prototype, for example, was a close second to a GT40 around the Ford testing ground handling loop. Even more interesting than the GT-500, but seldom seen since less than 50 were built, were the Shelbys powered by the 427 medium riser engine. The Shelby American Automobile Club reported that Shelby drove one such creation around the Goodyear track in Texas at over 170 mph.

In spite of its bulk and weight, the GT-500 received a reasonably positive press review. *ROAD & TRACK* noted, "It looks something like a racing car, yet it isn't. It also has something of the flavor of a luxurious Grand Touring machine, but it isn't quite that either." *CAR AND DRIVER* was somewhat more positive, maintaining, "All the viciousness had gone out of the car without any lessening of its animal vitality."

Changes for the 1968 were relatively minor, a typical example being a new fiberglass hood with wide and low twin scoops near its front edge. There were also new names for 1968: Shelby Cobra GT-350 and Shelby Cobra GT-500 plus, for the first time, a convertible body style. The 306 hp, 289 cid engine was replaced by Ford's 302 cid V-8. Its output, with hydraulic lifters and a single 600 cfm Holley four-barrel, was just 250 hp. The Paxton Supercharger was still available, boosting that figure to 350, but only a few were sold.

The GT-500 was still alive and well thanks to the 360 hp provided by the Ford "Police Interceptor 428" equipped with cylinder heads from the 410 cid V-8 used by Mercury, a Cobra aluminum intake manifold and a 715 cfm Holley. Mixed in with these engines were a few GT-500's with 390 engines and another small batch of C-6 automatic transmissioned cars with the 400 hp, 427 engine.

At midyear, Shelby took advantage of Ford's introduction of the 428 Cobra Jet and brought forth his GT-500KR ("King of the Road"). These cars at rest were distinguished by their GT-500KR rocker panel labels and Shelby snake emblem. When the KR was put up in a grease rack, staggered rear shock absorbers were discovered along with extra bracing for the bottom of the front shock absorber towers. For all its underrated 335 hp, the GT-500KR wasn't as quick from zero to 60 mph or in the quarter-mile as the original GT-350. Under 7 seconds from zero to 60 mph wasn't pedal car caliber performance, but, obviously, weight and bulk had taken its toll.

The 1969 season was the last one for Shelby Mustang production. A new body style for the Mustang meant the same for Shelby and, with three NASA-type hood scoops, a neater front end plus the sleekness of the Mustang's new Sports Roof, the 1969 Shelbys were visually very exciting. Less stirring was their performance. The GT-350 powerplant was the 280 hp, 351 Windsor V-8, which was a shadow of the old 306 high revver. Brock Yates said it best in *CAR AND DRIVER:* "The GT-350 was now a garter snake in Cobra skin . . . a tiger is turned into a pussy cat."

The GT-500 with the Cobra Jet engine didn't come under this indictment but both cars, with overly long front ends and a general sensation of having compromised function for form, just didn't measure up to the high standards of past Shelby Mustangs.

None of this was really Shelby's fault. Ford itself, with its own proliferation of production offerings, had been a tough competitor and, as the market softened, it just made good business sense for Shelby to follow the shift away from all-out performance to milder mannered cars. To his credit, Shelby went out in style (new, unsold 1969 models were retailed as 1970's). As Richard J. Kopec wrote in his *SHELBY AMERICAN GUIDE,* "Shelby ceased production of the GT-350 and GT-500 when they were at the highpoint of their evolution. The motoring public would never see a Shelby as an anemic blob masquerading in stripes and spoilers and fake gimmicks. Rather, they would see nothing — and nothing would be better than that."

32. Studebaker

If the Age of Performance had a stepchild, it was Studebaker. In the years preceding World War II, Studebaker was a force to be reckoned with, both as a high stepping road machine with the power to eat up mile after mile at high speeds and as a competitor at Indianapolis. Studebakers held numerous speed records, thus obliging no Studebaker owner to be defensive about his automobile's capability.

This state of affairs changed rapidly in the postwar years. Studebakers, with their "new look," were visually impressive, but in no way demonstrated their predecessors proclivity for performance. Much of Studebaker's corporate behavior after 1945 was tainted with "missed the boat" overtones, and one of the best examples of Studebaker's shortsightedness was its new for 1951 V-8. Studebaker spent a bagful of money developing this engine and, from the viewpoint of durability, toughness and longevity, they got their money's worth, providing in the process, thousands of loyal Studebaker fans with many years of satisfactory service. But this engine, with bore and stroke of $3\frac{3}{8}$ inches x $3\frac{1}{4}$ inches and displacement of 232.5 cubic inches, was on the small size, even for 1951. Worse yet, especially when the horsepower race started to heat up, Studebaker's V-8 couldn't be opened up to the extent possible, for example, with the Oldsmobile and Cadillac engines. Thus, in the world of the 400 cubic inch heavyweight, Studebaker was a 300 cubic inch welterweight, perceived by the muscle car crowd as an automobile not to be taken seriously.

The problems posed by Studebaker's small, 120 hp engine weren't apparent in 1951, nor was there a sense of apprehension among its advocates when Studebaker unveiled its sensational 1953 coupes. "There's no doubt," said *ROAD AND TRACK* (September, 1953), "that this car marks a milestone in America car manufacturing." That, it most certainly was. Its styling will forever represent good taste and excellent form, but such attributes weren't enough to overcome an early reputation for poor workmanship plus the unappealing looks of Studebaker's sedans and (in 1954) station wagons that had to sell in fairly large numbers if the South Bend plant was to keep functioning. They didn't, as is well known, and Studebaker started hitting the skids. Meanwhile, the coupes were having problems of their own.

Below, 1955 Studebaker Speedster

They looked like sports cars but who ever heard of a modern sports car with a 120.5 inch wheelbase? Perhaps an automobile that size might get by masquerading as a Grand Touring machine in a different age and time, but certainly not in 1953. In this respect, though, let's take a look at the Studebaker's performance. Most contemporary road tests credited the 120 hp coupes with zero to 60 mph times hovering around the 16 second mark. *MOTOR TREND*, for example, reported in with a 16.9 second time for an automatic-transmssion model with a 3.54 rear axle. *ROAD AND TRACK* coaxed its Studebaker test car, equipped with overdrive and 4.55 axle, up to 60 mph in 14.9 seconds. This latter figure came close to matching the claim of Studebaker engineering that their car needed only 13 seconds to accelerate from zero to 60 mph. In any case, the typical Studebaker V-8 was a spirited, but by no means an exceptional, straight line performer.

More debatable was its handling competence. "The Studebaker," said *MOTOR TREND* (June, 1953), "has more feeling of a sports car than any other stock car today." *ROAD & TRACK* (September, 1953) was essentially in agreement with *MOTOR TREND*, concluding, "This car corners better than any of the cars in its class." Yet, these comments, complimentary on the surface, could also be viewed as examples of damnation through faint praise. Thanks to its fairly heavy engine, slow, $5\frac{1}{4}$ turns, lock-to-lock, steering and soft suspension, the coupe simply was not a sports car in regard to its responsiveness, roadability or handling. Yet, it was also apparent that the Studebaker coupe was a diamond in the rough. "South Bend has the basic ingredients," said *AUTO SPORT REVIEW* (July, 1953), "the body shell and the motor. A little hard work by the engineering department on the problems of handling, steering and road-holding and some real thinking by the body department on the details of seating, positioning of controls, and general quality of finish and you couldn't ask for a sweeter road car."

Unfortunately, both for Studebaker's future fortunes and its performance advocates, the company's lethargic leadership failed to pursue this line of action either in 1953 or 1954. Lethargy wasn't characteristic of American hot rodders, however, particularly one Bill Frick who earlier had mated a number of Ford sedans with Cadillac V-8's. Since the Cadillac 331 cid V-8 weighed just 13 pounds more than the 232 cid Studebaker V-8, there was no serious

impact upon the Studebaker's weight distribution. Even when Hydra-Matic transmission was used the total weight increase was no more than 100 pounds. Frick Motors did not simply drop in a 210 hp engine into the Studebaker and leave everything else unchanged. The Studillacs built by Bill Frick were carefully designed and built road machines. Some 20 man-hours alone were spent on each car correcting the misassemblies so common to Studebakers shipped from South Bend. More fundamental changes occurred in the areas of engine and transmission supports, braking (11 inch drums from the 1953 Mercury were used) and steering.

With Hydra-Matic, the Studillac was one of the fastest accelerating sedans in the world, needing only 8.5 seconds to accelerate from zero to 60 mph. Small wonder Tom McCahill (*MECHANIX ILLUSTRATED*, November, 1953) claimed, "The Studillac, a direct descendent of Frick's Fordillac, will even run away from an XK 120 Jaguar as if it were a highway sign."

Those who wanted more zip than the stock 120 hp Studebaker engine provided, but weren't sufficiently endowed financially to go the Studillac route, had another alternative, thanks to the McCulloch supercharger. Early in 1951, the McCulloch Company began development of a supercharger adaptable to the Ford and Mercury flathead V-8's. Shortly after they went on the market in 1953, a unit suitable for the Studebaker V-8 became available. Its use on a stock, automatic transmission Studebaker reduced the zero to 60 mph acceleration time to 11.9 seconds and provided a top speed in excess of 107 mph.

Studebaker obviously wasn't ignorant of all these goings on and, with its Speedster model of 1955, made a belated attempt to cash in on the performance potential of its slinky coupes. To read Studebaker's ad copy for the Speedster was to vicariously experience an automotive orgasm. It was, said Studebaker, "lightning on wheels." a car with "the action look of an Indianapolis 500 Special . . . acclaimed by test drivers the world over as the get-away star of 1955." This was a pretty heavy order for any automobile to make good on, and, with its 185 hp "Passmaster V-8," the Speedster didn't quite match its advertised virtues.

The Studebaker-Packard merger of 1954 had numerous ramifications, most of them bad, but it also provided Studebaker with the wherewithal to make a strong run for the performance gold with its coupes. The old Speedster name was given the deep six, replaced by the Hawk, or, more appropriately, by four Hawks: Golden, Silver, Power and Flight. Of these, the most muscular was, of course, the Golden Hawk. In regard to its appearance, few could deny the Golden Hawk looked like a powerful piece of machinery. An aggressive front grille suggestive of earlier Lancia sports cars, plus only mildly subdued rear fins, were blended into the basic lines of the 1953 vintage body shell with a minimum of discomfort. Purists didn't shower the Golden Hawk with accolades but, since they hadn't flocked to Studebaker showrooms when the less adorned coupes were offered, you can't blame Studebaker for changing its game plan. Similarly, in a year when engine sizes and power rating were on a big upswing, Studebaker couldn't really be chastised too severely for installing the 352 cid Packard V-8 in the Golden Hawk. With a single Carter four-barrel carburetor and a 9.5:1 compression ratio, the Golden Hawk's engine was rated at 275 hp. Studebaker touted the Golden Hawk as having the best power to weight ratio of any American car and claimed it was capable of zero to 60 mph in 8.7 seconds. This figure was never matched by Golden Hawks available for road testing purposes. A more typical time for an overdrive equipped Golden Hawk was 9.2 seconds, with the Ultramatic version reaching 60 mph in approximately 10 seconds. Neither the Packard V-8 or Ultramatic were designed as high performance items. Durability and smooth operation were their forte and, thus, they weren't the ideal engine-transmission combination for a supercar. As installed in the Golden Hawk, Ultramatic did not have the electric pushbutton operation featured on the 1956 Packards. It did, however, offer the driver some control over its operation. When the transmission selector was placed in the "lo" range, the transmission would remain in first gear until the selector was moved to "low drive" or "high drive," then it would shift into second and then into high.

Around the Studebaker-Packard test track, a factory tuned Golden Hawk lapped at speeds approaching 130 mph so there was no doubt it had lots of push at the top end. Getting there on anything else besides a straight road was less a stirring experience than it was a startling one. The Packard engine and transmission weighed over 900 pounds and, road ready, the Golden Hawk tipped the scales to over 3,700 pounds. Of this weight, 2,200 pounds, or 59%, sat on the front wheels. In the turns, the Golden Hawk lost its composure as the body leaned at a dreadful angle and understeer reigned supreme. It's fairly common knowledge that the lower priced Sky Hawk with the 289 cid, 210 hp Studebaker V-8 was a far more roadable car but, without big cubes and a high horsepower rating, its appeal as a performance machine was limited.

The horrendous collapse of Studebaker-Packard's fortunes in 1956 brought not only a near brush with bankruptcy but also the end of the Packard in its true form. This tragic end to the history of one of America's greatest automobiles brought with it a dilemma for Studebaker. In spite of its shortcomings, the Golden Hawk had kept Studebaker at least in the running as far as performance was concerned and, without a minimum of 275 horsepower, its 1957 version powered by the familiar 289 V-8 would be nothing less than a sham. The solution wasn't exactly original but, with Ford embracing supercharging for 1957, Studebaker's decision to do likewise put it in with good company.

More importantly, the Golden Hawk with a McCulloch supercharger breathing into a single Stromberg, two-barrel carburetor was a far better automobile than it had been a year earlier. Except for new front shock absorber mounts the Hawk's suspension was little changed from 1956. It was hardly sophisticated, being cast in the classic American front coil/wishbone/rear leaf springs mold, but, in heavy-duty form, freed from the Packard engine's weight, it provided the Golden Hawk with acceptable road manners, while the supercharged engine provided acceleration and top speed comparable to the standards set by the 1956 model.

In this form, the Golden Hawk was carried over into 1958, receiving only some cosmetic changes in the process. A production mark of less than 900, along with 588 Packards Hawks that were its mechanical twin, seemed to justify the Golden Hawk's demise at the end of the model year. The execution took place on schedule but at the last moment a reprieve was granted to the Golden Hawk's sidekick, the Silver Hawk. Both in 1957 and 1958, the lower priced Silver Hawks with pillared hardtop styling and a choice of either a 186 cid or 289 cid V-8 had been reasonably good sellers. However, the top engine available for the Silver Hawk in 1959 was a small, 259 cid Studebaker V-8. Its top horsepower rating was a modest 195, hardly enough to

satisfy appetite of anyone accustomed to a menu full of 300-400 cubic inch entrees.

Known only as the ''Hawk,'' the Studebaker coupe existed in a kind of automotive limbo in 1960 and 1961. The 289 V-8 with either 210 or 225 horsepower was available but was hardly capable of providing performance equal to the supercars from the Big Three.

Studebaker was gearing up for its last harrah under Sherwood Egbert who became its president in 1961 but, between the Hawk's power slump and arrival of the Avanti and its fabled R type engine, the spunky little Studebaker Larks took a fling at racing that was short but also rather sweet. Prior to the 1960 Sebring 12-Hour Race, 27 American and foreign compact cars lined up for a 2-hour match around the 5.2 mile circuit. The winner was Walt Hangsen driving a Briggs Cunningham 3.4 Jaguar but Hangsen's success was by no measure a walkaway. Hot on the Jaguar's heels were three, very hot and loud Lark V-8's handled by Curtis Turner, Ralph Moody and ''Fireball'' Roberts. At race end, the top four were: Jaguar, Lark, Jaguar, Lark. Admittedly, the Studebakers were a bit tattered around the edges after their two hour workout. Turner's second place car, for example, finished with its left front tire in shreds.

The Holman and Moody prepared Larks made an encore appearance at that fall's ''Little Le Mans'' race at Lime Rock, Connecticut, and drove away with first place, but, as far as Studebaker's public image was concerned, these achievements were small flashes in the pan. What was needed at South Bend was something new and flashy, an automobile that would draw second glances from those who it passed on the highway.

Sherwood Egbert moved dramatically to provide Studebaker with a double dose of this type of automotive stimulant. Brooks Stevens was given the assignment to

Above, 1963 Studebaker Avanti with Raymond Lowey (left) and Sherwood Egbert

refurbish the veteran Hawk with a new suit of metalwork and Raymond Loewy received the greenlight to create what would become the Avanti.

Both Steven's Hawk GT and the Avanti were design successes. The Avanti was visually controversial and, like the earlier 1946 and 1953 Studebakers, broke with conventional American styling. The Hawk, on the other hand, offered little that was new in terms of styling innovations but that was a deficiency of little importance. The final product borrowed from many different sources yet looked fresh and right, the way the Hawk should have appeared initially.

From a commercial viewpoint, the GT Hawk was a success, the Avanti, a terrible disaster. Whereas the redesigned components Stevens developed for the new Hawk blended together with ease and in the process actually reduced its production cost, the production of the Avanti was an unmitigated nightmare, an automotive Black Hole that sucked up never-to-be-seen-again money that Studebaker could hardly afford to lose. Yet, this economic Dunkirk had one redeeming part to it: the creation of the greatest Studebaker engines of all, the R types.

As it had done in 1957, Studebaker turned in 1962 to supercharging as the quickest way into the performance big leagues. This time they went as far as to purchase Paxton Products, an offspring of the original McCulloch supercharger products. In announcing Studebaker's acquisition of Paxton, Mr. Egbert noted, ''If the customer wishes to buy more horsepower than he can use, he will be able to buy it from Studebaker.''

This final performance episode for Studebaker lasted only from April, 1962, when the Avanti debuted at the New York International Auto Show, to December 9, 1963, when the dreaded announcement was made that automobile production in South Bend would cease. During that short time span, by a clever combination of puff and real huff. Egbert made the R engines highly regarded performance powerplants.

When the news broke early in 1962 that an R2 Supercharged Avanti had set a two-way flying mile record of 168.15 mph, some initial responses expressed disbelief, but the cynics soon had to accept the reality of the Avanti's achievement, much to the satisfaction of Studebaker's hardcore advocates. Initially, Studebaker demurred when pressed for details of the R engines' horsepower output. Instead of providing factual data, it coyly replied that they produced "more than enough" power. Eventually, bowing both to public interest and pressure from the N.H.R.A., Studebaker formally announced their power rating.

The basic R1 engine, like all the versions, was based upon the virtually vintage 289 cid V-8. With a single four-barrel carburetor and 10.25:1 compression ratio, it produced (according to an SAE paper by Eugene Hardig, one of the greats of Studebaker engineering) 240 hp at 4800 rpm. Studebaker later endorsed Hardig's figure but pegged it at 5000 rpm. The 280 hp R2 engine, again with 289 cubic inches, had a lower, 9.0:1 compression ratio to accomodate its Paxton supercharger that delivered a maximum boost of 4.5 psi.

Whereas the R1 Avanti with the Borg-Warner "Power-Shift" automatic transmission, which allowed manual control of first gear, accelerated in a respectable 9.1 seconds from zero to 60 mph, the automatic transmissioned R2 accomplished the same feat in 8 seconds. The use of a 4-speed manual gear box allowed the R2 Avanti to nudge the 7 second zero to 60 mph mark.

Although Studebaker described the Avanti as "a high performance prestige car," it was often judged by critics as a sports car. Like all Studebaker V-8's, the R1 and R2 Avantis were nose heavy, thus making comparisons between the Avanti and the typical sports car a rather one-sided affair. Still, with front disc brakes that probably gave the Avanti the best negative acceleration performance in the industry, plus quick acceleration, it was a unique blend of luxury, power and originality.

In late January, 1963, the relatively familiar R2 Avanti was joined by two new, and rather interesting, R2 Studebakers, the Super Lark and Super Hawk, for some high speed exercise at Bonneville. All three supercharged Studebakers, with manual transmissions and running with air cleaners and mufflers in place, recorded these very creditable top speeds:

R2 Super Lark	—	132 mph
R2 Super Hawk	—	140 mph
R2 Avanti	—	158.14 mph

The $581.70 Super Hawk package included, in addition to special medallions, power front disc brakes, heavy-duty shocks and springs, rear radius rods and anti-roll bar, limited-slip differential, tachometer and 6.70 x 15 four-ply tires. If the R1 engine was desired, the Super Hawk features carried a $371.70 price.

The R2 Super Hawk was a unique automobile, described by MOTOR TREND (June, 1963) as, "a formidable opponent for any car on the road . . ." With power-shift, the Super Hawk's time from zero to 60 mph was a satisfactory 8.5 seconds.

Joining the R engine lineup in 1963 was its ultimate supercharged version, the R3. This was as rare an engine as any of the age. Most Studebaker authorities have settled on 9 as the magic number for the total production run of R3's. The initial plan called for a 299 cid for the R3 but, after March 1, 1963, all were of 304.5 cubic inches, the ultimate overbore of the Studebaker V-8. Incidentally, at least three Avantis were powered by the early, 299.4 cid R3 engines since that number participated in runs at Bonneville in August, 1962. Andy Granatelli's R3 maintained an average of 168.24 mph for 10 miles. The R3 engine was built by Paxton, originating as a basic 289 engine block from which Paxton bored an additional 0.093 inches. A cylinder head with larger ports and valves (1⅞ inch intake, 1⅝ inch exhaust) was used along with a 276° duration cam. To say that the R3 was carefully tended to by Paxton would be an understatement; better to suggest they were exquisitely assembled. Prior to their release, every R3 had to produce at least 335 hp at 5350 rpm. When installed in an Avanti or Lark, the R3 package also included a heavy-duty suspension that gave handling very competitive to that of the typical American supercar. MOTOR TREND (August, 1963) tested an R3 with automatic transmission and reported it was capable of a quarter-mile time and speed of 102 mph and 14.3 seconds. Its zero to 60 mph time was a strong 6.7 seconds. At Bonneville, HOT ROD magazine found a speed of 150 mph within the reach of an R3 Lark.

At the Bonneville introduction of the ill-fated 1964 Studebakers, a special "Due Cento" Avanti with an R5, dual supercharged engine equipped with a Bendix-Novi fuel injection system sped through the flying kilometer at 194.35 mph. A production R3 Avanti set new Class C records for supercharged cars, reaching a maximum speed of nearly 171 mph.

Before the roof fell in, Studebaker, late in 1963, took the R engine evolution one step further to the R4 configuration. Essentially, this was the R3 without a supercharger but with dual Carter AFB four-barrel carburetors, high-rise manifold, 12.0:1 compression ratio, and 308° duration cam. The R4 engine was very strong at higher rpms and, while Studebaker rated its output as 280 horsepower at 5000 rpm, it probably did nearly as well as 6000 rpm.

If rarity equals desirability, then the R4 Studebaker is the most desirable supercar of them all. Exactly one was built and it powered a 1964 Lark Daytona two-door hardtop.

Undoubtedly, Studebaker had envisioned a slightly more ambitious R4 production run but, in the "rationalized" post-South Bend world of Studebaker, there was no provision for Super Larks, Super Hawks, R engines or Avantis. Thanks to a South Bend Studebaker dealer, Nate Altman, the Avanti enjoyed a remarkably successful rebirth as the Avanti II but, for all time, the book closed on Studebaker's performance era.

Whatever the key factors behind Studebaker's time of troubles (and one suspects historians will never fully agree on them), its limited economic resources made competition with the big three in the performance car market very, very difficult most of the time Studebaker was outclassed but it did have a few, all too brief moments of glory. When the limited extent of Studebaker resources was measured against the scope of its accomplishments they stand out as minor miracles.